Six Philosophical Appetizers

Dale Jacquette

Boston   Burr Ridge, IL   Dubuque, IA   Madison, WI   New York
San Francisco   St. Louis   Bangkok   Bogotá   Caracas   Lisbon   London   Madrid
Mexico City   Milan   New Delhi   Seoul   Singapore   Sydney   Taipei   Toronto

McGraw-Hill Higher Education

*A Division of The **McGraw-Hill** Companies*

SIX PHILOSOPHICAL APPETIZERS

1 2 3 4 5 6 7 8 9 0 DOC/DOC 0 9 8 7 6 5 4 3 2 1 0

ISBN 0–07–365934–7

Editorial director: *Jane E. Vaicunas*
Sponsoring editor: *Monica Eckman*
Developmental editor: *Hannah Glover*
Senior marketing manager: *Daniel M. Loch*
Project manager: *Joyce M. Berendes*
Production supervisor: *Laura Fuller*
Freelance design coordinator: *Pam Verros*
Cover photograph: © *Musee D'Orsay, Paris/Lauros-Giraudon, Paris/SuperStock*
Compositor: *Shepherd, Inc.*
Typeface: *10.5/12 Times Roman*
Printer: *R. R. Donnelley & Sons Company/Crawfordsville, IN*

Library of Congress Cataloging-in-Publication Data

Jacquette, Dale.
    Six philosophical appetizers / Dale Jacquette. — 1st ed.
      p.   cm.
    Includes bibliographical references and index.
    ISBN 0–07–365934–7
    1. Philosophy—Introductions. I. Title.

BD21 .J33 2001   00–028754
100—dc21   CIP

www.mhhe.com

for Scott K. Templeton

Let the stoics say what they please, we do not eat for the good of living, but because the meat is savory and the appetite is keen.

—Ralph Waldo Emerson
"Nature," *Essays* (1844)

Contents

Preface

PHILOSOPHY À LA CARTE

Are you curious about philosophy, but unsure about how to begin? This book can help you get started by offering a selection of bitesize philosophical reasonings to sample. If you are new to philosophy, then these appetizers in just a few pages present a concise overview of some of the main problems and methods of philosophy. Here you can savor small quantities of several ways of doing philosophy. As in an exotic restaurant, where you may not even recognize many of the items on the menu, you are wise to try a variety of appetizers before you order a main course of unfamiliar dishes. The chapters in this book are intended as table starters to whet your appetite for more specialized, in-depth philosophical inquiry.

This book invites you to think systematically about some of the most intellectually challenging and personally important problems of philosophy. The book will pose questions and propose answers to a series of philosophical questions, illustrated by means of examples from everyday life, along with many imaginative thought experiments. The appetizers investigate philosophical problems that all thoughtful persons consider at some point in their lives. The topics include the meaning of life, the possibility of knowledge, the concept of mind as it relates to the freedom of will, the existence and nature of God, the difference and reasons for choosing between moral right and wrong, and the practice, scope, and limitations of philosophy itself, in the philosophy of philosophy, or metaphilosophy. To concentrate on these problems, the book does not refer to philosophers by name or to other philosophical writings, and assumes no background in philosophical methods or in the history of philosophy.

The book develops a connected line of argument that follows a natural progression of topics linking theme to theme as you work through the chapters from beginning to end. Nevertheless, the chapters can be read in any order, according to your interests, as you might choose appetizers from a tray. The discussion of metaphilosophy appears in the final chapter, where it raises philosophical issues about the conduct of philosophy that can best be appreciated after you have seen several types of philosophy in action. However, if you want to know more about the subject matter and methods of philosophy before you take the plunge, you might read this chapter at least lightly as a prelude, then again when you have encountered particular philosophical problems firsthand from the contents of other chapters.

A collection of readings, *Philosophical Entrées: Classic and Contemporary Readings in Philosophy,* is published by McGraw-Hill as a companion for use with this text. *Six Philosophical Appetizers* can be combined with these readings, designed to accompany the book to create customized reading and discussion programs. *Philosophical Entrées* offers a natural complement to *Six Philosophical Appetizers.* Divided into six corresponding sections, the supplementary readings in *Philosophical Entrées* provide historical background and carry forward in more detail some of the major themes explored in *Appetizers.* The selections have been chosen from among the most important writings of classical and contemporary philosophers to illustrate the variety of philosophical styles associated with each of the six main topics introduced in these chapters. *Appetizers* can also be enjoyed at a more leisurely pace as an introduction to philosophical problems entirely on its own, with ample opportunity for exploring the philosophical questions it raises, or in conjunction with another choice of readings.

I am grateful to the students in my Basic Problems of Philosophy courses at The Pennsylvania State University, who provided both the occasion and inspiration for these introductory studies. They are the audience for whom this book was originally intended, along with their counterparts at college and university introductory philosophy courses everywhere. I owe a special debt of thanks to Sarah Moyers and Monica Eckman, my editors at McGraw-Hill, for believing in this project when it was only a concept in development, and for encouraging me to pursue my aesthetic as well as philosophical vision for the book.

CHAPTER ONE

The Sojourner's Question

Midway on life's journey, I went astray from the straight path and awoke to find myself alone in a dark wood.

—Dante
The Inferno, Canto I, 1–3

WHO AM I?

If you stop to think about it, no matter what you are doing, you are on a journey. And stopping to think about it is the whole point. Life is a journey, from birth to awakening as a person, to death, and, as some people believe, before and beyond. Even if you try to remain perfectly still, you cannot avoid moving in time and space as a passenger on planet Earth and through the series of life's experiences. A sojourner is someone who pauses along the way while traveling from place to place. A sojourn, then, is a rest stop, during which the traveler enjoys a brief time out from normal activities. A sojourn makes it possible to regather energy, to reflect on what has come before, and to prepare to set out again and continue traveling wherever it is you have decided to go. A sojourn can help you take the next step in a carefully considered direction.

JOURNEY OF A LIFETIME

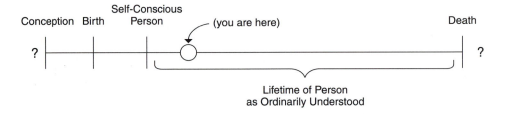

The sojourner's question concerns both the traveler and the meaning—the point or purpose, if any—of the journey: Who am I? What am I? Why am I here? What is the meaning of life and—more important, perhaps—what is the meaning, if any, of *my* life? How should I think about the existence of the universe and my place in it as an individual? Am I just an animal or a conscious biological machine that has come about through a chance sequence of events through the forces of nature? Or is there a larger plan, which it might be my responsibility to discover and in accordance with which I should try to live my life? Is there a deeper meaning to be found, or is life altogether meaningless and devoid of any purpose? Is life, after all, as we might have heard some people say, absurd? The sojourner's question arises only when we slow ourselves down enough to ask it, and only then, if we allow ourselves sufficient time to consider possible answers.

How can we answer such questions? What can we know, and how can we rely on the truth of any of the answers that may present themselves? How can we separate the correct solutions to these age-old enigmas from merely wishful thinking, especially if the true answers are not especially comforting or flattering to our sense of the importance of human destiny? Where can we begin?

THE MEANING OF LIFE

So far, we have been multiplying rather than answering questions or solving problems. This frequently happens in philosophical investigations, especially at the beginning stages. At some point, we must take stock and try at least provisionally to draw some general conclusions about these weighty matters. But at the outset it is worthwhile to clarify the questions themselves and to try to state as precisely as we can just what it is we want to know. That is the goal of this first philosophical appetizer. We should not be disappointed if we cannot simply pour forth a predigested solution to a problem as challenging as the meaning of life. We must first try to understand the problem and get a sense of the preliminary topics we might need to investigate in order to get a firm handle on the sojourner's question.

That task will occupy us in this and the next four chapters. We will venture one sort of answer to the problem of the meaning of life only when we return full circle in the last chapter for our sixth and final philosophical appetizer, when we are in a position to make use of all the ideas we have considered. Along the way, we will get a sampling of some of the other categories of philosophical problems in which philosophers are interested, and we will see a number of styles of philosophical inquiry in application.

All this will take some time. That is another sense in which the meaning of life is a sojourner's question. We need to abstract ourselves from ordinary concerns in order to engage in serious philosophical reflection. A sojourn can occur in many ways. The necessary ingredients are time, a desire to ask difficult questions, and the commitment to follow the answers in an open-minded spirit wherever they lead. The amount of time needed for a satisfactory consideration of the sojourner's question might come about through various changes of circumstance. It is not time alone that is important, moreover, but a temporary withdrawal from everyday cares and concerns. If you are fully absorbed in an ongoing pattern of life, it might simply never occur to you to question who or what you are, or whether life has meaning beyond the attainment of short-range goals. Instead, you might be inclined to take such things for granted.

If you are healthy and happy and moving toward the objectives you have set for yourself, then you might not be motivated to question the meaning of life. We should be grateful to the extent that life goes well for us, and naturally we want to live well and succeed at whatever we choose to do. But experiencing a rich and fully rewarding life might also demand of us occasional self-examination, to think about our lives in more ultimate terms with regard to their deeper significance. Are we sure that what we are doing is right, that it makes sense to us? Or are we merely following along in a path laid down for us by others, which we have never personally thought through? Are we living without having deliberately chosen our own way because we have never questioned the meaning of life? Have we ever seriously considered whether there are alternatives to the way we are living and, if so, what they are? Do we have good reasons to continue what we have been doing, or have we blindly accepted a lifestyle and an attitude toward living that are easy because they are familiar or expected of us by parents, teachers, friends, and others in society, or because they are what other people in our acquaintance have chosen?

PURPOSE AND ACHIEVEMENT

Although we do not desire misfortune, it is a fact of life that two of the things that can awaken us from our complacent acceptance of what life has offered us are the frustration and suffering that come through various kinds of failure. Everyone experiences setbacks at some point in life—some more than others. If life is a journey, then one way in which a sojourn can be imposed on us is to undergo a mishap or to encounter an obstacle to the achievement of something we had hoped to attain.

The philosophical reason for this might seem obvious enough. There is no call to examine life or the purpose of life as long as everything is going smoothly. It is primarily when something goes wrong that we are upset from our endeavor and capsized momentarily in midstream. This sort of event can cause us to wonder whether we had been going in the right direction in the first place. Was the effort we were making really worth it, if the plans of a lifetime can be so easily overturned? Or should we not use the opportunity to reconsider our goals and perhaps choose another way, and, in extreme cases, an entirely different walk of life?

An extraordinary example of this type of enforced sojourn occurs when someone experiences a health emergency. A person feels healthy and well, and life seems good. The person has the ordinary expectations that life will hold the usual rewards that come about through luck and hard work. Such a person sees the future as involving receiving support from a loving family, enjoying sports and outdoor activities, falling in love and having a fulfilling personal relationship with a significant other, getting an education, working toward a career, learning to appreciate the arts, following current events and participating in political affairs as a good citizen, and perhaps raising a family, seeing one's children grow into happy, healthy, mature, responsible people.

Along life's way, there can be other respectable goals. Some of these might be valuable as ends in themselves, and others as means to an end. There are career objectives of many different kinds pitched at many levels of personal ambition. You already know some of the possibilities, and you might have already set your sights on goals of this kind. You might know exactly what you want to do, or you might be considering several options or freely exploring your abilities to see what finally captures your interest or what you happen to fall into. You might want to become a professional sports player, doctor, journalist, lawyer, artist, scientist, historian, politician, soldier, or other worthwhile and personally satisfying occupation. You might want to own a home, raise a family, have an automobile and travel to interesting places, cultivate a circle of friends, learn foreign languages, support a worthy charity, earn a pilot's license, share your life with a small menagerie of pets, write a best-selling novel, memorize all of Verdi's operas, help save the rain forest, or work toward racial equality, social justice, and world peace.

All of these are good things; some of them are noble. It is natural to suppose that the meaning of life consists of deciding on such goals and purposes, the ones that seem right for us, and working toward them. Of course, we do not expect everything always to go our way. A mature person recognizes that there are likely to be minor or even major reversals from time to time and understands the need to be strong enough to persevere and to remain focused on one's goals, and being inventive in meeting life's challenges by finding ways around temporary obstacles and adversities. Then, with determination, we can bounce back and continue toward the attainment of the most important purposes that we think of as constituting the meaning of our lives. According to such a picture, the meaning of life just is or consists of choosing and struggling to achieve these ends. It is being part of a family, going to school, preparing for a career, having a family of one's own, enjoying the pleasures we cultivate for ourselves, doing good for others, and in general experiencing the ups and downs of human existence in the social world we inhabit.

SURVIVING A CRISIS

There are occurrences that do not fall under the category of setbacks and challenges but are of such a nature as to cause us to question the meaning and even to doubt the meaningfulness of life. It is probably not psychologically healthy to dwell on the possibilities that can ruin life by thwarting even its most basic purposes. But it is also naive to pretend that such things do or cannot happen, and it represents a certain undeveloped understanding of life not to recognize that there can be overwhelming threats and disasters that disappoint even the most reasonable objectives of good persons who are trying to enjoy the best of what life has to offer. We see others who are deprived of such things, not through any fault of their own, but through simple bad luck. Let us not obsess about the miseries that life inflicts on some people, and might yet hold in store for us, but consider a simple example.

An athlete, let us say, on the way to a promising career, is struck down by an incurable disease or is injured in an automobile accident. Up to this tragic point, everything in and about the athlete's life might have been clear, and the road to the future might have seemed all laid out, with nothing more to do than follow a sensible plan with persistence and make the most of whatever opportunities present themselves. Now, however, a totally unforeseen hand has been dealt, and there is nothing to do but play it out the best one can. Unfortunately, what this entails for the individual in question is to abandon what had been the central purpose of life until the time of the misfortune.

Life can be perceived as having an overall purpose, for which we pursue our talents, and we build the rest of our existence around doing what we believe is most important and for which we are naturally suited. When this central core of meaning is suddenly taken away through no fault of our own, or of anyone at all, just because that is the way things happen, then life in retrospect before this reversal, as well as toward the future, can seem empty and meaningless. After the pain, disappointment, and shock of realization have subsided, a sojourn along life's way might then take place. An illness or a hospital stay might provide the unwelcome occasion for this kind of sojourn. The experience forcibly removes us from the flow of past events and expectations for the future that had previously constituted our existence. Think of what the athlete in our example might experience. With everything radically changed, and with such a central part of life's purpose rendered impossible, it becomes necessary to rethink how the rest of life might continue, what to do and how to live now that so much has been undone.

We need not feel unduly sorry for the athlete in the example. We know that similar and even worse things happen to people every day. More important, we should suppose that the athlete has the same reserves of personal courage that other unfortunate individuals have demonstrated in like situations. Many people have faced life's trials bravely and have made the most of whatever fate has handed them. We can expect that we would do the same if we were were to suffer a similar disaster. People rebuild their lives with extraordinary pluck and do not usually need or want pity. Now further imagine that the permanently incapacitated athlete not only begins to redesign a life in the aftermath of illness or accident but also is sent on a respite from life's journey in which to reflect on whether life has any deeper meaning. In other words, the athlete begins to question whether life has an overarching context of purposes in which the defeat of a personal goal—such as to become a professional athlete—can be understood as meaningful.

In such a situation, it is tempting to ask what all the athlete's previous effort and training could possibly have been worth. If in the end it does not produce the desired result, but is so easily taken away, then what was the meaning of it all? Surprisingly, we can experience that same kind emptiness when we succeed at something toward which we have worked for a long time. When we have overcome obstacles, when the struggles that have defined our purpose have at last been defeated, and we look back from our victory over all the hard work and anxiety the effort has cost us, we may find ourselves wondering whether it has all been worth it, whether there can still be a meaning to our existence now that we have actually arrived at the goal we fought so hard to attain. The psychology of such occurrences, in turn, can cause a person to see in these individual circumstances a kind of metaphor for the overall human condition. Even if we are luckier than the athlete in the example and are not struck down in the prime of life before we realize our dreams, are we not in any case doomed someday to die?

MEANINGFULNESS AND ABSURDITY

All that we have worked for and all that we have learned will eventually be lost. The greatest scientists, artists, religious leaders, political figures, military heroes—all the people who have struggled to achieve a certain place in life, regardless of their success or failure—will finally be reduced to worms and ashes, and even the worms and ashes will not endure forever. If the meaning of life is to develop one's talents and work toward having a career, a family, a house, and interesting experiences, what is the value of such activity, when in the end it will all come to nothing and it seems we must all perish along with all our hopes, ambitions, and fulfilled or unfulfilled goals?

Such considerations have led some people to reply that the real meaning of life must consist not of what any individual can do or try to do for himself or herself but, rather, of much larger cultural contributions to society and, on a smaller scale, of the perpetuation of the species, one person at a time, by raising a family. This is something even the athlete in our example might be able to do, depending on the severity of disability. Having children and contributing in this way to the odyssey of the human species might be understood as the more important biological purpose or meaning of human life. It is a purpose, moreover, that transcends the fate and fortunes of any particular individual. After all, people sometimes sacrifice themselves for a nobler good, which is often a larger social unit. Parents sacrifice themselves for their children, soldiers do so for their battalion, and citizens do so for their country and sometimes for the good of humanity.

Does this not testify to a greater purpose or meaning of human life that goes beyond whatever happens to any particular person? Does it not also neatly solve the problem we have thus far been pondering, of understanding and making sense of the meaning of human life in light of the fact that the best laid plans can be completely overturned? Moreover, there are many possible ways of contributing to the higher purposes of human life. Even if the athlete we have been considering cannot have children after tragedy strikes, he or she can serve as an example of courage and determination to others in a way that might contribute to the progress and survival of humankind and, on a more local scale, can help other family members live happy and productive lives. No doubt something like this type of reasoning could enter into the thinking of the athlete during the sojourn we are imagining in redesigning a goal and purpose for life. Is this a satisfactory answer to the question of the meaning of life?

Skeptics might observe that the limits of individual human life apply also on a slightly different time scale to families, societies, nations, cultures, civilizations, and even the entire human species. Go to a natural history museum and contemplate the demise of the dinosaurs. Once the most powerful and biologically successful creatures on Earth, the dinosaurs are now extinct, surviving only, if we are to believe the theories of some zoologists, in their feathered descendents, the birds. Then consider the rise and fall of great empires and the tremendous efforts of will that have gone into the building of cities, the clearing of forests, the erection of monuments, the creation of art, the harnassing of power sources, the mining of ores and fossil fuels, the discovery and implementation of technologies, the preparation for war, the enslavement and liberation of peoples, all the glory and misery of human history—the partly mad, partly divine human comedy. The ancient Assyrians, Babylonians, and Egyptians have come and gone, as have a long succession of Chinese dynasties, the ancient Greeks and Romans, and countless others. These civilizations, in Shakespeare's words, have strut their hour upon the stage of human history, and some have left behind impressive artifacts of their cultures, including recorded expressions of the knowledge they gained in their time to be passed along to future generations. But, for all their exertions, they are no longer here. In many cases, they would not necessarily approve of the ways in which the world has inherited and changed the things they strived to achieve.

When we consider that our own civilization, which, to complicate matters, has also discovered and manufactured monstrous weapons of mass destruction, will also eventually succumb and take its place among the relics of history, it is hard to understand what real or ultimate value all our daily worry and concern can have, whether our individual and collective contributions to society in the modern world could possibly constitute the meaning of life. Imagine a museum of the far distant future, if there is a future for humankind, in which a few remnants of the material culture of our times are displayed. There might be a television set, an automobile, a few tarnished coins, and a hard disk drive from a computer. All are rusted and caked with encrustations from where they have been excavated many miles below the surface of the Earth by future archaeologists. If that image puts our present human existence in a certain perspective, ask if from any long-term standpoint it really makes sense to suppose that the meaning of human life consists of investing our time and energy—the very substance, so to speak, of our souls—in the material trappings of our society.

Neither does a shift of focus necessarily improve our view of the human condition. Can the meaning of life involve, instead, the more regional purpose of reproducing and raising a family? If anything, here the futility of human endeavor is often more easy to discern, no matter how personally rewarding and important it may be for individuals who love their children and grandchildren and the wider network of all their relatives. A family can die out much more quickly than a society or civilization. There are countless instances in which parents have labored intensively to secure a future for their children, only to have their children lost to disease, war, accident, or foul play, or to prove themselves unworthy in some way to inherit all that their parents have built for them. At best, family goals cannot reasonably be expected to succeed for more than a limited number of generations. After a few seasons, one's progeny will ultimately share the fate of the evolving society and civilizations to which they belong, together with their final destruction.

None of this is to say that we should not want to have children or raise families. We should not be discouraged just because our progeny will not continue indefinitely into the future. Neither should we choose not to become athletes, merely because, like the person in our story, we might fall victim to a disabling illness or accident. There are strong natural desires to enhance the quality of life in these and other ways, none of which comes with an ironclad guarantee. The question is, rather, whether such purposes, subject as they are to frustration and defeat, can possibly constitute the meaning of life or whether the meaning of life, if life has meaning, must be something different, something more. The point is not to become depressed about the prospects of life. Some philosophers have nevertheless concluded that reflecting on death and the futility of human endeavor can provide a source of profound philosophical insight. The issue is whether the things that give us pleasure or the things we feel compelled to do to complete our lives can themselves constitute the meaning of life, whether the meaning of life is something else, or whether life has any meaning at all. If none of these possibilities provides the meaning of life in a sense that we can accept, and if there is no better alternative, then no matter what happiness we find in life, life itself must be meaningless.

Life may strike us as absurd when a series of unrelated events tragicomically conspires to thwart our aspirations, or when persons whom we deem undeserving of special honors or privileges succeed outrageously in spite of themselves through sheer dumb luck. How absurd, we say, when someone who is in every way unqualified for the job is elected mayor just because she has a winning smile. And how absurd when a busload of children is picked up by a tornado, transported across county lines, and deposited on a road far away with no one injured. How can there be any plan or meaning in such events? Life can often seem to be nothing but a succession of random occurrences. The absurdity of life in the absence of any recognizable meaning is experienced precisely in those circumstances when things go inexplicably right or wrong, and there no longer seems to be any rhyme or reason to the universe, when the world proves to be painfully indifferent to our interests and concerns. The idea that life is absurd is not new, and it is not one that impresses us with equal force at all times in our lives. It might do so especially on those occasions when the meaningfulness we have otherwise taken for granted comes apart at the seams. When we are disappointed, we see that not everything in the world is designed for our happiness, and we might think that we glimpse reality as it is independently of the delusions of order and meaning in the universe with which we ordinarily try to console ourselves. On a quiet night, the planets and stars can seem cold and distant in the vastness of space, and those of us living here on Earth can seem utterly alone when we look to them for answers about the meaning of life, so unrelated to events elsewhere in the cosmos.

It is not unless or until we are drawn into a philosophical sojourn that we are likely to doubt the meaning of the universe. The sojourner's question is so-called not only because it arises mostly when we are abstracted from life's journey and given both the opportunity and motivation to reflect on the meaningfulness or absurdity of life. It is appropriately the sojourner's question because it is specifically a question about life's journey, about the nature of the journey and the traveler, and about whether life itself considered as a whole is but a sojourn along a larger, more meaningful journey. The sojourn is an inseparable part of the journey, so that, if the journey altogether lacks meaning, then so does the sojourn. By the same token, if the sojourn has meaning, then the journey taken in its entirety cannot be totally absurd.

BLUES AND GREENS

Let us now modify the sojourner's problem. Imagining someone whose life plans have had to be abandoned or drastically changed through a catastrophic occurrence is one way to understand the point of view of some philosophers who consider life to be ultimately meaningless. But there are others. Instead of contemplating a terrible reversal through illness or accident, let us consider a fictional society at war with its neighbors. The two factions are the Blues and the Greens.

The Blues and Greens have fought throughout their long history. Religious differences divide the two peoples. The Blues not only ardently believe that God is blue but also maintain as part of their ancient faith that God demands a daily sacrifice of green peas. The Greens believe that God is green and requires a weekly offering of blueberries. As fate would have it, peas grow only in the valley territory of the Greens, and blueberries can be found only on the mountain slopes inhabited by the Blues. The armies of the Blues and Greens are consequently engaged in repeated raids across one another's borders, partly to harrass and test each other's weaknesses and partly to prepare for an eventual full-scale invasion. The immediate purpose of their daily forays, however, is not to conquer and subjugate their age-old enemies but to pilfer precious peas or blueberries, according to the requirements of their respective religions. Occasionally, one side takes the other by surprise and gains a temporary advantage, only to be beaten back at a later date and suffer similar losses themselves. On the whole, however, the military prowess of the Blues and Greens is roughly evenly matched by compensations of different sorts. The Blues have a better mountaineering corps, for example, as one might expect, while the Greens have a superior cavalry.

The two societies strive to injure one another in whatever way they can. For the greater glory of their two nations and, it turns out, for the personal profit of the arms dealers and weapons suppliers, both sides stand ready to provoke hostilities. The exploits of the most heroic Blues and Greens are celebrated in their homelands by statues and public monuments, and by stirring patriotic songs that all schoolchildren are taught from the time they are old enough to speak. By their eighteenth year, the young among the Blues and Greens have received extensive military training, and some have distinguished themselves sufficiently to qualify for officer cadet academies, where they study the latest military science and techniques of campaign strategy, and prepare for careers as valiant soldiers dedicated to fighting for their sacred heritages of peas and blueberries.

Now enter the scene a philosophically reflective young female cadet in the army of the Blues. She is a brave soldier, skilled in all the martial arts, fearlessly dedicated to the Blues cause, and poised if necessary to give up her life for peas in the valley of the Greens. One day, the woman is on maneuvers deep behind enemy lines, in the land of the Greens. She is cut off from the rest of her patrol, finds herself unexpectedly face-to-face with a solitary infantrywoman of the Greens, out reconnoitering for signs of incursions by the Blues. When they first spot each other, they are less than arm's length apart, rounding a cliffside edge of rock and almost bumping into one another without warning. They stand within reach, and their first thought, or perhaps the reflex reaction they have been taught as the result of their military training, is to draw their weapons. Nevertheless, the situation is so unexpected that at first neither moves a muscle. Instead, they stare at one another for a few seconds, trying to assess the danger they might be in; then, as though on cue, each suddenly turns back to find her own company and says not a word about the encounter to her compatriots.

Later that night, the Blues soldier turns the incident over and over in her mind. She cannot get over the idea that the Greens soldier was in many ways just like herself, despite the fact that she belonged on the other side. She did not appear at all to be the monster she had always been told the Greens were. To see her in their abrupt near collision was almost like looking in a mirror, seeing someone very much like herself but in a differently colored uniform. There was a woman of approximately the same age, trained to hate and fight her people, the Blues, just as she had been trained to hate and fight the Greens. The more she thinks about the similarities and differences between them in that fleeting eye-to-eye contact in the valley, the more she begins to wonder how and why and by what accident of chance she happened that day to be a soldier of the Blues and not of the Greens. Why, for that matter, did the soldier she stumbled on happen to be born and raised a Green rather than a Blue? What rational justification could there be for any individual to have one affiliation rather than the other? Why Blue and not Green, or Green and not Blue? Why Green or Blue? Why anything at all? Why does anything happen the way it does, and, if there is no satisfactory reason anyone lives on one side rather than on the other of any of the countless kinds of fences that divide people, why should people let their particular station influence in any way how they think and what they do? Is it not finally absurd to devote one's life and energy to any pursuit whatsoever if no adequate rationale can be found for it? But, then, why do anything at all, if any of the decisions by which we shape our lives can be made to seem equally absurd?

The fable of the Blues and Greens is meant not only as a political satire. It can also symbolize any of the distinctions that separate people into different groups. There are men and women, white people and people of color, rich and poor, workers and employers, teachers and students, officers and enlisted men and women, soldiers and civilians, customers and waiters, waitresses and cashiers, persons who live on one side of the railroad tracks and persons who live on the other side, drivers and pedestrians, carnivores and herbivores, old people and young, academics and nonacademics, doctors and patients, them and us. Why it is so and whether it should be so are other questions. For the moment, what is of interest is only that such divisions exist. But, in thinking about any of the ways in which we are divided from others, the question posed by the example of the Blues and Greens remains what reason there can be for us to find ourselves on one side of an invisible border rather than the other. If there is no satisfactory answer, then, thinking of myself only as a person, I might as well be on one side as the other. Indeed, I could just as easily be on one side rather than the other, if only I had been born at a different time and in a different place under different circumstances, to different parents, speaking abstractly, also living different lives. No matter who I am, and no matter where I find myself in life, when I think of myself as an individual human being, there is a sense in which I can imagine myself being exchanged for any other person experiencing any other kind of life. So why am I living the particular life I am living? Why am I a white man rather than a black woman? Why am I a twentieth-century philosopher rather than a medieval cleric? Why am I a civilian rather than a soldier? Why am I a Blue rather than a Green, or a Green rather than a Blue? Why am I one of us instead of one of them?

If there is no good answer to the question of why we find ourselves in one role rather than another in life, then, given the extent to which such distinctions determine how we live and think about our lives, what, if any, is the real meaning of life?

Like the soldier in the story, all of my energy might be devoted to thinking of myself and my place in the grand scheme of things as a soldier for the Blues. In somewhat the same way as the athlete of our previous example, if I am the Blues woman, then, when I consider that I might as well be a civilian among the Greens, I must ask what meaning my life as a Blues soldier can have. What does it mean that so much of my life and what I try to do, the goals I set for myself and the ways in which I judge my success or failure in these endeavors, is predicated on my belonging on one side of a number of divisions between myself and others, that could have been just the opposite from what they are?

The point is not merely to make us more sympathetic to other people who are not on the same side as we are, although it is also that. The fable of the Blues and Greens is supposed to make us question the meaningfulness of any of the ways in which we think of our lives insofar as our lives depend on our being one thing rather than another. We know that, in a different world, we might discover ourselves to have different values and different purposes by virtue of playing a very different part in the oppositions that constitute our lives. If everything could have been different, how can the meaning of life depend on the way things accidentally happen to be? What, then, would be the purpose of our lives? What could be the purpose of life in more general terms for all human beings if so many individual purposes are bound up in the them-or-us oppositions in which we stand in conflict with other people? How can the purpose of life for human beings be doing either what the Blues do or what the Greens do, when in the final analysis the purposes of the Blues and Greens cancel each other out? The purpose of life cannot be both to help the Blues fight the Greens and the Greens to fight the Blues. That would be absurd. But, then, some philosophers conclude that life, insofar as it is defined by the purposes we find and the energy we devote to participating in one side of such ultimately groundless oppositions, is equally absurd.

WHEN OPPOSITIONS MATTER

Or is it? Life is absurd if it requires that we participate without good reason in one side of oppositions that are as artificially pointless as that between the Blues and Greens. The example is deliberately constructed so as to embody a superficial difference that makes no difference to us as outsiders. If the Blues win and the Greens lose or the Greens win and the Blues lose, it is all pretty much the same. Why should we care?

But are all oppositions as meaningless as that between the Blues and Greens? Would it not be worthwhile and lend genuine meaning to our lives if we were to struggle to defeat a tyranny that degrades its citizens and causes terrible human suffering, to discover a cure for a devastating disease, or to create a new style of art? If there is no rational justification for participating on one side rather than another of any opposition, then life as a whole insofar as it involves such commitment and participation is ultimately meaningless and absurd. But it does not follow that life is absurd if we can involve ourselves in a truly worthwhile activity.

The question becomes whether good reasons can ever be given for our being on one side rather than another of any opposition.

Returning to our example, after a political coup, a dictator emerges in what had previously been the underdog Jade Party among the Greens. The dictator abolishes free elections, the free press, and freedom of religion, together with all the liberties traditionally enjoyed by both the Blues and the Greens. The dictator begins persecuting a scapegoat ethnic subgroup of his own citizens, the Emeralds, as well as any who dare to speak up against his rule. The Jade Party kidnaps dissidents in the middle of the night, sets up concentration camps, and takes the Greens' military power to unprecedented heights. The intelligence reports gathered by the Blues suggest that the Greens are planning an attack, with the objective of taking over the Blues territory and imposing their new style of military dictatorship before destroying them in a campaign of genocide. At an alarming rate of escalation, the Greens prepare to take action against the Blues in a life-or-death struggle. The Blues mobilize their forces and assume first a defensive position, while steadily making plans of their own for a preemptive strike against the Greens for the sake of their own security and to liberate the oppressed minorities among the Greens who have been the victims of merciless oppression by the Jade Party. The old days of feuding between the Blues and Greens are over, and each side sees itself as locked in mortal combat in an epic battle for the future of their respective ways of life.

The Blues infantrywoman of the previous story, who in the meantime has resigned her commission in the army, is considering whether to reenlist. She begins to think that what has happened and what appears about to happen among the Greens may now have given her something worth fighting for. She feels an obligation to go up against the Greens Jade Party, which she identifies as the forces of evil. She wants to be part of her nation's defenses and to be involved in the liberation of the Greens political prisoners. Suddenly, she feels, life has a purpose. There is something important to do. It is not just a matter of stealing green peas for a religious ceremony. The purposes now are to assure the survival of her people and to alleviate the misery of persecuted individuals in another land. It is something she can help to do that will make a difference in the world, something she believes she must try to do. The opposition is still the Blues against the Greens and Greens against the Blues, but the stakes are higher because of a change of events, and now she is drawn into the conflict with the sense that everything she does must contribute to the downfall of the Jades. When this purpose is accomplished, she thinks, she will have achieved something vital for the good of the world. She reconsiders what she had previously thought about the meaninglessness of life as involvement in either of the equally irrelevant sides of a pointless opposition.

Although some oppositions might cancel each other out and, as such, fail to offer a meaningful choice for commitment to action, others, maybe most or even all others when seen in the right light, cannot be ignored but require every thinking person to become engaged in the events of their time. There are always urgently important, vitally valuable things to do. Taking a stand against the Jades is just one such mission, but there must be countless others. Fighting the Jades is not just a negative or an oppositional purpose but a positive effort to promote essential values.

OBJECTIVITY IN THE SEARCH FOR MEANING

The meaning of life can be understood as fulfilling a succession of vital purposes, doing what is right according to our strongest moral feelings or even what we may believe to be commanded by God. The idea is not to become entangled in meaningless oppositions but to become involved only in those that are important, the ones that make a difference and that collectively give meaning to life by providing an opportunity to affirm whatever we find valuable.

All this might seem perfectly reasonable, but there are other aspects of the problem to consider. How do things look from the standpoint of the Greens? Their green God equally commands them to do what they are doing, and they might equally believe with the same heartfelt conviction that what the Jades are doing to destroy the Blues is their moral duty. Thus, the question arises once again about the real meaning of the opposition. The difference in the antagonism between the Blues and Greens as it has developed in some ways is more a matter of degree rather than a difference of a new kind. It is just another level of opposition. But, wherever there is opposition, there are people ranged on opposite sides. And this does not happen unless people on both sides believe themselves to have good reasons to oppose the others. Why should one side be regarded as ultimately more important than the other?

The only conceivable answer is that there must be an objectively correct side in any opposition. The Jades must be wrong and the Blues who oppose them must be right, despite the fact that participants on both sides believe themselves to be right. Is it necessarily wrong ever to oppress others, as the Jades are doing? Is it indisputably correct for the Blues to have decided to defend themselves against the Greens in order to defeat the Jades? The important point is that it cannot be enough to be strongly convinced of the justice of one's position, since all parties, including the Greens, might believe this. Then we are right back where we started, effectively in the same situation as originally for the Blues and Greens, before the tyranny of the Jades. If you are a Blue, on reflection you can imagine yourself to be a Green, with all of the Greens' beliefs and animosity toward the Blues; if you are a Green, you can imagine yourself to be a Blue, with all of the Blues' beliefs and animosity toward the Greens. The moment of abstraction needed for such introspection might be found, for example, in the soldier's encounter with her counterpart in the valley, or in an unguarded hour while thinking in general terms about the meaning of life. If there is a basis for choosing one side over another in any opposition, it must be the objective rather than merely the subjective outcome of having been raised and indoctrinated in one set of beliefs rather than another.

However, if one side in such a dispute is truly objective, why is there disagreement and opposition in the first place? Why have both sides not come to the same point of view—why do they continue to oppose each other? The answer might be that, if the Blues are objectively right, then the Jades and their supporters among the Greens are simply mistaken, or they have not considered the issues with sufficient care in order to see that they are wrong. If they were to think about the problems aright, then perhaps they would arrive at the same objective conclusion and would abandon their aggression. Is this believable? Most people would say that the Jades are acting as they are because they believe that they have something to gain, and because they have the will to do morally wrong things on the assumption that they are likely to succeed if they act decisively and overwhelm their enemies. If they can get away with it, they will profit from their actions, and that is what they hope to achieve. The Blues, for their part, sense a danger to their lives and way of life and are determined not to let the Greens win. Thus, under the circumstances, there is an opposition that can be resolved only by armed confrontation.

The Blues will fight the Greens—but to decide what? Suppose that the Blues win. Does that mean that they were right? Wars are won or lost because of strength, preparedness, and sheer chance. None of these things determines the moral rightness or wrongness of the issues about which two peoples go to war. Suppose that the Greens win because they are more ruthless and reckless in battle. Would that mean that they were right? If you ask some of the Blues who have decided to fight, they might say that it does not matter whether they win or lose, that they have no choice but to take arms against the Greens. If they do not, the Greens will overpower them and they will be lost anyway. They believe their cause is just, and they will fight as hard as they can. But they do not confuse might with right, and they do not expect the battle to decide who is right. They already know in their hearts that they are right, and that is why their position is worth fighting for. But, if the outcome of the struggle does not determine whether the Blues or Greens are right, what else can? There must be a way of judging these matters that is equally available to both sides of any opposition, whether or not they choose to follow it and whether or not they would be willing to abide by its conclusions. But, even if such a method exists, it is clear from the example that the pursuit of objective judgment is not the only way in which a person's life can attain meaning by commitment to one side of an opposition. After all, the Jades and most of the Greens are as strongly motivated to do something desperate as the Blues are to try to stop them, and both cannot be proceeding according to the same objective decision-making method or they would not have reached and be ready now to fight for completely opposite positions.

To say that we do not need to follow an objective method in order to find at least a superficial kind of meaning in life only reinforces the assumption that there might be no deeper meaning. For, if trying to find meaning in life involves having a good reason to devote one's energies to one side rather than another in an opposition, and if there is no really good reason to do so, then there is no ultimate meaning in life. The existence of an objective method for deciding whether or not to adopt some purpose might offer a basis to make life more meaningful by providing a definite reason that goes beyond the chance or otherwise unjustified agreement with a position that could just as easily be reversed. Then we could say that life can ultimately be meaningful for those who have such reasons, and not for those whose purposes are only superficially meaningful because they are not motivated by sound reasoning. Now, if reasoning is supposed to supply the meaning of life, then philosophy has a central role to play in the solution to the sojourner's question. But, before we can examine such a possibility in detail, the fact that it is not always necessary to give an objective justification for decisions about what to do with our lives suggests that, even when we can provide a reason for what we do, the reason by itself cannot be enough to motivate action in a particular direction. We could have such a reason but still choose not to act on it, and we might choose to act in a certain way even when we have not worked out the reason.

Consequently, it could be argued that some people who have thought about the sojourner's question might have identified the meaning of life in trying to do what they believe to be good, which they might even think is morally obligatory as God's will. There is enormous potential for self-deception in this kind of search for meaning, because the issues are so personally important. When we are convinced by a chain of reasoning that what we have chosen to do is morally right or mandated by God, we feel a strong compulsion to believe that the meaning of life is to follow such convictions wherever they may lead. The attitude is reasonable enough until we reflect that the Blues and Greens might experience the same strong sense of conviction, drawing them in opposite directions. If only objective reasoning adequately justifies such a commitment, then presumably the Blues and the Greens cannot both be correct in their chosen mutually incompatible courses of action, yet they might be equally convinced of their rightness. If each side truly believes that it is morally obligated or commanded by God to do what it is doing, then we are back once again to a situation like the original confrontation of the Blues and Greens. It is not so different for a Blue to realize that, except for an accident of birth, she would have been a Green, as to realize that, but for a similar kind of accident, a completely different set of reasons than those that now move her to oppose the Greens could have persuaded her instead as one of the Greens to oppose the Blues. A Blue could as easily have been born a Green, and a Green could as easily have been born a Blue. A line of reasoning capable of persuading a Blue thinker under the right circumstances could also persuade a Green thinker, and conversely.

We are left only with the possibility that the meaning of life might be found in doing what is objectively right or truly commanded by God. For this criterion to be applicable, we must be able to distinguish between (1) what is actually right for us to do and what God may actually command and (2) what may merely seem right or what we merely believe God requires us to do. If we cannot draw such distinctions correctly in practice, then we might be involved only in self-deception about the higher justification for what we have decided to do anyway, possibly for hidden or self-serving reasons. It is too easy to persuade ourselves—as the history of human conflict shows—that what we want or what it would be to our advantage to do is objectively morally obligatory or commanded by God. Such discriminations are notoriously difficult to make, partly because they concern questions of value rather than simple matters of fact, partly because they involve projections of future actions, and partly because self-interests can cloud our judgment. If we cannot distinguish between what is objectively morally required or truly commanded by God and what we merely believe to be morally required or commanded by God, then, if the meaning of life is to do what is morally obligatory or to obey the will of God, we might be fulfilling the meaning of life and not know it. But how can such a highly abstracted sense of the meaning of life be meaningful for us? Could life have a purpose without our being able to know its purpose or whether its purpose is being fulfilled? If not, then life itself by yet another more circuitous route can be seen as absurd. To have a purpose and to act with a purpose entail acting intention-ally,which further entails knowing what we are doing and why. It is logically absurd to imagine that life could be meaningful but that no one could know its meaning or whether its meaning is being promoted or impeded. It would be the equivalent of life's being meaningful or having a purpose that no human being could deliberately choose.

TRANSCENDENT RELIGIOUS MEANING OF LIFE

It is worthwhile to reconsider the idea that the meaning of life depends on the exis-tence of God. We have already seen that the Blues worship a blue God, while the Greens worship a green God, and that each side believes that its God requires it to do conflicting things, leading to open warfare. The antagonism between the Blues and Greens is an allegory of the way religious believers historically have fought against one another. As examples, think of the warfare between Christians and Muslims during the medieval Crusades, or of Protestant and Catholic Christians who waged some of the bloodiest battles that ever occurred, in the full conviction on both sides that they were obeying God's will, during the Thirty Years' War in seventeenth-century Europe.

These conflicts highlight the frequently made point that it is difficult, if not impossible, to know whether or not God exists and what, if anything, God wills. Once again, we run up against the problem of distinguishing between what is objec-tively morally required or demanded of us by God and what we may merely be con-vinced of for personal or even self-serving reasons is our duty. Many today, with the distance time affords, condemn the religious wars of the past as nonreligious and even antireligious. The Crusades, for example, can be seen as a decidedly non-Christian effort to exploit religious zeal for the sake of profit, plunder, and politics. At the time, however, the religious factions preparing for war were not much dif-ferent in outlook than the fictional Blues and Greens. Are we so certain of our own good motives that we can say without hesitation or fear of contradiction that, although the Crusaders and the Infidel did not understand the religious meaning of life, we do today? Then, what exactly does God command, and how do we know? If we have a special way of determining anything so precious and difficult, why were the Crusaders and their Islamic counterparts left in the dark? Why were the Protestants and Catholics less enlightened during the Thirty Years' War? Why does God not act in mysterious ways to reveal identical truths to the Blues and the Greens?

Suppose that God exists. It does not necessarily follow from the existence of God that God has a moral nature, that God as creator and sustainer of the universe is good, or that God is not evil or manifests some more humanlike mixture of good and evil. Neither does it follow that God, even if possessing moral properties, takes any interest whatsoever in the affairs of human beings. It may be that God is infinitely good but simply does not care whether human beings are good or not. God might be indifferent to our morality in much the same way, for example, that we do not necessarily care whether the fish in an aquarium, over which we hold the godlike power of life and death, are morally good or not, whether or not they are virtuous, or whether or not they treat each other fairly according to their imaginable fishy moral standards. Again, for the sake of argument, let us suppose not only that God exists but also that God has a moral nature and takes an interest in the morality of human beings. Then God might have a plan for the universe in which every person has a purpose. The meaningfulness of the world in this conception depends on the assumption that the universe is an artifact of God's will. If God creates the world, then the meaning of life is connected with whatever purpose God has for the universe. If we can find out what this purpose is, then we might be able to conduct our lives accordingly. There are difficulties in discovering what God wills, as the fable of the Blues and Greens illustrates. But there are also logical philosophical problems entailed by the idea that the meaning of life derives from the existence of God and the world as God's purposeful creation.

The first thing to observe is that, if the meaning of life is a function of God's plan for the universe, then the meaning of life transcends all human purpose except insofar as human beings bring their will into agreement with God's. This is what many religions teach, and there is nothing objectionable about philosophy reaching the same conclusion. But the religious meaning of life, if it can be upheld philosophically, is something external to natural human purposes, imposed on us from without by the supernatural agency of God. God's plan, whatever it is, is *God's* plan, and the best we can do is to accept and agree with it. It need not be a purpose that we would have arrived at for ourselves. If God is the dominant force in the universe, and if we owe our very existence to God, then it may be reasonable for us to go along with whatever higher purpose God has for the universe, and to try to bring our actions into conformity with God's plan. But could a decision to accept the purpose of a higher being give *our* lives purpose, as we ought to think of the purposefulness that would save us from the absurdity of a meaningless life's journey?

An analogy may be helpful. To accept God's plan for the universe as the meaning of human life is like being an employee in a company and making the company's purpose one's own as a condition of employment. On my own, I would not necessarily care about whether a certain business prospers, about whether a certain production quota is met, or about any of the other things that must happen in order for a company to be solvent and continue to employ a workforce. But, if my livelihood depends on the company's succeeding in meeting its purposes, then, insofar as I am a good employee, insofar as I may recognize that my economic survival and happiness depends on the company's thriving, and insofar as I may be grateful to have a job that enables me to keep body and soul together and support my family, I may be willing to make the company's purpose my own, at least during business hours. The company's purpose is not one that I would ordinarily have adopted, but it is rational for me to do so under the circumstances. In a traditional employer-employee relationship, I do not have any input in determining the company's purposes. I can either comply with the company plan and keep my job, or not comply and risk being fired.

The analogy with God's plan for the universe as the meaning of human life should be obvious. There is a direct similarity between the idea that worshipping God according to the right religion contributes to our well-being and might be rewarded with heaven and avoidance of the eternal punishments of hell in an after-life, and an employee's situation in accepting the company's purposes in order to remain in the boss's good books. To complete the argument, a more relevant comparison for the ancient and medieval world in which many of today's world religions first arose involves the relationship between a feudal lord and his vassals, rather than a company boss or board of directors and the employees, in which the dependency and adoption of an external purpose as one's own from a higher authority is enforced by the lord's power over a vassal's life and death.

The analogy is enhanced by considering differences in attitudes toward the imposition of purpose from an economically powerful entity to those who are dependent on assimilating its directives. Some people genuinely adopt their company's purposes and do not merely pretend to do so, or they switch their allegiance on when on the job and off when on their own free time. It is similar for serfs who owe a debt of gratitude to the feudal lord. Others, particularly in a thriving economy or where feudal allegiances are more fluid, might shift their loyalties from one company to another or one feudal lord to another, depending on what they perceive to be more conducive to their interests. They can be just as good and loyal workers for one company or feudal lord as for another, depending on who is currently willing to offer them the best overall package of rewards. Something similar occurs in the religious attitudes of certain believers. Some people are so devoted to a particular religion that they cannot conceive of converting from one faith to another. Religion is too serious a proposition for them, and too much a part of what they see as their personal identity. As such, religion is too fundamental a part of what they regard as inextricably connected with the meaning of life. In the ancient world, by contrast, especially among polytheists, who worshipped multiple gods, it was a frequent practice to change religions even more freely than one might change from one employer to another, looking for a better god or God in much the same way that one might look for a better job or a more profitable arrangement with a friendlier suzerain. Even today, and even among people of monotheistic faith, this type of shopping for a religion still occurs, which by implication is shopping for a different god or different conception of God corresponding to a different conception of God's plan for the universe and a different conception of the meaning of life.

The fact that some people are fickle in their religious faith does not by itself entail that the religious meaning of life is false, but it does suggest a philosophical problem. It is in a way again the problem of the Blues and Greens. Just as any of the Blues with sufficient effort should be able to conceive of being a Green and vice versa, if we strain thought a little, then, if we are Christians, we can imagine being Jewish, Islamic, Buddhist, or any other religion, and equally in the opposite direction. If the circumstances of our lives, the accidents of birth that brought us into one society and culture rather than another, had been different than they happened to be, then we might have been raised in a different religion, which we might then accept as ardently as we do the one to which we in fact belong. We may feel very strongly that the religion we accept is the only true faith and that our particular religion's teachings hold the key to the meaning of life, but so do the Blues and Greens. Can even the most powerful religious emotion provide a philosophically adequate basis for preferring one set of religious beliefs over another? In philosophy, we are guided to accept or reject beliefs on the basis of reason, reflection, and argument. This means that, unless we can put together sound reasoning with the feeling that a certain religion must be right, the mere feeling that the religion in which we have been raised is true or which we have since chosen through conversion is not a philosophically adequate basis for concluding that that religion provides an answer to the question of the meaning of life.

CAN THE MEANING OF LIFE COME FROM WITHOUT?

If God's plan constitutes the meaning of life, and if we as God's subjects are not contributors to the plan and are not even consulted in the matter, then the meaning of life is not of human origin but comes from a supernatural being outside ourselves and beyond our control. Thus, the most we can do is adopt God's external purpose derivatively as our own in somewhat the way that the most devoted employee can accept a company's goals and try to act accordingly.

We are not to imagine any sort of coercion on the part of the author of the universe, so we need not be troubled by the idea that the meaning of life is to be forced on us against our choosing. On the contrary, the model is one in which we somehow come to learn what God has ordained for the universe—the purpose for which the universe including ourselves and all other life was created—and we either accept it and conduct our lives in conformity with the divinely authorized meaning of life, or we do not—just as we suppose ourselves to be free to act or not to act in accord with the meaning of life, however it is interpreted—if the meaning of life should turn out to be the propagation of the species, the development of our talents, or any of the other possibilities that might be considered.

The problem is whether it makes sense to think of the meaning of life as independent of human purposes. Can God's plan for the universe determine the meaning of our lives? Can it be meaningful for us simply to accept what another intelligence has decided is right for us? Here we find the underlying rationale for much of the history of religious and secular strife. It is the struggle between devout acceptance of the authority of God's will and the defiant assertion of human reason in interpreting the meaning of life. The sojourner's question is as much a continuation of this ongoing religious and philosophical dispute as it is a simple attempt to decide whether life has meaning or is absurd and, if meaningful, what meaning it has. Do we human beings even so much as have the right to choose a purpose for ourselves as constituting the meaning of human life, or should we just passively accept and acquiesce to the will of a supernatural being? It is not an easy question, but one over which many of the world's great religions and philosophies are sharply divided.

The comparison with the loyalties we might have toward an employer or feudal lord is relevant. While I might decide to give up some of my personal freedom in exchange for financial gain by agreeing to work for someone else and, in doing so, make that person's purpose and plan partly my own, I do not and perhaps I cannot decide to abandon my whole purpose in living to another being. However much I like my job and however much I believe myself to gain by channeling my energies in directions predetermined for me by my boss or the company's board of directors, I do not substitute my employer's will for my own in every aspect of my life. In particular, I do not do so where such fundamental issues as what I take to be the very purpose of my life are concerned. Working for a living is just a means to an end. The end is something independent of what I must do in order to live. At least this is how we usually think of things. It would be a perversion of interests for me to allow my boss to decide everything that I am to do and all the reasons. If I were to allow that kind of intrusion into my life, there would be nothing left of me as an individual, and it would no longer be my life.

Is the same thing true if I accept God's plan as constituting the meaning of life? If God has determined the purpose of my life in every aspect and every detail, then in what sense is it still my life? This is a point of serious controversy, because some religions maintain that, in order to achieve salvation, we must totally surrender our selfish individual will and allow ourselves to be entirely absorbed in mystical union with God. The religious annihilation of the self is a desirable religious necessity to some, as the only way of achieving the meaning of life. For others, though, it is an abhorent idea that would amount to the degradation of everything that makes us human. We cannot easily settle these difficult issues here, but we can at least note the problem presented by the collision of religious and philosophical perspectives on these fundamental matters, and can begin to think about the implications of the opposed positions. What is entailed by accepting God's purpose in place of any purpose of one's own, as determining the meaning of each person's life in all its dimensions? We might accept God's plan on its merits because we agree with it and choose to live in accord with it. In that case, we retain our individuality and preserve our distinctive personhood. We are, then, in a sense, like the person who freely chooses to work for a particular employer or to serve under a particular feudal lord because it seems advantageous to do so. In that event, even if we understand the meaning of life as predetermined by God, we do so in principle by making God's idea our own, in the way that we could freely choose to accept the advice or good example of another person in making any other kind of decision, about which we could always later change our minds.

Could this basis for adopting God's purpose constitute the meaning of life? A possible objection is that the motive for accepting God's plan for the universe cannot be the exercise of free rational choice. Then the decision is comparable in every way to the decision that an employee might make to work for a certain company or that a vassal might make to serve a certain feudal lord. Here the assumption is that a person exercising rational free will makes such a decision only if the benefits are sufficiently attractive, while remaining free to seek employment or patronage elsewhere if conditions change, or if another, more favorable, opportunity arises. This cannot be the meaning of life, because the attitude of the person who accepts God's purpose for the universe on this model does so merely as a means to another end. The end is to live in a certain way or to gain certain benefits, possibly an eternal existence with God in heaven or the avoidance of eternal damnation and punishment in hell. But, then, these more ultimate goals are really the meaning of life, for the sake of which we freely choose to follow God's plan for the universe as a way of achieving that end. The decision to act in accord with God's purpose in that case is not itself the meaning of life but is merely a means to attaining the real meaning of life.

MEANING OF LIFE IN THE AFTERLIFE

It might be said that it is part of God's plan that, if we live as God commands, then it is possible that we will attain eternal life in heaven. Accepting God's purpose as the meaning of life can then include the end as well as the means to achieving the end as part of a single concept. However, the question still remains of whether on the present assumption about our motivation for following the will of God we can be understood as choosing to adopt God's purpose as our own purpose in life.

It seems that our purpose is to do as well as we can for ourselves, whatever opportunities prevail. If God offers immortality and eternal bliss, and if this is the best or even the best conceivable offer, then we may freely choose to accept it. But we do so only with the understanding that, if something better were to present itself—say, if the limits of what we find conceivable should be extended and another offer better than any from God we had previously considered were made to us—then we should feel free to accept it instead. The situation is much the same as when we think we have found the best possible employment. At first we are satisfied, but after a few years we may discover that we could find a better job or could serve a more generous feudal lord.

There are other difficulties with the idea that God's purpose could constitute the meaning of human life. The assumption implies that God, who is usually thought to be all powerful, could have a purpose for the world, the completion or satisfaction of which depends on the apparently free-will decisions of human beings either to act or not to act in accord with the divine plan. But how can an all-powerful being require the cooperation of fallible lesser agents in the created universe, and how can the purpose of an all-powerful being be left to chance fulfillment by the cooperation or noncooperation of human beings acting out of free will in conformity or disharmony with God's purpose? Theologians have ingenious things to say about these kinds of puzzles. Their reactions begin with the uninteresting answer that God's will is inscrutable and that it is a kind of impiety or blasphemy to question the nature of God. But they also include subtle efforts to distinguish between God's imposition of divine purpose on human beings and God's perfect knowledge that, in the end, human beings will freely choose to cooperate. If God's will is inscrutable, then human beings cannot know what God's purpose or plan for the universe requires of them, so they cannot bend their will to God's in adopting God's purpose for the universe as the meaning of life. If God knows in advance that some human beings will cooperate with the divine plan for the universe, then how can their cooperation be freely chosen? How can human agents fail to do anything that God knows they will do if, as it seems, that would falsify God's perfect knowledge?

However these problems might be resolved, it is clear that there is no obvious way of understanding God's will as the meaning of life. The model whereby human beings choose to accept God's purpose for the universe as their own embodies a significant disanalogy with the attitude they might take toward an employer or a feudal lord. Whatever the meaning of life is—if, indeed, life has any meaning at all—it must be the end for which we do everything else; it cannot merely be the means to another end. Is it possible, then, to have the ultimate purpose of life, as opposed to having a means of achieving that ultimate purpose or end, handed down to us from another being, even if it is the all-powerful, intelligent being God is believed to be? If God's purpose for the universe is supposed to be the end and therefore the meaning of life, and not merely the means to an independently chosen end, then we cannot freely choose to accept God's purpose for the universe as the meaning of life. To do so for the sake of heaven reinstates a human objective as the meaning of life, a goal that we can decide to accept or, however unwisely, not to accept. It might be God's purpose that we freely choose such an end, but, if we do, then it can only be as a means to realizing a human desire for eternal happiness or satisfaction, in which case God's plan or purpose for the universe does not constitute the meaning of life.

The unthinking acceptance of God's purpose, as an aspect of unconditional faith in God, is required by many religions in order to enter fully into the spirit of the religious way of life. But philosophers must ask whether such a view of the religious meaning of life is conceptually coherent or whether it harbors a hidden logical inconsistency. The problem is that, in attributing purpose to someone, we generally suppose that the person deliberately or intentionally adopts a particular goal. If my will merges with God's, then in a sense I no longer continue to exist as a distinct person, capable of intentionally adopting any goal. A worse difficulty is that, if my will mystically merges with God's in uncritically adopting God's purpose for the universe as the meaning of life, then it appears that I cannot do so for any good reason. If I were to accept God's plan as the end of life, then my reason could only be that I agree with it or somehow find it advantageous. But I can do so only if I understand where the universe is going and apply my own standards of judgment in accepting its direction. Otherwise, I must adopt a life's goal that I do not fully comprehend, which for that reason could not be a purposive, deliberate choice that I can accept as the meaning of life.

If we are candid, we must admit that we do not know the outcome of the universe. Much of the motivation for those who want to accept God's plan for the world as the meaning of life is that we must do so purely on faith, without reason or justification. If I adopt a religious interpretation of the meaning of life, then I may prefer to place my trust in a supernatural authority, precisely because I do not know where the universe is going or what my place in it is supposed to be. I may desire to leave things in the infinitely more capable hands of the creator of the world, whom I may believe knows and can do whatever is needed to enable the universe to achieve its purpose, far beyond my limited knowledge and abilities. However, for this very reason, the blind acceptance of God's purpose could not constitute the meaning of life, for it would lack all personal meaning, and so would not be the purpose of my life.

LIFE AS A SOJOURN FROM BIRTH TO DEATH

At last we are in a position to consider the second interpretation of the sojourner's question. According to this reading, the meaning of life might be understood in terms of all of life as a sojourn. If life itself is a sojourn, then it is merely a way station along life's path from birth to death and, perhaps, to an afterlife.

The meaning of life in such a conception is fulfilled only after we have died and gone on to another existence. We have already examined the idea of the purpose of life as preparation for death and judgment, as a trial by which we may prove ourselves worthy of eternal life in heaven and avoidance of hell. When Dante in the epigraph to this chapter speaks of coming upon himself midway through life's journey in a dark wood, he is speaking metaphorically, even if he did arrive at a moment of self-reflection while walking in a forest. The metaphor is descriptive of the somber mood in which he begins to think seriously about the meaning of life, as we might, whether, like Dante, we are at midpoint or only beginning our lives. Neither is it accidental that Dante in this way introduces his three-part *Divine Comedy,* in which he considers the soul's fate after death in hell, purgatory, and heaven. If life is but a sojourn in the soul's journey from conception or birth to our final destination in heaven, hell, or somewhere inbetween, then the meaning of life might be to prepare ourselves for whatever is to follow. We will not try to address this possibility definitively for now but, having posed the question, take note of the philosophical issues raised by the concept of life as a temporary sojourn on the way to a more meaningful existence in God's greater scheme of things.

The mystery of individual human existence and the challenge of deciding how we are to live is the sojourner's question. Are we simply animals with a biological nature and biological destiny, or is there something more to life than birth, satisfaction of immediate needs, procreation, and death? The sojourner's question concerns the path of life and its meaning for each individual, and it is the kind of question we can ask only when, like Dante, we have reached a midway point along the journey. We must be far enough along to know what it means to be on the path, to have already had experiences to reflect on, with a bit of distance from the journey itself and the leisure to pause and consider these matters. There are fundamental philosophical problems about the direction we must choose in each step we take along the path of life, and about the direction and meaning, if any, of the path itself. If life is a journey, where is it headed, and what are we to think about it along the way?

These are difficult questions, among the most difficult we could ask. Whether there is a higher purpose to life than pursuing our perceived needs and wants is a topic that takes us beyond the scope of all the other kinds of problems we ordinarily try to solve. We spend a great deal of energy in training for a career, finding a mate, raising children, accumulating wealth and material goods, building and outfitting a home, seeking pleasure and entertainment, maintaining health, and, if we are lucky enough to survive to this point, retiring and making our old age as comfortable as possible until we die. This sequence of events consists both of choices we make and things that happen to us that are largely out of our control. If we are faced with choices at each step along the path, how are we to decide what to do, and what sorts of considerations should guide our decision making? As we move forward through life, should our attention be fixed on what we need to survive and prosper in a purely material sense, or is it reasonable to suppose that our activity should also, at least sometimes, be directed toward higher goals? What higher goals could there be, how could we know or find out about them, and what does it mean to think of them as higher?

It might be said that, although life is meaningless in that there is no single, universal purpose that gives meaning to everyone's life, life nevertheless is meaningful in a more important sense, because each person can give meaning to his or her life in an individual, personally satisfying way. This is potentially comforting, but it does not solve the philosophical question of whether or not life is meaningful in providing an ultimate purpose for the lives of all intelligent beings, regardless of their success or failure in satisfying their particular desires under particular circumstances.

We have not yet tried to answer the sojourner's question, but we have already brought together some important clues. We have considered and discovered difficulties in the following suggestions. The meaning of life, it has seemed reasonable to suppose, might be found in developing our talents and abilities, in biologically reproducing ourselves and contributing to the continuity of the species, in trying to live a morally correct life, in setting and achieving personally satisfying goals, and in obeying the will of God and preparing our souls for judgment and eternity. In order to pursue any of these possibilities, we must first decide whether we can know anything at all and then, more specifically, whether we can know anything about the meaning of life, about who and what kinds of things we are, about the existence and nature of God, and about what is morally right and wrong. Thus, we embark on a preliminary philosophical investigation that will take us through the remainder of this book as we determine the kinds of answers we can give to the sojourner's question. We must investigate the concept of knowledge to determine what, if anything, we can know and how we can know it. We must investigate the concept of mind in order to understand what kinds of beings we as thinking things are, and to decide whether we can make free and morally responsible choices. We must investigate the concept of God, the problem of whether it is possible to prove or disprove the existence of God, and what, if anything, can be known about God's nature. We must investigate the concept of virtue, moral good and evil, and the considerations that motivate us to do what is morally right. Then, having explored these ideas and gained experience in several kinds of philosophical reasoning, we can turn more reflectively toward philosophy itself and can examine its scope, limits, and proper methodology. Finally, if we make progress in all of these areas, we may at last be in a position to return to the sojourner's question and to try again, with more powerful philosophical methods at our disposal, to answer the question of the meaning of life.

CHAPTER TWO

Knowledge and Skepticism

Our treasure lies in the beehive of our knowledge. We are perpetually on the way thither, being by nature winged insects and honey gatherers of the mind.
—Friedrich Nietzsche
The Genealogy of Morals, 1887

CONCEPTS OF KNOWLEDGE

What can we know? Is it possible to attain knowledge? If so, how do we go about discovering what can be known? To begin to answer any of these questions, we must first try to define the concept of knowledge, to understand what it means to know something. If it turns out to be impossible to acquire knowledge, if we cannot really know anything, then it may be pointless to continue our philosophical journey.

To make progress in trying to answer the sojourner's question, we first need to decide whether and what we can come to know about ourselves, our lives, the world, and the meaningfulness or absurdity of life. That is the task of this chapter's inquiry into the nature of knowledge and skepticism. We must try to clarify the meaning of knowledge and to decide whether and how it is possible to know. Then we can apply these general lessons more specifically to the problem of knowing whether life is meaningful and what, if anything, we can know about the meaning of life. The philosophical study of the concept of and conditions for knowledge is referred to as theory of knowledge, or epistemology, from the Greek word *epistêmê,* which means knowledge.

We can begin by considering the things we claim to know and the circumstances under which we attribute or deny knowledge to ourselves and others. We might be mistaken in making these judgments, so we must be prepared to withdraw them if they turn out to be unjustified, but they are as good a place as any to start our investigation. Typically, we say that we know many kinds of things. We know, or perhaps we should say that we believe we know, that we are human beings, that red is a color, that $2 + 2 = 4$, and many other things. What can we say about the knowledge we seem to have about these matters?

Knowledge appears to be something that we as knowing subjects add to the world by virtue of having certain mental states. If I know something, then I am in a psychological condition with respect to a presumed fact or state of affairs, such as the fact, if it is a fact, that I am now sitting out on my back porch watching hummingbirds drinking snapdragon nectar. What is this psychological condition? I suppose that I am in a particular mental state or that I have a particular attitude toward the presumed fact that I am here observing the hummingbirds. Knowing is something a psychological subject does, and knowledge is something a psychological subject has by virtue of being in a certain psychological state. The psychological state that constitutes knowledge might be described as a special kind of belief. If I know that there are hummingbirds here, it must be because I believe that there are hummingbirds, provided that my belief has certain further characteristics.

Of course, not all beliefs qualify as genuine knowledge. I might believe that I can benchpress 350 pounds. But, if I am unable to do so, if my belief is false, then surely I do not know. If someone believes that aliens from outer space built the great pyramids of Egypt, but the belief turns out to be false, then the person cannot correctly be said to know that the pyramids were built by aliens. We have many beliefs, some of which constitute knowledge, and others of which do not and are only beliefs. To speak of knowledge is to refer to a special kind or category of belief. A belief must satisfy additional requirements in order to qualify as knowledge. Since we refuse to grant that a false belief is knowledge, we can now add the qualification that knowledge is not just any belief but, more particularly, a true belief. If we claim to know something, but it turns out that our belief is false, then, if we are intellectually honest, we ought to withdraw our claim to know and to admit that we only thought or believed that we knew—or thought or believed that we had knowledge—but that we did not actually know.

KNOWLEDGE AS TRUE BELIEF

Accordingly, we can consider the proposition that knowledge is true belief. Does this qualification provide an adequate definition of knowledge? Is anything else missing, or is the idea now complete?

Again, we can test the analysis by asking whether there are instances of true belief that do not constitute knowledge, even if all instances of knowledge are true beliefs. When we question a definition in this way, we are asking whether its conditions are correct, or whether it is subject to *counterexamples.* A counterexample tries to show that there is a lack of agreement between the terms of a definition. A definition always consists of two main parts—a term or concept or a set of terms or concepts being defined, and a term (or, more usually, a phrase or set of terms or concepts) that provides the meaning of the term or concept to be defined. It is customary to link the two parts of the definition or conceptual analysis by means of a kind of identity sign, =df, which says that the term or terms on the left of the sign are being defined by the term or terms on the right. We can read this symbol as saying "is defined as" or "is identical by definition with."

There is a technical way of referring to the components of a definition. The term to be defined on the left of the =df sign is standardly known as the *definiendum,* and the term, phrase, or set of terms or concepts on the right of the sign, which provides the meaning of the term to be defined, is known as the *definiens.* The general form of a definition can be represented schematically in this way: *definiendum* =df *definiens.* A counterexample to a definition or conceptual analysis tries to find a situation in which the *definiendum* of a proposed definition is satisfied but the *definiens* is not satisfied or, oppositely, by a situation in which the *definiens* is satisfied but the *definiendum* is not satisfied. When we deny that knowledge is simply belief, on the grounds that a false belief does not constitute knowledge, we are already making use of the counterexample method. Specifically, we are putting forward a counterexample to the proposed definition that knowledge =df belief, in which the *definiens* of belief is satisfied by a false belief, but the *definiendum* knowledge is not satisfied.

Philosophers often give painstaking attention to the definitions of certain terms, because they want to understand the concepts that can lead to philosophical problems. Otherwise, they believe that we might reach false conclusions based on misunderstandings of basic ideas. Accordingly, philosophers usually want to clarify the most fundamental concepts as a necessary preliminary to elaborating a philosophical theory or explanation, or to arriving at a sound philosophical view of any problem. When following a philosophical argument, and in undertaking philosophical inquiry of our own, we must be patient with the process and try to understand how, in this case, the definition of knowledge might be further refined. We can use the counterexample method to test the analysis of knowledge as true belief to see if the revised definition stands up to philosophical scrutiny. If we cannot find a counterexample to the definition, then we can at least provisionally conclude that the definition may be acceptable. If, on the other hand, we discover a counterexample to the analysis, then we must reject the definition and try to redefine the concept in such a way as to avoid objections. The process can continue indefinitely, unless or until we are satisfied that we have arrived at an adequate analysis and are ready to accept and make use of the concept.

We should therefore try to criticize the new and improved definition, by which knowledge =df true belief. Is this definition counterexample-proof? Can we think of a case in which we have knowledge but it is not a true belief? Probably not, since we have already agreed that knowledge is the particular kind of mental state ordinarily referred to as belief, and we have seen that if a belief is not true then it cannot qualify as a genuine instance of knowledge. What, then, about a counterexample occurring in the opposite direction, for a situation in which we have a true belief that is not knowledge? Are there circumstances in which a true belief does not yet constitute knowledge?

Suppose that I visit a fortune teller. Madame Rosa examines the lines and creases in the palm of my hand and predicts that I will soon meet a tall dark stranger. My faith in fortune tellers might be such that I come away with the belief, or even the firm conviction, that I will soon meet a tall dark stranger. Tall dark strangers abound, and it is not that hard to meet one, so suppose further that my belief turns out to be true. I do, in fact, meet a tall dark stranger, just as Madame Rosa said I would. Thus, I had a belief—as it turns out, a true belief—that I would meet a tall dark stranger. But did I *know* that I would meet a tall dark stranger? Did I have *knowledge* that such a thing would definitely occur, and did my true belief that I would meet a tall dark stranger constitute *knowing* that this would happen? Most persons on reflection will deny that the fortune teller really knew such a thing but that, at most, she made a lucky guess. It follows by implication, then, that I did not acquire genuine knowledge from the fortune teller by believing what she claimed to discover in reading my palm.

The reason the fortune teller's hocus pocus does not confer knowledge, even if it induces true belief, is that we do not expect that consulting the lines in a person's palm determines any connection with the events that will happen in the future. More generally, we can say that it seems to be entirely accidental that I happened to meet a tall dark stranger after being told by the fortune teller that I would. The fortune teller was either guessing or mistakenly believed certain implications of the palm reader's craft that later just happened to make my belief true. What is absent from this situation to prevent true belief from qualifying as knowledge is a good reason, or *justification,* for believing what later by chance turns out to be true. Where someone genuinely knows, we expect the person not only to have a true belief but also to have sound justification for what he or she believes. Interpreting the natural contours and crevices in the palm of a hand is not regarded, except by the most gullible, as a good enough reason for believing what the fortune teller predicts, because there does not seem to be any direct connection between patterns in the skin and what will happen to a person in the future.

There are several ways in which we can disprove the fortune teller's methods. We are reminded of the frequency with which tall dark strangers are encountered and of the fact that there does not seem to be any causal relation between the patterns and texture of the inside of the hand and the occurrences in a person's life, whereby one could serve as reliable evidence of the other. We can also perform a simple experiment to verify the unreliability of fortune telling. We can accompany someone with a very different configuration of palm lines whom Madame Rosa has predicted will not meet a tall dark stranger, and observe in either case, whether we both meet or do not meet a tall dark stranger, that at least one of the fortune teller's predictions will turn out not to be true. The ability to tell the future by such techniques is surely a superstition with no basis in science or common sense. By contrast, we expect knowledge to rest on something more secure, to carry with it at least a reasonable degree of justification for a true belief to count as knowledge. The same applies to reading tea leaves, gazing into a crystal ball, or laying down tarot cards. None of these practices provides knowledge, even when they give rise to the most sincerely held beliefs, and even when such beliefs happen to turn out to be true in a remarkable series of coincidences. If, on the contrary, a fortune teller were always right in predicting very specific matters with no other explanation of how the correct answers were obtained, we might be tentatively inclined to ascribe knowledge to whatever true beliefs the fortune teller inspires. As it is, however, from the standpoint of our general background understanding of how the world works—and, in particular, of the kinds of events that can provide good evidence for predicting another set of events—we do not regard palm reading and other kinds of fortune telling entertainments as providing the justification needed to constitute knowledge.

KNOWLEDGE AS JUSTIFIED TRUE BELIEF

If, however, the fortune teller counterexample defeats the definition of knowledge as merely true belief, the question then becomes, What is missing from the analysis? What must we add to the concept of true belief in order for true belief to qualify as knowledge? In other words, how can we prevent the fortune teller counterexample from refuting a strengthened, even newer and more improved definition of the concept of knowledge?

The suggestion that might be inferred from the counterexample is that true belief is not enough for knowledge in the absence of a good reason, justification, or warrant in support of the belief. If we incorporate this additional condition in the revised definition of knowledge, then we can consider an amended version of the analysis, according to which knowledge =df justified true belief.

This is a definition of knowledge that has had a wide following in the history of philosophy. But it, too, is unacceptable. The more sophisticated the definition of a concept becomes, the more sophisticated the counterexamples to it must also be made in order to discover a mismatch between *definiendum* and *definiens*. This is certainly true in the case of the definition of the concept of knowledge. We have now refined the original crude definition to the point at which it contains three separate conditions, stating that knowledge is (1) justified (2) true (3) belief. The definition in this form covers many of the standard cases in which people appear to assert correctly that they know or are in possession of genuine knowledge. In such cases, individuals have beliefs that are not only true but are also such that they have good reasons for accepting their beliefs as true. We might even wish to say that in ordinary cases this is just what it means to say that a person knows. However, the search for counterexamples often requires us to consider the most unusual imaginable kinds of problem cases. We want a correct definition to stand up to the most extreme type of counterexamples, and this requires that we consider extraordinary situations that push a definition beyond the limits of its ordinary intended applications.

Such cases are strange but not difficult to imagine. Philosophers who criticize definitions spend a lot of time and energy trying to find obscure situations in which the *definiendum* but not the *definiens* of a definition, or the reverse, is satisfied. Following is a problem that philosophers have discussed at length with respect to the once widely accepted analysis of knowledge as justified true belief. Suppose that someone paints a gold coin with gold-colored paint made out of a nongold substance. The person shows me the coin, and because it looks gold, exactly like other gold coins I have seen, I believe that the coin is gold. In fact, the coin is gold, so my belief is true. I am also justified in believing that the coin is gold because it looks gold, having been painted that color, and because I have no reason to believe that any kind of hoax has been perpetrated. All told, I have a justified true belief that the coin is gold. But do I *know* that the coin is gold? It appears that I do not know that the coin is gold, despite having a justified true belief that it is gold.

The reason why I do not know the coin is gold is that I believe the coin is gold only because of a very peculiar kind of evidence. I see the gold-colored, nongold, painted surface of the coin, but this evidence is irrelevant to the fact that the coin beneath the paint is actually gold. I have no evidence in seeing only the painted surface of the coin that the coin is actually made of gold, because I do not see the gold metal of the coin underneath the layer of paint, which does not provide any part of my justification for truly believing that the coin is gold. The problem is that I have justification for my belief that the coin is gold, but my justification is of such a kind that what makes my belief true, seeing the painted surface of the coin, is not good enough evidence for the fact that the coin beneath the paint is actually gold. The coin beneath the paint, for all that I know in perceiving the surface, could be a substance other than gold. In ordinary cases, we expect that when we know something, there is a connection between the state of affairs that justifies a true belief and the state of affairs that makes the belief true. If there is any disparity between the two, we are reluctant to credit a justified true belief as an instance of knowledge. In this case, the counterexample depends on the fact that it is just a lucky accident that my belief that the coin is gold is true, even though I have good (but not good enough) justification for believing that the coin is gold. The coin is, in fact, gold, but I could not be said to know that it is gold on the basis of seeing its gold-colored, nongold, painted surface, which might, after all, disguise any other kind of metal.

Admittedly, the counterexample is arcane. We do not ordinarily expect anyone to paint a gold coin with gold-colored, nongold paint. But the fact that such a thing could logically happen is enough to challenge the definition of knowledge as justified true belief. We can imagine many other variations on this theme in which we would otherwise be deluded into thinking that we have genuine knowledge when we have only justified true belief that falls short of knowledge. In all such cases, we would be wrong, because the evidence we take as justification does not entitle us to know that the belief we have accepted is true. If I see a neighbor drive away in a BMW every day, I might come to believe that the neighbor owns a BMW. This belief might also be true if the neighbor, in fact, owns a BMW. Seeing someone drive that kind of car out of her garage every day further justifies accepting the belief. But, if the neighbor owns a BMW other than the one I see driven, and the one I see the neighbor drive is not the one she owns but is, instead, rented or borrowed, then I ought to conclude that I do not really know that my neighbor owns a BMW, even though I have a justified true belief that she owns a BMW.

The problem in this case, as with the painted coin, is that the evidence that justifies my belief is irrelevant to the facts that make the belief true. As far as the evidence that justifies accepting the belief goes, it is purely accidental that the belief happens to be true. There is no relevant connection between the state of affairs that justifies me in believing what I believe and the state of affairs that makes the belief true. I have justification, so I satisfy the amended definition of knowledge as justified true belief, but I do not have enough, good enough, or the right kind of justification, for knowledge.

KNOWLEDGE AS RELEVANTLY JUSTIFIED TRUE BELIEF

As before, in light of this more elaborate counterexample, we must now ask what is missing from the definition. What additional condition should be added to close the gap in the analysis, so that the counterexample cannot arise?

If we can answer this question, then we will be in an excellent position to refine the definition of knowledge so that it comes even closer and may finally perfectly satisfy the requirements of a correct definition to express an exact match between the concepts of the *definiendum* and *definiens*. A definition that successfully avoids all counterexamples is sometimes said to be bulletproof, so we can say that we are in search of a bulletproof refinement of the analysis of the concept of knowledge.

One obvious way to proceed is to strengthen the requirement of justification so that the counterexamples are avoided. This could be done by demanding that, in order to know something, a true belief must be so strongly justified that there is no possibility of being mistaken. This suggestion turns knowledge into absolutely certain knowledge, which seems to be a different concept. We will see that such a revision is too strong for the way in which we ordinarily think of knowledge. To avoid the painted coin and rented BMW counterexamples to the definition of knowledge as justified true belief by strengthening the concept of justification to infallible justification might, therefore, make the concept of knowledge too far distant from the way we generally think about knowledge. Thus, I might be said to know that I have five fingers on my right hand, because I can see them as clearly before me as I can see anything else, I have good reason to believe that I am not hallucinating or dreaming, and other people who have been reliable in their judgments in the past also inform me that they perceive no more and no fewer than five fingers on my right hand. What more proof, what better justification, could I want? However, even in this knowledge claim it remains possible that I am mistaken. I might after all be hallucinating or dreaming, even though it does not seem that way, no matter how vivid my experience and no matter how unlikely it appears that I could be deceived when I look at my hand directly before me and hear the corroborating testimony of other people who also express the belief that my hand has five fingers. Thus, it appears that, if we are going to say that we know any of the kinds of things we think we know, then defining knowledge as requiring infallible justification is too extreme a way of avoiding the gold coin and BMW counterexamples. A definition of that sort would err on the opposite side by making the *definiens* so hard to satisfy that virtually none of the things we suppose ourselves to know would constitute genuine knowledge. If we get desperate enough, we might reconsider this solution, but before we reach that point it will be worthwhile to investigate the alternatives.

A better possibility is to introduce a category of fallible justification, in which there is a direct connection between the state of affairs that justifies someone in accepting a true belief and the state of affairs that makes the belief true. Clearly, there are both types of justification: one in which the connection holds—as in ordinary, unproblematic cases of justified true belief that qualify as knowledge— and another in which the connection does not hold, as in the painted coin and rented BMW counterexamples. The difference in the two kinds of justification is straightforward. We need only find an appropriate terminology to distinguish the two, so that we can require that knowledge involve only the sort of justification in which a connection exists between the state of affairs that justifies us in accepting a true belief and the state of affairs that makes the belief true. Justification in which an evidential connection exists between the state of affairs that justifies the knower in accepting a true belief and the state of affairs that makes the belief true is called *relevant justification,* as opposed to irrelevant justification or just plain, good old-fashioned unqualified justification. Then we can redefine knowledge as relevantly justified true belief: knowledge =df relevantly justified true belief. All that remains to complete the analysis is to explain the concept of relevant justification. In effect, we need to define relevant justification, so that we can plug it into the newly redesigned definition of knowledge.

We now say that relevant justification is justification in which a particular kind of connection exists between the state of affairs that justifies someone in accepting a true belief and the state of affairs that makes the belief true. The only question is how we should think of this connection. There are several possibilities, which we may briefly consider before settling on what appears to be the appropriate condition.

We could say that relevant justification requires that the state of affairs that justifies someone in accepting a true belief and the state of affairs that makes the belief true must be identical. Or we might prefer to say that relevant justification entails a rather different kind of relation, something weaker than identity. What is the result if we define relevant justification in terms of a strict identity holding between the state of affairs that justifies someone in accepting a true belief and the state of affairs that makes the belief true?

Identity may be too strong a relation for relevant justification. The state of affairs that justifies me in believing that there is a gold coin before me is that I see a gold-colored coin and that I have no reason to believe that the color I am seeing is not the color of the metal substance of the coin. The state of affairs that makes it true that the coin is gold is that the coin is, in fact, made of gold. These states of affairs are obviously not identical, and this may make it tempting to conclude that the counterexample is best avoided by stipulating that such states of affairs be identical in order to provide relevant justification.

However, we should not rush to judgment. Before we adopt this definition of relevant justification, we would do well to consider what happens in ordinary cases in which there is genuine knowledge. Suppose that I see an unpainted gold coin and conclude from the evidence that the coin is gold. Does it make sense to say that the state of affairs that justifies me in believing that the coin is gold is identical to the state of affairs that makes it true that the coin is gold? Not at all, because the state of affairs that justifies me in believing that the coin is gold is my perceiving the gold color of the coin, which is not the same as the coin's being gold or being made of gold. The state of affairs of my seeing the gold color of the coin is not identical to the coin's being gold or being made of gold. There is rather another kind of relation between the two states of affairs, in which my seeing the gold color of the coin provides evidence for my belief that the coin is gold. Consider, as another example, the relation that holds between a sudden change in a barometer taken as justification for the belief that there will soon be a storm. The fact that there has been a drop in the barometer, let alone the fact that I see the barometer's needle or the column of mercury in a tube fall dramatically, is plainly not the meteorological state of affairs that makes it true, if it is true, that a storm will soon begin. Yet the change in the barometer or my seeing the change in the barometer is ordinarily regarded, against a background of independently justified beliefs, as good justification for knowing that a storm is likely to occur.

We should therefore explain relevant justification not as identity of the state of affairs that justifies a true belief with the state of affairs that makes the belief true but, rather, as a relation in which the state of affairs that makes the belief true also makes it evident that the belief is true. We can call this an *evidentiary* relation. If we emphasize, as some philosophers have done, the fact that it is always a person's perception of a state of affairs, rather than the state of affairs itself, that directly justifies psychological belief states, then the state of affairs that makes a proposition true will virtually never be identical to the states of affairs that justify the person's belief that the proposition is true. The fact that I see my neighbor drive a BMW is usually sufficient empirical evidence to know that my neighbor drives, even if she does not own, a BMW. But my seeing such a state of affairs by itself is not the state of affairs that makes the proposition that my neighbor drives a BMW true. There is, instead, an evidentiary relation between my neighbor's driving a BMW, my seeing my neighbor drive a BMW, and my coming to believe the proposition that my neighbor drives a BMW. As a result, the concept of relevant justification requires a condition in which the state of affairs that makes a belief true provides sufficient evidence to justify someone in believing that it is true.

We are now in a position to redefine knowledge as relevantly justified true belief. Where the relevant justification of a true belief is understood as a relation in which the state of affairs that makes a belief true also provides good enough evidence to justify believing that the proposition is true, the painted coin and rented BMW counterexamples cannot arise. I am justified but not relevantly justified in believing, as happens to be true, that the painted coin is gold, because the state of affairs that makes the coin gold does not provide the evidence that justifies me in believing that the coin is gold. My belief is nonrelevantly justified only by my perceiving its nongold gold-colored coat of paint. I am justified but not relevantly justified in believing what happens to be true, that my neighbor owns a BMW, because the state of affairs that makes it true that the neighor owns a BMW is not the evidence by which I come to believe that my neighbor owns a BMW. In order to arrive at relevant justification in the two cases, I would need to examine the true metal of the coin beneath the surface of paint to know that it is gold, and to check with the register of motor vehicles to know that my neighbor owns a BMW other than the one I see her drive.

If our analysis has been correct, then we now have a very powerful, if not absolutely bulletproof, definition of knowledge. The content of the definition reinforces the importance of clarifying the concept of knowledge before trying to make further progress toward the solution to other philosophical problems, such as the sojourner's question. The problem in this instance is so vital in understanding the meaning of human life and our place in the universe that only knowing the answer, knowing that there is no answer, or knowing that we cannot know the answer, will satisfy our desire. As we now see, having struggled with the definition, only *knowledge*—not mere belief, or even true but unjustified belief, or justified but not relevantly justified true belief—as *relevantly justified true belief,* can offer the answer we seek. We want to *know* whether life has meaning or is absurd, and we want to *know* what meaning, if any, it has.

SKEPTICISM AND CERTAINTY

Now that we have a good working definition of knowledge, we can ask whether knowledge is possible. This is not something to be taken for granted. Many philosophers have doubted whether we can know anything. There are numerous challenges to the possibility of knowledge, all of which collectively are classified as various forms of *skepticism.* Skepticism is the view that knowledge is unattainable. We will discuss three main sources of epistemological skepticism: (1) the problem of certainty, (2) a dilemma about acquiring knowledge, and (3) the diallelus, or problem of the circularity of epistemic criteria for true beliefs.

Some skeptics regard knowledge as impossible, because they believe that the concept of knowledge implies *certainty,* and because they further believe that certainty is impossible for human epistemic agents to achieve. What do we mean by certainty, and do or should we require knowledge to be absolutely certain? There are several kinds and degrees of strength of certainty. Certainty can be distinguished into two main categories, *psychological* and *epistemic.* Psychological certainty is merely a state of mind. We are certain of something in this sense when we feel a deep conviction that a belief we hold is true. I say, for example, that I know that my father once owned a horse. When someone asks, "Are you sure?" I may reply that I am sure, I am certain, or, for special emphasis, I am *absolutely* certain. By this, I mean that there is no question in my mind about the truth of my belief. In some cases, I strongly believe that a proposition is true, while, in other cases, I strongly believe that a proposition is not true; in still other cases, I do not strongly believe that a proposition is true or false, and I might or might not incline toward belief or disbelief.

When I strongly believe something, I might express the degree of my lack of psychological hesitation or sense of compulsion in accepting a proposition by saying that I am certain that it is true. In this situation, I might experience no nagging doubts; on the contrary, I might feel psychologically driven to affirm the truth of my belief. In the case of my belief that my father once owned a horse, I might find my belief reinforced by a mental image of my father with a horse or memories of my father and other people speaking of his having owned a horse, together with photographs or other kinds of documents that testify to my father having owned a horse. These memories might be so vivid and compelling that, when I reflect on the proposition, I find that they leave me no choice but to believe that my father once owned a horse. In terms of our analysis of the concept of knowledge, my memories might provide what for me at the time appears to be the strongest possible evidence of both the truth and relevant justification of my belief that my father once owned a horse. This overpowering psychological sense that a belief is irrefutably true is the psychological sense of certainty.

In addition to psychological certainty, there is another sense called epistemic certainty. Psychological certainty is subjective, because it depends on one's internal feelings about the truth or justification of a belief. No matter how strong our sense of psychological certainty, by itself it does not guarantee the truth or justification of a belief—except, perhaps, the belief that we believe something. There is no contradiction or inconsistency in the idea that, despite my psychological sense of absolute certainty that my father once owned a horse, in fact, my father never owned a horse. I believe it is true with all my heart, but it might turn out to be false. The photographs and vivid memories that contribute to my unshakable personal conviction that my father once owned a horse might be mistaken—in which case, perhaps they can all be explained in a way that did not occur to me while I was in the grip of my overpowering sense of psychological certainty. Maybe a brother actually owned the horse but always allowed my father to use it. And perhaps my father, who badly wanted a horse of his own, frequently spoke of the horse as though it were his, thereby setting in motion the false word-of-mouth testimony that he owned a horse, spreading through the family as part of our folklore, where at last it reached me to influence my belief.

If psychological certainty is a subjective state of mind, and if it is no guarantee of truth, then there does not seem to be a good reason to require that knowledge must be psychologically certain in addition to being relevantly justified. In this light, psychological certainty appears only to color the strength of the belief we have in a given proposition, but it does not add anything to the question of whether the belief is true or relevantly justified. Knowledge does not seem to require that we accept a belief to any particular degree of psychological conviction. As long as we believe a proposition, the question of whether the belief qualifies as knowledge does not seem to depend on how fervently we believe it. Furthermore, as we have just seen, the most ardent acceptance of a belief by itself does not confer knowledge status on the belief. It may happen that when we know something we also experience a sense of psychological certainty about its truth or relevant justification. But the examples suggest that this is the purely accidental accompaniment of a psychological state that arises in a secondary way when the conditions for the truth and relevant justification of the belief are satisfied. When my belief is true and relevantly justified, these facts—depending on my personality, among other things—might reinforce the strength of my conviction in the truth and justification of the belief to the point of psychological certainty. However, since psychological certainty can be a mistaken guide to truth and relevant justification, and since I can rightly be said to have knowledge even when the degree of conviction of my belief does not amount to psychological certainty, provided that the belief is true and relevantly justified, it seems best not to superadd psychological certainty as a further requirement of knowledge.

Therefore, skeptics who have wanted to challenge the possibility of knowledge have generally avoided psychological certainty and instead have proposed that epistemic certainty is an unattainable requirement of genuine knowledge. The concept of epistemic certainty implies that a belief, regardless of the degree of psychological certainty or lack thereof that happens to accompany the belief, cannot reasonably be rejected. Whereas psychological certainty is subjective, epistemic certainty is objective. We can define epistemic certainty not as a subjective state of mind or feeling, but as an objective condition by virtue of which no possible circumstance could justify us in rejecting a belief.

A THOUGHT EXPERIMENT

I believe with an overwhelming sense of psychological certainty that I have a body with a head, torso, arms, legs, and two hands with five fingers each. But is my belief also epistemically certain? The answer is that the belief is not epistemically certain if I can imagine circumstances that could justify me in disaffirming the belief. But could anything possibly cause me to reject the belief that I have the two hands I see directly before me?

Philosophers try to address these kinds of questions by engaging in *thought experiments.* A thought experiment is literally an experiment, but one that is carried out in the imagination rather than in a laboratory with test tubes and particle accelerators. Thought experiments can be as fictional and as distant from our ordinary assumptions about the way the world actually is as the counterexamples by which we critically evaluate the adequacy of definitions. Indeed, the two methods, counterexamples and thought experiments, often go hand-in-hand. Let us try to imagine a thought experiment in which I believe with psychological certainty that I have the two hands I now see before me, but also in which conceivable circumstances would lead me to recant or at least to question my belief, showing that I do not thereby have epistemic certainty.

The thought experiment is going to be a little farfetched, but the point is to describe a logically possible situation that could cause me to reverse my judgment that I have two hands. The greater the sense of psychological certainty I have in a belief, and my psychological certainty that I have two hands is naturally very strong and powerful, the more bizarre the thought experiment must be to cast doubt on my belief. Thus, imagine that, as I was crossing the street earlier today, I was run down by a speeding car and instantly lost consciousness. A medical emergency team rushed to the scene and quickly put me on a state-of-the-art life support system while I was taken to the university research hospital. At the hospital, there happened to be visiting a brilliant neurosurgeon from Scandinavia who had just perfected a new surgical technique whereby the brain and spinal cord can be kept alive and functioning normally, even when detached from the rest of the body.

The accident leaves me so thoroughly damaged that no part of my body can be salvaged except my brain and several feet of spinal cord. The surgeon preserves this neurological tissue in a glass fishtank filled with special salts and electrically stimulated by electrodes. There my brain continues to function more or less as it would if it were still housed within my body and connected to all my sense organs and muscles by way of the nervous network. The surgeon and her assistants do not want me to experience a severe psychological trauma by discovering too suddenly that I have lost all the rest of my body, so they introduce a carefully prescribed series of chemical agents directly into the liquid in which my brain and spinal cord are immersed. The chemicals are chosen to stimulate the cortex of my brain directly so as to induce in me a continuous sequence of sensations precisely like those I would have experienced if the rest of my body had never been destroyed. The laboratory assistant adds substances to the chemical bath in which my brain has been placed that give me indistinguishably the same sensations I would have undergone if I had not been struck by the automobile but had continued safely on my way across the street and through the rest of my day.

The world for me as a brain in a fishtank is no different to me than what I would encounter in a typical afternoon. I cross the street and never see or hear the car that hits me. I walk to the library, look up a book that I want to read, check my mail and see if there are any letters I need to answer immediately, have lunch at a taco stand and drip pepper sauce on my shirt, and finally meet with some of my friends at the gym to play racquetball. I am as psychologically certain of all of these things actually happening to me as I am that my five fingers are still on each hand. However, in fact, I have done none of these things, because I no longer have most of my body. What is left of me is only my brain and spinal cord floating in a fishtank of chemicals and being gently jolted by electrical wires, sitting on a shelf in the laboratory at the university research hospital. I did not cross the street. I did not go to the library. I did not have a taco for lunch and drip hot sauce on my shirt. I did not meet my friends at the gym to play racquetball. To do these things, I would need a head and a torso, with arms, legs, hands, and feet, whereas, on the present assumption, I have none of these body parts. I merely believe with psychological certainty that I have them because of the way in which my brain in the fishtank is reacting to the chemicals that have been added.

Then the surgeon and her assistants want to begin to make me aware that I have lost almost all of my body and have become only a brain in a fishtank. They inject a special chemical dose that gives me the sensation of hearing my friends at the gym talking about someone who was run down by a car earlier that day and had experimental surgery to save his brain and nervous system in a tank of liquids by a brilliant Scandinavian brain surgeon. Finally, they get around to mentioning the name of the person, as well as all of the things that the person was artificially caused to believe had happened to him. I begin to come to the startling realization that, in fact, I am the victim of the automobile accident and the benefactor of the surgeon's technique. In due course, I further realize that, although I had been psychologically certain that I had two hands in front of me, along with all the usual body parts, in point of fact I have no fingers or hands, and I have not done all of the other things I had previously believed with psychological certainty I had done.

Of course, I do not need to be a brain in a fishtank in order for the possibility to cast a shadow of doubt on my psychologically certain belief that I have fingers and hands and that I might not actually be doing the things I am psychologically certain I am doing. The mere possibility of being mistaken in these judgments alone proves them to be less than epistemically certain. The thought experiment shows that, despite all the present psychologically compelling evidence of my senses and the psychological certainty they produce in me at this moment of the existence of my hands, for all that I know, I could be no more than a brain and spinal cord in a fishtank with no hands or other body parts whatsoever. All of the visual and tactile evidence to which I appeal in trying to justify my belief that I have two hands, each equipped with five fingers, together with the verbal or written corroborating testimony of others that they see and feel the same thing, could equally have been artificially manufactured for me in the absence of any corresponding reality by the right chemicals being added at the right time to the solution enveloping my brain in the fishtank. I can therefore have psychological certainty about the truth or justification of some of my beliefs without having epistemic certainty, let alone absolute epistemic certainty.

ELUSIVENESS OF EPISTEMIC CERTAINTY

What else do we learn from this thought experiment? Does the example have any implications for the question of whether we ought to include epistemic certainty as a requirement for knowledge?

It is clear that, if we require knowledge to be epistemically certain, then, as some skeptics have concluded, it is virtually impossible for anyone to have genuine knowledge of anything. Even such widely accepted beliefs as the proposition that

$2 + 2 = 4$ in simple arithmetic need not carry epistemic certainty, because we can imagine that, if we were to accept other beliefs, then we would have to reject the belief that $2 + 2 = 4$.

We can imagine that everything we have learned about arithmetic has no basis in the truths of mathematics but are just beliefs artificially induced in us, like those of the brain in the fishtank. It might still be true that $2 + 2 = 4$, but the relevant justification by which the true belief constitutes knowledge will then be cast in enough doubt to deprive the belief of epistemic certainty. The same thought experiment can be invoked to describe an imaginable situation in which all the experiences that seem to justify the belief that $2 + 2 = 4$ are unreal. These include hearing a teacher explain the laws of addition, observing and memorizing addition tables, learning the algorithms by which elementary additions are performed, adjusting our work with numbers to what we take to be the approval of others in getting what we take to be the right answers when counting pairs of pairs of objects or making change, and so on.

All of these supposed experiences on the basis of which we believe that $2 + 2 = 4$ do not correspond to anything in reality if we are brains in a fishtank. They are merely produced in us by direct chemical and electrical stimulation of the brain's cortex. It might be said that the laws of arithmetic provide a relevant justification for a true belief that $2 + 2 = 4$, regardless of where or how we acquire them. But we can easily imagine someone who believes the addition, not because of the laws that the person never understood, but because of the authority of the teacher who explains the rules of arithmetic or the textbooks by which the rules are illustrated. We cannot reasonably deny that teachers and textbooks constitute relevant justification for many of the beliefs we have, even if the beliefs they support are not epistemically certain. Yet all of these kinds of evidence for the psychologically certain belief that $2 + 2 = 4$ might be completely false if we are only brains in a fishtank. And how do we know that we are not?

The implication is that, if knowledge entails epistemic certainty, then we cannot be said to know much of anything, if anything at all. If not even the simple truths of arithmetic can be known with epistemic certainty, and if epistemic certainty is needed for knowledge, then knowledge is immeasurably more difficult to attain than we would ordinarily suppose. This is precisely the radical conclusion of skeptics who advocate certainty as a requirement of knowledge, and who are not embarrassed by the fact that such a result is in direct conflict with what many people say. After all, what people say is only an expression of their less than epistemically certain beliefs—which, by the skeptic's high standards, fall short of genuine knowledge. If knowledge is (virtually) impossible, the skeptic argues, then we will just have to live without it. We should not tinker with the definition in order to make knowledge falsely appear to be possible when, according to a correct definition, it is not. Having set aside psychological certainty as irrelevant, this makes it necessary to confront the question of whether or not knowledge entails epistemic certainty. What should we say about knowledge and epistemic certainty? Is epistemic certainty a requirement of knowledge, or is it too strong a condition for a proper analysis of the concept?

One problem is that those who maintain that epistemic certainty is required for knowledge cannot by virtue of their own position consistently claim to know that epistemic certainty is required for knowledge. At most, they can believe it only with psychological certainty as something that is true and relevantly justified. But the defenders of knowledge as epistemically certain cannot claim to know that it is true or relevantly justified that knowledge entails epistemic certainty. To put the point more rhetorically, we might wonder whether skeptics who believe that epistemic certainty is required for knowledge and who base their skepticism on the belief that epistemic certainty is required for knowledge and that epistemic certainty is virtually impossible ought not consistently to be skeptical about whether epistemic certainty is required for knowledge, whether epistemic certainty is virtually impossible, and, hence, whether they ought not also consistently to be skeptical about the grounds of their own skepticism.

Another difficulty is whether, according to skepticism, it is necessary for a knower to know that a belief is not epistemically certain in order to cast doubt on its truth or relevant justification. Is it enough for the skeptic that a believer not be in a position to be epistemically certain that there is no possible basis for doubting a belief, or must a believer be epistemically certain that there is a definite possible basis for doubting a belief, in disqualifying a relevantly justified true belief as knowledge? This may seem like splitting hairs, but the distinction is important. It is one thing to say that we cannot have knowledge and that, therefore, skepticism is justified, even if we cannot know that skepticism is correct, because we cannot have epistemic certainty about virtually any of the things we claim to know. It is altogether another thing to admit that we know some things that possibly we might not know and that epistemic certainty as a condition for knowledge merely calls attention to the fact that we might not know some of the things we do in fact know. In the first case, knowledge is impossible; in the second case, knowledge is not only possible but actually exists, even though it is possible that we do not know what we think we know. After all, the possibility that is supposed to undermine the claim to knowledge in the case of the person contemplating the existence of two clearly visible hands is the extraordinarily farfetched fictional scenario by which the person might be a brain in a fishtank.

There are examples that may cast at least a shadow of a doubt on what we would otherwise regard as genuine knowledge in situations in which we have relevantly justified true belief accompanied by psychological certainty. We might imagine the knower being a disembodied spirit subject to deceit about the existence of the objects of immediate sensation by illusion, hallucination or dream, or active interference of another, more powerful spirit able to induce false beliefs. But how seriously should we take these fanciful possibilities? Since, moreover, according to the skeptic, we cannot know or be epistemically certain that there is even the possibility that a relevantly justified belief might be false, the skeptic merely asks us to consider one set of beliefs as refuting another. Why should we place more weight on the belief that our knowledge claims might be false than on the beliefs that provide the content of the knowledge claims themselves? If we cannot know that there is a possibility of our knowledge claims being false, why should we be concerned about, and impressed with, the mere possibility of skepticism as the mere possibility that the knowledge we believe ourselves to possess might not actually be knowledge? In other words, why should we suppose that knowledge requires such an excessively strong condition as epistemic certainty?

If I do not know with epistemic certainty that I am not a brain in a fishtank, I might still know all of the things I think I know through experience, if I have no positive reason to believe that I am in fact a brain in a fishtank. It is only a question of whether my belief that it is possible that I am a brain in a fishtank should have more, less, or equal weight in assessing whether I can know the things I believe I know. This is like asking in a courtroom which side of a dispute has the burden of proof. Should I give more credence to the belief that it is possible that I am a brain in a fishtank than to the belief that I am not a brain in a fishtank? Why? What would justify such an extraordinary conclusion? If it is more reasonable to give more or even equal credence to the belief that I am not a brain in a fishtank, or that I am dreaming or hallucinating, then skepticism does not meet its burden of proof in trying to persuade us that knowledge entails epistemic certainty and, as a result, is impossible.

In that case, we can neutralize the threat of skepticism from the standpoint of epistemic certainty. We can reasonably continue to accept the definition of knowledge as relevantly justified true belief without adding epistemic certainty as a further condition. We can reasonably continue in the commonsense view that knowledge is possible, that skepticism that tries to foist onto the concept of knowledge an unfulfillable requirement of epistemic certainty does not undermine the attainability of knowledge, and that we do, in fact, have knowledge whenever we have relevantly justified true beliefs, regardless of their epistemic certainty or uncertainty.

DEFEASIBLE JUSTIFICATION AND KNOWLEDGE WITHOUT CERTAINTY

To conclude that knowledge does not require epistemic certainty, just as it does not require psychological certainty, is to accept a concept of knowledge that is based on what is sometimes called *defeasible* justification. This means that knowledge so conceived is not absolute but is based on relevant justification that might possibly or imaginably be overturned or defeated by contrary facts.

If I know that I have two hands, but my relevant justification is only the defeasible justification that I see my hands clearly before me, then I should acknowledge the remote possibility that something could, in principle, cause me to retract my belief that I have two hands. In other words, I should admit that, although I believe myself to know that I have two hands, it is at least logically possible that I might be wrong. As a knower, I recognize my fallibility. It could turn out that a particular belief I believe to be true and relevantly justified is not actually true or relevantly justified. If an overriding knowledge-defeating belief of this sort comes to light, then I ought to withdraw my claim to know what I believed or thought I knew. Typically, in such a situation, I will do so at the same time that I withdraw the belief itself, along with the belief that the belief is true or that the belief is relevantly justified. If knowledge is fallible rather than certain because relevant justification is defeasible, if knowledge can be defeated by contrary facts if such should ever appear, then my knowledge is not as secure as logically possible. But, since I am only a finite creature with finite cognitive abilities, finite sensation, finite memory, and finite reasoning, I do not expect anything more absolute in my efforts to arrive at knowledge. I could give up the word *knowledge* to satisfy skeptics who demand that knowledge entail epistemic certainty, but I do not see any good reason to do so.

The propositions I believe myself to know might be both true and relevantly justified. I might, after all, know many or even all of the things I believe myself to know. The fact that knowledge does not come with an absolute guarantee against all logically possible refutations does not mean that knowledge is impossible, only that it is fallible rather than epistemically certain, because justification is defeasible. By discounting skepticism based on a requirement of epistemic certainty in the analysis of knowledge, we as knowers do not avoid the responsibility of exercising our cognitive abilities to the utmost in trying to determine beyond a reasonable doubt, even if not beyond the faintest imaginable shadow of a doubt, that the beliefs we claim to know are true and relevantly justified. On the contrary, the fact that knowledge appears as a possibility for human knowers makes it even more important that, in claiming to know, we hold ourselves to the highest standards of truth and relevant justification, which will nevertheless inevitably fall short of the excessive demands of epistemic certainty.

CAN WE ACQUIRE KNOWLEDGE?

If we agree to define knowledge as relevantly justified true belief, excluding epistemic certainty from the concept of fallible knowledge with defeasible justification, there are nevertheless other kinds of skeptical challenges to the possibility of knowledge. It is worthwhile to consider some of the most influential types.

Skepticism arises when critics maintain that it is impossible to arrive at knowledge because of a dilemma. The dilemma has two parts, or *horns*. Either we already know or we do not already know that which we seek to know. If we already know what we seek to know, then we cannot acquire knowledge, because logically we cannot acquire what we already have. If, on the other hand, we do not already know that which we seek to know, then we cannot acquire knowledge, because we will not know what to look for and we will not recognize it if we happen to stumble upon it. The first horn of the dilemma seems to allow that we might somehow start by having knowledge but cannot reacquire it later. However, if we already have at least some knowledge before we try to acquire more, then we might be saved from at least the most virulent kinds of radical skepticism that deny the possibility of any knowledge whatsoever. The possibility of having knowledge before we try to acquire it raises an interesting question of its own. Can we have knowledge that does not need to be acquired?

Epistemologists sometimes distinguish between two general categories of knowledge. Some knowledge depends on experience of the world and is known as *empirical* or *a posteriori* knowledge, because it comes after, or posterior to, experience. Other knowledge is described as independent of experience and is known as *innate* or *a priori,* on the assumption that it comes before, or is prior to, any experience of the world. If it is possible to have knowledge independently of experience, then perhaps we can know some things prior to any effort to acquire knowledge about them in a very strong sense of *a priori* knowledge.

The first horn of the dilemma seems to allow that there can be *a priori* knowledge. But many theorists believe that all knowledge must be acquired through experience and that *a priori* knowledge is, instead, a kind of knowledge that does not require experience more specifically for its justification than for its acquisition. As examples, they cite such knowledge as the truths of logic and mathematics. Instances include the proposition that either today is Tuesday or today is not Tuesday, that $2 + 2 = 4$, and so-called analytic truths, such as the proposition that all triangles are three-sided plane geometrical figures, or that all bachelors are unmarried male adults. Logical and mathematical truths are not justified by experience in the ordinary sense, even if their knowledge must be acquired experientially, because we do not need to know whether or not today is Tuesday and because to know what day it happens to be does not help us know the purely logical truth that either today is Tuesday or it is not the case that today is Tuesday.

Similarly, in the case of mathematical propositions, we do not need and it does not actually help in any way to investigate the basic truths of arithmetic by checking to see whether every two things added to any other two things always equals four things. The propositions of mathematics are not essentially about the objects encountered in experience but, rather, are truths of a different kind concerning abstract entities, the numbers 2 and 4, and the abstract function of addition. In the cases of analytic propositions about triangles being three-sided plane geometrical figures and bachelors being unmarried male adults, their truth follows by definition, as a consequence of the meanings of concepts. The property of being a three-sided plane geometrical figure predicated of triangles is said to be contained within the concept of being a triangle, or to be such that the property can be analyzed as belonging to the concept of being a triangle. The property of being an unmarried male adult predicated of bachelors can equally be said to be contained in the concept of being a bachelor, or to be such that the property is analyzed as belonging to the concept of being a bachelor. We do not need to justify these beliefs by appealing to any particular kind of experience. It will not help to conduct an opinion poll, to check on each triangle to see if it has three sides, or to go door to door with a questionnaire, trying to satisfy ourselves that every bachelor is an unmarried male adult. The propositions are true because of the meanings of the words involved, as explicated in an analysis of the corresponding concepts.

The existence of *a priori* knowledge, which seems to be countenanced by the first horn of the skeptical dilemma as knowledge possessed prior to any attempt to acquire knowledge, defies skepticism. If we can have *a priori* knowledge, then we can at least have knowledge of logical, mathematical, or analytic truths. Yet this may be small comfort in view of the first dilemma horn, for, if the dilemma is sound, then it means that we cannot acquire any knowledge, so we can know only whatever knowledge does not need to be acquired. We cannot know whether we have hands; we cannot know whether today is Tuesday; we cannot know whether grass is green or snow is white; we cannot know whether any of the propositions of natural science are true. This is still a very powerful skeptical objection against the possibility of much of what we believe we know and, in particular, of the most important and most useful kinds of knowledge to which we otherwise reasonably lay claim. This makes it necessary to consider the second dilemma horn.

The second dilemma horn states that, if we do not already have the knowledge we seek to acquire, then we cannot acquire it, because we will not know what to look for and will not be able to recognize it, even if it were to appear. Is this version of skepticism a serious cause for concern? Is it true that if we do not already possess knowledge then we cannot look for or recognize it? This skeptical position on examination seems very problematic. I can acquire many kinds of things purely by accident, without deliberately seeking them out. Often knowledge seems to come to us in just this sort of way, in what is sometimes called serendipity—which is to say, by luck. The discovery of penicillin as an antibiotic was made accidentally in this fashion, when researchers happened to notice that bread mold on a culture dish retarded and destroyed the bacteria growing there. The researchers were not looking for an antibiotic, because at that time they did not even know that there was such a thing to be discovered. Many other examples could as easily be multiplied from the history of science as from ordinary life. As a kind of thought experiment, suppose that there is an extremely rare coin, perhaps the gold coin previously discussed, which no one knows about because no one has ever noticed it and which has never been cataloged. I cannot set about to acquire such a coin, because by hypothesis I do not know that it exists. But does that mean that I cannot acquire the coin? Clearly not, since I might receive the coin by luck or accident with my change at the newsstand, or I might find it on the sidewalk or while digging in the sand at the beach. After I acquire the coin, I can then go on to study it and draw certain conclusions about it, thereby adding to my knowledge. But, even in discovering the coin through sheer accident, I acquire knowledge that I did not previously have, the knowledge that such a coin exists.

The same thing might be said by analogy with respect to the information that comes unbidden to me, like the lucky gold coin. The knowledge can simply appear to me without my seeking it in the form of the sensations I experience of the outside world. When I open my eyes, I do not necessarily know in advance and have no control over what I will see. This is even more obviously true in the case of infants using their sense organs for the first time. The world presents itself to perception and thereby conveys information to the mind. But, in order for this to occur, we do not suppose that we must first choose or already know what we will find; neither do we already need such knowledge in order to recognize the information about the world that can lead to true or relevantly justified belief. If we do not already need to possess knowledge in order to acquire it, then the second horn of the skeptical dilemma does not hold, and so poses no danger to the possibility of acquiring *a posteriori* knowledge.

DIALLELUS, OR SKEPTICAL CIRCLE

Yet another challenge to the possibility of knowledge has to do with the way in which beliefs are justified. How can we determine when a belief is true or relevantly justified? Which among all our beliefs are relevantly justified as true, and which are not? This question asks nothing less than that we be able to distinguish which of our beliefs qualify as knowledge and which are mere beliefs. We need a method for distinguishing knowledge from its opposite, for dividing beliefs into two categories representing those that are relevantly justified and those that are not relevantly justified.

How can this be done? The concern of some skeptics is that, for logical reasons, the requirement cannot be satisfied. The problem is that, in order to decide which of our beliefs constitute knowledge, we must determine which of them follow from correct epistemic principles. But, in order to decide which among a variety of alternative epistemic principles are correct, we need to know which of them imply all and only the beliefs that qualify as knowledge. Thus, it appears that we need to satisfy both of these requirements simultaneously. We need correct epistemic principles in order to judge which beliefs are knowledge, and we need to know which beliefs are knowledge in order to judge which epistemic prinicples are correct. Since we need to satisfy both of these vital requirements at the same time, and, worse, we need one in order to satisfy the other, it looks as though we cannot satisfy either requirement and, hence, that we cannot know which of our beliefs constitute knowledge or which epistemic principles are correct.

This dilemma is sometimes known as the *diallelus,* or wheel, because it describes a circularity in the requirements for determining true beliefs by correct epistemic principles. We go around and around, trying to find solid footing for knowledge, which persistently eludes us, because we can judge true beliefs only by a correct epistemic principle, and we can judge the correctness of an epistemic principle only by true beliefs. How can we possibly get off of the wheel? It might be supposed that we could do so if we had access to a special epistemic principle that we could know to be correct without first having to judge its ability to justify all true beliefs or, alternatively, if we had at least some epistemically theoretically unprincipled true beliefs that we could know to be true and relevantly justified without first appealing to a correct epistemic principle. Of these possibilities, the second seems more promising than the first. It is easier to suppose that there could be true beliefs that do not need to be justified by epistemic principles than to suppose that there could be correct epistemic principles independently of any true beliefs. There may appear to be a natural process whereby belief and true beliefs come first, and the principles that justify the beliefs arise only secondarily and in retrospect as a way of codifying the methods that we otherwise use unreflectively and un-self-consciously in arriving more naively at intuitively true beliefs. A correct epistemic principle may then be needed for higher theoretical purposes, but not in order to arrive at relevantly justified true beliefs. We complete one half arc of the diallelus if we begin by accepting a correct epistemic principle, for then we must already have the relevantly justified true belief that the epistemic principle is correct and that it is an epistemic principle.

Can there be true beliefs that do not stand in need of justification by a correct epistemic principle? If so, there may be a way out of the diallelus; if not, we may be driven to a very strong form of skepticism. The problem of arriving at theoretically unprincipled true beliefs is similar to the same difficulty that occurs in connection with the previous skeptical dilemma. There we considered the possibility of acquiring knowledge that we did not already possess—in light of the objection that, if we do not already know that which we seek to know, then we will not know what to look for, and we will not recognize it if we happen on it accidentally. The problem at first seems complicated, but we may conclude that it is logically no more difficult to acquire previously unidentified knowledge than it is to acquire a previously unknown rare coin.

The situation with respect to attaining true beliefs without appealing to correct epistemic principles is much the same. We acquire beliefs naturally, almost against our will. I do not decide to believe that there appears to be something red before me when I behold a rose; the belief arises irresistibly, uncontrollably. Neither do I need to invoke correct epistemic principles in order for a belief I hold to be true. A belief is true just in case the content of the belief is satisfied, or just in case what the belief claims corresponds to the way things actually are. Such a correspondence will either exist or not exist, independently of any attempt I make to apply a correct epistemic principle. Truth, like belief, is out of my hands. I cannot make any of my beliefs true or false by correctly or incorrectly applying a correct or incorrect epistemic principle. I do not and do not need to invoke a correct epistemic principle in order to justify my true belief, even if I later adduce such a principle to correlate my empirical experiences with the belief states that they evoke. The point is that, although I may bring forward a correct epistemic principle afterward to justify my true belief in retrospect, I do not need the principle in order to accept the true belief and the grounds for its relevant justification in order to know. Without making use of any theoretical epistemic principles, I can accumulate a large number of theoretically unprincipled but relevantly justified true beliefs for the sake of justifying higher-order epistemic principles.

There is a crucial difference between the existence of a correct theoretical epistemic principle that could be brought forward in order to justify a true belief and an epistemic agent's being aware of and making use of such a principle in justifying a belief. I can have a true belief without trying to justify it by a correct epistemic principle, and there can be a correct epistemic principle of which I have no knowledge at the time that I accept a theoretically unprincipled true belief, but which I might later learn about and choose to invoke in looking back at and trying to justify previously unjustified true beliefs. The problem of the diallelus is the problem of acquiring knowledge in real time, where at a certain phase of my cognitive activity I cannot have access simultaneously both to all and only true beliefs and to the correct epistemic principles that would justify my true beliefs. However, if I can have at least temporarily epistemically unjustified true beliefs, then I can break out of the circle by building up a body of true beliefs that does not require justification by correct epistemic principles in order to be believed, to be true, or to be relevantly justified. Admittedly, such epistemically theoretically unprincipled true beliefs will not yet include higher-order theoretical epistemic principles. But, as I acquire enough knowledge, I can use it as a basis against which to measure the adequacy of the principles I might later try to formulate in order to understand the epistemic status of my relevantly justified true beliefs, and which I can apply to extend my knowledge in more theoretical ways.

ATTAINABILITY OF KNOWLEDGE

Knowledge as relevantly justified true belief falls between two extremes of absolute certainty and radical skepticism. If the analysis we have developed is correct, then knowledge is neither certain nor impossible, and it is possible precisely in part because it does not need to be certain. We find knowledge in all categories to be a special psychological state that is accessible to human thought.

We can know many things. The valuable truths discovered in mathematics, science, history, and philosophy are among the treasures of knowledge. Yet the possibility of attaining knowledge does not rule out the possibility that we may be wrong when we believe ourselves or claim to know something, even with psychological certainty. Since knowledge on the present analysis does not entail epistemic certainty, it is possible that we may not actually know what we think we know. This awareness may have a salutary effect on our efforts to acquire knowledge, and especially on our assertions of what we know or think we know. The refutation of skepticism in the several forms we have considered opens up the possibility of knowledge and allows us to take seriously the challenge of acquiring and enhancing knowledge. But there is a healthy skepticism that should caution us in the manner of a nagging voice of conscience, to prevent us from believing and claiming that we know something unless or until the belief in question stands up to the most rigorous scrutiny we can provide. We must constantly test our ideas and be prepared to modify or reject them if they do not satisfy the highest standards of truth and relevant justification.

By refuting skepticism, we make knowledge possible, but we do not thereby make knowledge easy. Knowledge does not signify a category of epistemic appraisal that is entirely beyond human reach but, rather, one that indicates a true belief that we have very good reasons to accept. We have also seen that mere psychological certainty in the truth of a belief is no guarantee that what we believe is true. The role of psychological certainty in epistemic practice is complex. It is one thing to observe, as we have, that psychological certainty is neither necessary nor sufficient for knowledge, and another to understand the importance that psychological certainty may have as one source of fallible evidence about the truth of what we believe. There is no denying that a sense of psychological certainty sometimes accompanies knowledge, even if it is not essential for it. When we know something, psychological certainty often emotionally reinforces the coldly rational and experiential grounds for knowledge that relevantly justify that what we believe is true.

A commonsense approach is to say that psychological certainty, although not an adequate proof of knowledge, can be a positive if not always decisive indication of knowledge. When we experience a sense of psychological certainty, it might reinforce or otherwise lead us to take seriously the possibility that we know whatever it is we feel certain about. Thus, the sense of certainty can provide us with a kind of mental barometer for knowledge. It does not rain every time an aneroid barometer indicates falling atmospheric pressure, and we do not always have knowledge whenever we feel psychologically certain that something is true. But an aneroid barometer is fairly good evidence that it will rain, since rain frequently occurs when the atmospheric pressure suddenly decreases. Similarly, although greater significance should not be attached to its occurrence, the sensation of psychological certainty can provide positive evidence that one has knowledge. The important thing is not to confuse the evidence with the fact for which it may be evidence. There is less risk of doing this in the case of the barometer and the weather, because no one would reasonably mistake the behavior of the needle or the column of mercury in a barometer with the conditions outside of sunshine, cloud, or rain. In the case of psychological certainty as evidence of probable knowledge, there is a more natural excuse for conflating the two, since both involve mental states.

There is a principle by which we can distinguish between knowledge and psychological certainty as evidence of knowledge without running them together. We can reasonably take psychological certainty as a sign of knowledge, provided that we do not rely on psychological certainty by itself as justification for the truth of what we believe. Psychological certainty as a sign of knowledge arises as it should when we are persuaded of the truth and justification of a belief, but psychological certainty does not justify or make what we believe true. Thus, while psychological certainty can motivate us to satisfy ourselves that we have knowledge, it must not be allowed to replace the need to investigate the truth of our beliefs or their objective justification. We fall into error only when we delude ourselves into thinking that having psychological certainty by itself demonstrates the truth or constitutes relevant justification for a belief, even when the belief in question happens to be true and relevantly justified. To do so is to put the cart before the horse. Psychological certainty should occur when and because we have good justification in hand. We should not try to replace the requirements of truth and justification by psychological certainty. By analogy, we should not try to water the garden with an aneroid barometer, even when it indicates falling atmospheric pressure. If we can satisfy ourselves on objective grounds that our beliefs are true and that there is good justification for us to believe that they are true, then, if we find ourselves psychologically certain of the truth and justification of our beliefs, we will not base the appraisal of our beliefs as knowledge merely on the subjective experience of psychological certainty, but we will have solid, independent reasons for appraising our beliefs as knowledge.

MODES AND METHODS OF JUSTIFICATION

What kinds of objective justification can we have for true beliefs? If we distinguish between *a priori* and *a posteriori* knowledge, as previously suggested, then we can identify two main kinds of objective justification, each of which provides reasons for accepting beliefs in these separate categories.

An *a priori* proposition is one that is true or false by virtue of truths that do not depend on the existence or nonexistence of any empirical facts. Such facts are said to be *contingent,* meaning that if they are true they might logically not have been true, and if false they might logically not have been false. A contingent fact, for example, is the fact that snow is white, that grass is green, or that falling barometric pressure indicates the likelihood of rain. These facts happen to be the case, but if the world had been different in particular ways, they would not be true and are not among the facts of alternative logically possible worlds. We can also include as contingent facts certain states of affairs that happen to be false, such as that snow is green, that grass is white, or that falling barometric pressure indicates the likelihood of winning the lottery. These are contingent falsehoods, because, although they do not hold true in the actual world, we can imagine an alternative logically possible world in which they would be among the facts or truths that make such a world different from the actual world. The truth or falsehood of contingent truths depends, or is contingent, on the way the world happens to be.

A priori truths, such as those we have discussed, are true independently of any contingent states of affairs. To say that either it is raining or it is not raining is to state an *a priori* truth, because its truth does not depend on the actual state of the weather but is, rather, an implication of pure logic. To say that rain is the atmospheric release of liquid water droplets from clouds is to state an *a priori* truth, because its truth does not depend on the actual state of the weather but is, rather, an implication of the definition of the concept of rain. It might or might not be raining, but what it means for it to be raining is for there to occur an atmospheric release of liquid water droplets from clouds. It might be objected that even these kinds of truths depend in some sense on contingent states of affairs, because our language, logic, or conceptual framework might have evolved differently than it did. The standard and quite reasonable reply to this concern is that logic, by virtue of being logic, cannot be different than it is, even though we might disagree with or be mistaken about some of its principles, and that, in all such judgments of possibility and contingency, we must hold our language and conceptual framework constant, or we cannot make sense of any philosophical claims whatsoever.

If we adopt the usual distinction between *a priori* and *a posteriori* knowledge, then we can further distinguish between two main modes of justifying beliefs. We can try to justify *a priori* beliefs by applying the rules of logic and by working out the analysis of the definitions of particular concept terms, much as we did earlier in this chapter in defining the concept of knowledge. It is something we can know *a priori,* if our analysis of the concept of knowledge is correct, that knowledge implies truth, that if we know something then we believe it, and the like. It is also something we can know *a priori,* again if the analysis is correct, that it is not the case that knowledge implies psychological or epistemic certainty, or that it is false that we can know something false or something we believe to be false. These are truths that we can know without appealing to any contingent truths about the world as evidence to justify the belief that the propositions in question are true. Like all *a priori* truths, they are true independently of the facts of the world. Logic and conceptual analysis provide the methodology for *a priori* knowledge, the route by which we can justify beliefs in this category of propositions as true.

The method of *a priori* knowledge by contrast also establishes a method of *a posteriori* knowledge. *A posteriori* knowledge is knowledge the justification for which depends on contingent facts. We must look at snow to know that it is white, and we must look at grass to know that it is green. We must study the empirical correlation between the behavior of an aneroid barometer and the weather in order to know that rising barometric pressure as indicated by the barometer can be used to predict the probability of rain. It will not do to consider pure logic or conceptual analysis as a way of trying to justify any of these items of *a posteriori* knowledge. At most, logic and the definition of terms may serve as a preliminary for empirical inquiry into the truth of these kinds of propositions. By themselves, logic and definition do not relevantly justify the acceptance or rejection of any *a posteriori* knowledge claim. The methods of *a posteriori* knowledge are those that have been most thoroughly developed for the natural sciences. They include observation, tests of explanatory hypotheses by further observation, and repeatable public experiments with control factors to eliminate possible extraneous causes, along with all the devices developed by scientists to divest nature of its secrets.

ON THE WAY TO KNOWLEDGE

In chapter 1, having raised questions about what we can know and how we might try to obtain knowledge about the meaning of life, it became appropriate and even unavoidable for us to address in more general terms what we mean by knowledge and whether and how it is possible to acquire knowledge. The concerns here are global. We need to decide what knowledge is, and how the concept of knowledge is to be defined, before we can seriously inquire into what we can know about such a difficult and important topic as the meaning of life.

Accordingly, this chapter has sought to explain the concept of knowledge, to investigate some of the ways in which knowledge can be discovered. There are difficulties about the possibility of knowledge, supporting different versions of skepticism. We have tried to answer skepticism arising from the unattainability of epistemic certainty, a dilemma that precludes knowledge both if we already know and do not already know that which we seek to know, and the problem of the diallelus. If knowledge survives these skeptical challenges, then we can begin to think about the form knowledge might take in our everyday, scientific, and philosophical thinking. The theory of knowledge that we have defended makes it possible, even if a challenging task, to acquire knowledge. We desire to know, and the analysis of knowledge we have examined implies that it is possible after all to attain genuine knowledge. A blueprint for a sound working theory of knowledge was also sketched, involving both analytic and logical, or *a priori,* and scientific experiential, or *a posteriori,* knowledge of the world. By refining these methods, we can increase and improve our knowledge, including knowing whether life is meaningful or absurd and, if meaningful, what meaning it may have.

Before we can try to solve the problem that got us started in the first place, we need to make additional inquiries into the nature of the knowing subject, the existence or nonexistence of God, and the principles of and motivations for morality. Only then will we be able to return with greater insight into our effort to answer the sojourner's question. The conclusions we have reached thus far about the concept and possibility of attaining knowledge should nevertheless have assured us that we are not necessarily involved in a fool's errand, but that, by journeying in search of knowledge about the meaning of life, we aspire to something that, in principle, is an achievable goal.

Minds, Machines, and Freedom of Will

The mind is a strange machine which can combine the materials offered it in the most astonishing ways.

—Bertrand Russell
The Conquest of Happiness, 1930

If it is for mind that we are searching the brain, then we are supposing the brain to be much more than a telephone-exchange. We are supposing it a telephone-exchange along with the subscribers as well.

—Charles Scott Sherrington
Man on His Nature, 1941

The grand thing about the human mind is that it can turn its own tables and see meaninglessness as ultimate meaning.
—John Cage, "Where Are We Going? and What Are We Doing?"
Silence, 1961

WHAT IS THE MIND?

The sojourner's question asks, Who am I? We have been investigating the concept of knowledge, the challenge of skepticism, and the conditions under which it is possible to know. But knowledge as relevantly justified true belief is a special type of mental state, a property of the mind. Whatever else we might be, and whatever meaning or absurdity we might be able to discover in life, if potentially we are knowers, if knowledge is a kind of belief, and if belief is a mental state, then we are beings with minds. If we want to understand the concept of knowledge more completely and to progress further toward an answer to the sojourner's question, we must now try to decide what we can know about the concept of mind.

There is yet another way in which the sojourner's question requires that we delve more deeply into the nature of mind. We should consider an argument that many philosophers and scientists have debated, to the effect that life may be meaningless if the mind is not free to choose what it does or does not do but, rather, is determined by external factors to such an extent that we cannot control what happens in our lives. If the mind has no free will, then we are the helpless pawns of forces that cause us to behave in ways that we cannot change or prevent. What meaning can life have for me if I am not free to live as I choose? If whatever I do cannot be made different by what I will to do, then there is no point in wrestling with the difficult problems of life and deciding what I want to do or believe I ought to do. Instead, I should just let everything happen as it is determined to take place without concerning or involving myself. Why bother, if I cannot change my life anyway? Why suppose that life is meaningful if my life is just a more complicated playing out of the same kinds of determinations that equally unalterably affect all aspects of the behavior of nonliving things?

Determinism is a challenge to the meaningfulness of life in much the same way that skepticism challenges the possibility of knowledge. Yet the proper philosophical attitude is not merely to dismiss either skepticism or determinism because they have unwelcome consequences. Instead, we must open-mindedly consider the issues they raise, critically evaluate the arguments on all sides of the question, and follow whatever conclusions of the best arguments prevail, letting the chips fall where they may. Maybe knowledge is impossible; maybe the mind is such that the will is not free and all our actions are determined; maybe life is meaningless or absurd. We must think deeply about all these matters and try to decide what answers are correct, regardless of the consequences. In responding to the problem of skepticism, we have already done much to refute its objections to the possibility of knowledge interpreted as relevantly justified true belief. While engaged in the process of evaluating arguments for and against skepticism, however, we did not necessarily know in advance how things were going to turn out. Despite our careful inquiry, we should admit that we might have made a mistake that could invalidate our defense of knowledge and refutation of skepticism. Here, unless or until we can resolve the conflict, we are in a similar situation with respect to the problem of determinism as a source of opposition to the freedom of will and meaning of life. We must not prejudge the controversy but, rather, now that we know that knowledge is possible, try to discover the truth.

THOUGHT AND THINKING

The mind is something that thinks. What is meant by the word *mind* is either the thoughts we have, so to speak, as a sequence of mental occurrences in real time, bundled together by overlapping memories and expectations, or the subject of these thoughts, as a kind of substance or entity capable of thinking.

Thought is very important to us; in a way, it is how we identify ourselves in terms of having a particular stream of experiences, including our memories and expectations. For this reason, we might even believe ourselves to be essentially thinking things. We are souls or spirits that inhabit a human body, on such a conception, and we might even be able to survive the body's death in a persistence of the person and continuity of psychological experience both before and after death—as some, though certainly not all, philosophies and religions have affirmed. Whether or not the mind can exist without the body, to answer the sojourner's question and decide who or what we are, demands a careful exploration of the concept of mind. We must try to learn what kind of thing the mind is and what implications, if any, its properties have for understanding the meaning or absurdity of life. The mind is the knowing subject, as well as the subject of pains and pleasures, doubts and beliefs, sensations, emotions, and will. It is who we are, the agent of our decision making; as such, if we are responsible for our actions, the mind is also the touchstone of morality.

There are many theories of mind. The mind is sometimes identified with the brain and nervous system, or with the more abstract information-processing procedures that describe the brain's functions like those of a living computer. The first theory is known as *materialism* and the second as *functionalism*. If the mind is a material entity, then it is subject to the same natural forces and causal laws as any other physical system. The mind as identical with the brain is then no different in principle from material objects generally, totally determined in its behavior by the lawlike necessity of causation that prevails throughout the universe. The brain may be the most complicated physical entity we have yet discovered, but, if it is only physical, then it is no less governed in all its activity by the same cause-and-effect relations than even the simplest biological and even nonliving purely physical systems. If the mind is just the brain and nervous system, then free will and moral responsibility must be illusory. For in that case the mind is causally determined, and we as persons cannot act differently than we do. The implications of this conclusion for the meaninglessness or absurdity of human life have already been mentioned. But we are not yet in a position to know whether or not the mind is the same as or is something more than the brain or the information processing by which it functions. To decide this issue, we must consider the kinds of properties that can be associated with the mind, and whether these properties can be reasonably attributed to the brain.

MIND-BRAIN IDENTITY

The brain is a biological organ. It is a highly complex assemblage of about 1 trillion neurons. Each neuron is a living cell capable of transmitting or retarding an electrochemical signal across a microscopic gap between neurons called a *synapse.* The complex network of neurons in the brain and nervous system is made even more complicated by the fact that each neuron can be connected by synapses in different ways to as many as 10,000 other neurons.

The brain and nervous system should be considered not merely as a mass of tissue but as a biologically active colony of cells acting in harmony to channel neurophysiological substances through a network of neurons and synapses according to the same basic laws of physics that govern all other material entities in the universe. If the brain were magnified many times in size, we could think of it as a fantastically complex plumbing and electrical system, connected to eyes, ears, other sense organs, and nerves that deliver information about the world to the brain and from the brain to muscles whose movements nerve impulses can affect in various ways.

The human brain is one of the most marvelous and intricately well-adapted physical systems ever known. But is the mind identical to this living biological network of neurons and synapses? How do we decide whether or not two terms such as *mind* and *brain* refer to the same thing, or whether they are different? An *identity principle* that many philosophers follow is that A and B refer to or are names for the same thing if and only if all and only the objective properties of A are properties of B. This is to say that, if A and B are names for the identical thing, then any objective property of A is also a property of B, and any objective property of B is also a property of A. It is also to say that, if any objective property of A is also a property of B, and, if any objective property of B is also a property of A, then A and B are names for the identical thing.

The principle enables us to distinguish between A and B as nonidentical when A and B are not names for the same thing. According to the identity principle, this is what happens whenever A has an objective property that B does not have, or whenever B has an objective property that A does not have. For example, we can distinguish between Munich and Geneva on the grounds that Munich has the property of being a city in Germany, whereas Geneva does not have this property but, instead, has the property of being a city in Switzerland; equally, Geneva has the property of being a city in Switzerland, whereas Munich does not have this property but is, instead, a city in Germany. Thus, *Munich* and *Geneva* are not names for the same thing, and Munich is not identical to Geneva. We exclude subjective properties from the identity principle, so that we do not wrongly conclude that Munich is not the same thing as München just because someone believes, doubts, hopes, or fears that Munich is a German city but, through a misunderstanding, does not happen to believe, doubt, hope, or fear that München is a German city—where, in fact, *Munich* and *München* are different names for the same city.

If we try to apply the identity principle to mind and brain, can we judge correctly that *mind* and *brain* refer to or are two different names for the same thing, that the mind is identical to the brain? Or must we conclude that mind and brain are nonidentical? We can settle the question by showing definitely that mind and brain are nonidentical if we can find at least one objective property that the mind has but the brain does not have, or conversely. On the other hand, if we merely accumulate a list of objective properties that both brain and mind share, that is not enough to prove that mind and brain are identical. For such a conclusion, we would also need to know that the list of such properties is exhaustive, or that there are no other properties not on our list that we have not considered and that are not possessed identically by both mind and brain. In this sense, negative nonidentity determinations are easier to justify than positive identity determinations. From the fact that we cannot find any distinctions between mind and brain, it does not follow that they are identical. At most, it might contribute evidence that by itself would be inconclusive to support the proposition that mind and brain are identical, in lieu of conflicting evidence to the contrary. What, then, is the situation with respect to mind and brain? Can we find objective properties of the mind that are not also properties of the brain, or objective properties of the brain that are not also properties of the mind?

As we might expect, the issue is fraught with controversy. Some theorists believe that the mind has properties that the brain does not have, while others hotly dispute this claim. We should consider some of the most important efforts to distinguish between mind and brain as nonidentical and we should try to decide whether or not they are effective. One of the most common claims about the difference between mind and brain is that the brain has a definite location in space, whereas thought, and therefore the mind, cannot be located in any particular place. The brain is found in the skull, and the nervous system extends down along the spinal column in a branching configuration of nerve endings. Every part of the brain and nervous system can be located at a particlar place in space. But where is my thought that life is meaningful or that life is absurd, or that I might be a brain in a fishtank? Where do I look for thoughts? They do not seem to be anywhere in particular. Moreover, all the parts of the brain have a particular weight and color; if someone were so inclined, he could touch, smell, and taste them. But can anything like this be done with respect to the contents of a thought or to the mind considered as a whole? What color is my thought that I might be a brain in a fishtank?

Even if I am thinking of a particularly colored brain and a particularly colored fishtank, a thought about those imaginary things does not itself have those colors.

Neither does it make sense, many philosophers argue, to attribute weight to my thoughts. As an experiment—not a thought experiment, but an actual scientific experiment that could be performed in a physics laboratory—weigh an entire living human body on the most precise and accurate scale on two occasions under two different circumstances: first when the person whose body is being weighed is thinking that life is absurd and then when the person is thinking nothing at all. Or compare such weighings for a living person entertaining thoughts and the same person immediately at death or in a coma when the brain has ceased activity. If, as seems likely, the experiment reveals that there is no change in the body's weight, then, other things being equal, it appears that there would be good empirical evidence for the claim that thoughts, unlike every other physical entity, do not weigh anything. If this evidence is judged correct, then together with the identity principle we previously adduced, it would appear to follow that the mind is not identical to but distinct from the brain.

MENTAL AND PHYSICAL PROPERTIES

Other differences between mind and brain have also been hypothesized. Some who distinguish between body and mind maintain that, unlike the body, the mind cannot be divided into independently existing parts of the same general kind.

The body as a material entity can be split up into several smaller but simultaneously coexistent material entities, but the mind, it is said, cannot. The mind can expand or shrink by taking on or losing new information or memories, and we can even increase or decrease our mental capacities, learning new skills or forgetting things we once knew; in this sense, we can metaphorically change the shape and size of the mind. But it is more problematic to suppose that we could divide the mind into several smaller but simultaneously coexistent minds. If I suffer an accident and have a body part amputated, then the two parts can continue to exist at the same time, even if the severed part starts to deteriorate. I can continue to exist as one and the same scattered object after such an amputation, with some of my parts no longer fully integrated but now spatially separated. But can the same be true of my mind? This is doubtful, because the mind appears to have an essential unity that prevents it from being divided into other, simultaneously active minds. Of course, the brain can be so divided. Mind-body dualists emphasize this fact in denying that the mind is identical with the brain, on the grounds that the body can be divided into like parts, whereas the mind cannot.

Many efforts to distinguish body and mind on the basis of a distinction in their objective properties, nevertheless, seem to involve *circular reasoning*. In an argument, if we assume what we are supposed to prove, then we are guilty of *begging the question* or *reasoning in a circle*. An obvious example is when I try to prove that God exists simply by assuming that God exists. A more subtle form of the same circular reasoning is when I conclude that God exists because the Bible says that God exists, and then argue that we must believe what the Bible says because it is the word of God. Circular reasoning is to be avoided, not because its conclusions are generally false; indeed, the conclusions of many circular arguments are perfectly true. An example is if someone were to argue that snow is white because snow is white, or that grass is green, therefore grass is green. The trouble with circular reasoning is that the inference fails to provide a good reason for accepting the truth of the conclusion, given the truth of the assumptions, for anyone who does not already accept the conclusion. An argument is supposed to convince us of something that we did not necessarily already accept. However, in the case of circular reasoning, the argument works only to the extent that we are already committed to the conclusion's truth, without which we could not believe that the assumptions were true.

The danger in many of the arguments for the mind-body distinction is that the reasoning might be circular in an even more subtle way. Consider yet another proof for mind-body nonidentity. It states that the mind has objective properties that the body does not, because the mind, unlike the body, is capable of containing images many times larger than itself. We see evidence of this whenever we look about. The visual image we experience is much larger than the brain considered as a material entity in which the image is supposed to be contained. My visual mental image of the room I am in is clearly larger by volume than the size of my brain. The size of my brain measured purely in terms of its height, breadth, and depth is comparatively smaller than my mental picture of the room. But the many convolutions of the brain, with all its synaptic connections linking neuron to neuron, might and presumably does have enough space to register enough information from and about the room to enable it to constitute the visual image I am experiencing. Presumably, it must have enough information storage space with all its complex internal surface area to project a visual image of all of outer space in the great outdoors when I look up at the stars.

There is a more serious logical objection to this style of argument about the mind-body distinction. The argument requires that a property predicated of the mind but not predicated of the body shows that mind and body are distinct. The trouble is knowing whether or not it is true that a property predicated of the mind does not actually apply to the body, or the reverse, unless we assume from the outset, and thereby reason in a circle, that mind and body are nonidentical. If mind and body are identical, then, according to the same identity principle, we would be equally justified in concluding that any property truly predicated of the mind is also a property of the body, and that any property truly predicated of the body is also a property of the mind. If someone wants to defend the claim that body and mind are identical against this application of the identity principle, it is only necessary to maintain that it is circular reasoning to suppose that the brain cannot contain pictures of the same size as those experienced by the mind. If the brain and mind are identical, and if such pictures can belong to the mind, then the images not only can but must somehow equally belong to the brain.

Still, it is sometimes possible to draw distinctions on the basis of differences among the properties of nonidentical objects. Presumably, not all applications of the identity principle are deadlocked by circular reasoning. Sometimes it must be legitimate to distinguish among distinct entities on the basis of one's having an objective property that the other lacks. If we are going to make use of the identity principle in trying to solve the mind-body problem, then it may be necessary to consider whether or not we can specify a less objectionable distinction among properties of a certain type that are truly predicated of the mind but that cannot possibly be predicated of the body, or among properties of another type that are truly predicated of the body but not of the mind. Are there any distinguishing properties of body and mind that show, even more conclusively than the arguments we have so far considered, that mind and body are nonidentical?

ABOUTNESS AND THE INTENTIONALITY OF MIND

A class of properties that belong to the mind but are often said to be impossible for the body when considered only as a material entity is the category of *intrinsic intentional properties.* Intentional properties are properties of thought and its expressions—in language, art, and artifacts—by which a thought or its expression is *about* something, or *concerns,* or as we also say, *intends,* an object.

Thought is intrinsically intentional because, considered in itself, it is always about an intended object. If I believe that life is absurd, or if I doubt or fear that I may have become a brain in a fishtank, then I am thinking about or am directed in my thought toward life and the state of affairs according to which life is absurd, or I am thinking about or am directed in thought toward myself, my brain, a fishtank, and the state of affairs according to which I may be a brain in a fishtank. If I then express my thought in language or art, if I speak or write down the appropriate words in a particular language, or if I create an artwork to express my feelings that life is absurd or my fear that I might have become a brain in a fishtank, then I am transmitting my intrinsic intentionality to an expression of my thought, which thereby acquires *derivative intentionality.*

The terminology is suggestive. It indicates that the intentionality by which a use of language or work of art intends or is about or directed toward something is not a feature of the language or artwork considered only in itself but, rather, insofar as it is an expression of the more primary intrinsically intentional thoughts from which its secondary intentionality derives. It is possible in this conception for thought to be intentional without its intentionality being publicly expressed. But it is not possible for language or art to express intentionalilty by itself or for any material object to constitute a genuine use or instance of language or art, except insofar as it is the derivatively intentional expression of intrinsically intentional thought.

If intrinsic intentionality is a property of thought, and so, of mind, can intrinsic intentionality also be a property of the body—in particular, of the brain and nervous system? The question is contested by metaphysicians and philosophers of mind, but there are interesting arguments to show that, unlike the body, the mind considered only as such is intrinsically intentional, and that the body considered only as such, unlike the mind, cannot possibly be intrinsically intentional. That thought is intrinsically intentional—that beliefs, doubts, hopes, and fears are about something or that these mental states intend an object—is not particularly controversial, although philosophers have disputed even this seemingly innocent assumption. Among thinkers who regard thought as intrinsically intentional, some have sought to prove that the intrinsic intentionality of thought can be reduced to or explained away in terms of nonintentional properties. It would be a worthwhile study to consider these attempts to replace intentionality theoretically with something purely nonintentional. For the time being, we will observe that, unless intrinsic intentionality is an illusion or is reducible to nonintentional phenomena, it is impossible to suppose that a purely material entity—such as the body or, especially, the brain and nervous system—can ever be intrinsically intentional. If this is true, then mind and body do not share all their objective properties, so that mind and body are nonidentical.

Why is the body, the brain and the nervous system, considered only in itself, incapable of intrinsic intentionality? The argument has several components. In the first place, it might be said that intrinsic intentionality is an abstract relation between a thought and its intended object. Intrinsically intending or being intentionally directed toward an object is something an intending entity does, an act or activity in which it engages, as a result of which a particular object is intended or becomes something the intending act or activity is about or toward which it is directed. Some intended objects, moreover, do not exist. If I believe, doubt, hope, or fear that I am a brain in a fishtank, then my thought is about a nonexistent intended object, the nonexistent state of affairs in which I am a fully functional brain floating in a fishtank. If I am planning and taking steps, say, to go to law school, then I am intentionally directed in thought toward what is currently a nonexistent state of affairs, one in which I am enrolled in and attending law school and making progress toward obtaining a law degree. This state of affairs does not exist and, if I am unsuccessful in my efforts, may never exist. But I am thinking about it, orienting my activity toward trying to bring it about that I enter law school, and devoting some of my energy to making what is now a nonexistent state of affairs exist. My actions, the things I do to try to achieve a purpose, are intentional, because they begin with a decision to do something in which my thought intends what is at first a nonexistent state of affairs, which I then work to try to accomplish.

If the mind is physically embodied in the brain and nervous system, then intending, and even intending a nonexistent object, is something a body can do. But can the body—in particular, the brain—intend something entirely by virtue of being a material entity? The answer to this problem in the philosophy of mind may depend on what we mean by the concept of a material entity. Perhaps the most clearcut account of a material entity is that of an object all of whose properties can be explained by the laws of physics. The laws of physics describe causal regularities in the interactions of physical substances. The body is a complex system of physical substances, and all of its purely material properties can be explained in terms of the causal regularities encoded in the laws of physics. If intentionality is a property of the body, the brain, and the nervous system, considered only as purely material entities, then it must be possible to explain the intentionality of thought in terms of the laws of physics as a matter of causal regularities in the interactions of physical substances. However, this is precisely what cannot be done, because some thoughts intend nonexistent objects with which the brain cannot causally interact.

Cause-and-effect relations are lawlike regularities among physical events that take place in real time and involve existent physical substances. The fact that we can consider causal relations connecting nonexistent objects—such as imagining what would happen to the world economy if, contrary to the facts, the Stock Market were to crash today, or how a planet that does not really exist would affect the orbit of Neptune if it were to enter our solar system—is a tribute to the intentionality of thought and, in particular, to the intentionality of imagination, rather than an exception to the general truth that causation is a relation between existent events involving existent objects. The intentionality of thought enables us to imagine what would happen if the causal laws of physics were applied to nonexistent objects. But, if we are thinking of the brain and nervous system as a purely material entity or physical system, then the factors to which we might appeal in asking whether the intentionality of thought can be a property of the body considered as a purely material entity are limited to actual causal relations and actual physical interactions occurring between the brain and whatever other actually existent physical objects are deemed relevant.

If we think again of the identity principle we have invoked in trying to answer the mind-body identity problem, we might conclude that mind and body must be nonidentical. The mind actually intends existent and nonexistent intended objects and, so, has the property of being abstractly related to objects that do not exist. The body, on the contrary, considered as a purely material entity, has only such properties as can be explained in terms of actually occurring causal relations among physical events involving actually existent objects. I, which is to say my mind, can think about the nonexistent Fountain of Youth, or about the Lost City of Atlantis, but my body, brain, and nervous system cannot be causally related to any nonexistent objects. By this application of the identity principle, it seems to follow that my mind is not identical to, but distinct from, my body, and that my mind is not a purely material entity.

FUNCTIONALISM AND THE MIND AS MACHINE

The theory that the mind is a purely material entity has also been disputed on other grounds. There is a widespread objection that the concept of mind cannot be explained by reference to any particular material substance, because it appears possible in principle for mental properties to be instantiated by many kinds of physical stuff.

Thus, it happens that human brains and the brains of other animals on Earth are made largely of carbon, and we Earthlings generally are said to be carbon-based lifeforms. But, on another planet in another solar system, there might well be creatures who are chemically very different from the biological organisms we know of as having evolved on Earth. There could be silicon-based rather than carbon-based lifeforms equally capable of the kinds of thoughts that we experience. Then it would not be correct to identify, say, the sensation of pain with a particular electrochemical event as it may occur in the brain of a carbon-based terrestrial, if silicon-based extraterrestrials are also capable of experiencing pain with an entirely different biology determined by an entirely different body chemistry involving different material substances. This line of argument makes it unreasonable to identify the mind and mental properties with any particular kind of material entity or particular physical system, even if the mind is always necessarily embodied in a particular material entity.

If the material substance of the brain and nervous system is not essential to mind, then some theorists have postulated that what is important instead is whatever the material entity in question is able to do. The shift of emphasis from material substance to function marks one of the most crucial distinctions in contemporary philosophy of mind between materialism, which we have already considered, and functionalism. Functionalism understands the mind as a dynamically functioning information-processing system that could, in principle, be implemented on many kinds of material systems. The analogy that is frequently offered to explain the underlying idea of functionalism derives from modern computer technology. It is the concept of mind as information-processing software that could be made to run on many kinds of hardware and, in that sense, is transportable from one machine to another. By similar token, in general terms the mind is thought by functionalists to be a complex system of information input-output flow and control that might be implemented by different physical systems, including terrestrial carbon-based brains and, if there are intelligent exterrestrials elsewhere in the universe, by alien noncarbon-based brains.

The reference to silicon as an alternative material substance by which the mind's software program might be executed further suggests the possibility that thought might be supported by an appropriately designed computer. Information processing in today's technology is effected by miniature electronic circuits imprinted on silicon chips capable of carrying electrical signals that function in some ways much like the brain's neurons. It is the dream of artificial intelligence researchers to be able to design and build a machine that can operate the right sort of computer program so as not only to simulate or imitate human thought but also to actually duplicate thought in the sense of thinking for itself as a kind of mechanical mind. The enthusiasm for achieving artificial thought is reinforced by functionalism as a philosophical ideology that interprets the mind as itself a living biological machine. In this view, the mind is a complex software program for converting input to output signals in a rule-governed way, with the brain and nervous system as its hardware. The functionalist solution to the mind-body problem is to regard the mind as the software or real-time dynamic functioning of a software program and the body, especially the brain and nervous system, as the hardware of a complicated machine. An extraterrestrial or the right sort of computer could then have the same or similar software implemented by a very different nonhuman, non-carbon-based brain or information-processing system; as such, to that degree of sameness or similarity, it would thereby constitute the same or similar kind of mind.

The advantage that many thinkers see in the functionalist concept of mind is that it accommodates some of our ordinary beliefs about the distinction between body and mind without resorting to any supernatural view of the mind as a kind of soul or spirit that could carry on thought in a disembodied existence after the body's death. Functionalism offers a scientific theory of mind by appealing to impressive advances in computer and information-processing technology. Machines are capable of doing many of the kinds of things that people in the past

have assumed only minds could do. Computers can perform more difficult calculations more quickly than even the most prodigious human mathematicians, and they can store, access, and combine information to produce output inferences in the same kinds of decision-making operations in which human reasoners engage. The implication seems to be twofold: (1) in principle, information-processing machines are capable of being minds, of having mental states in more or less the same manner as human minds; and (2) together with recent scientific discoveries about the neurochemistry of brain and nervous system neuromechanisms, the mind itself is a machine, interpreted as the mechanical functioning of software executed by the living machinery of the brain and nervous system.

If the mind and brain are related, as functionalism implies, then it might even be possible for the mind to enjoy a kind of immortality. If functionalism is true, then in principle it should be possible for the mind's program to be lifted from the brain and implemented on another brain or transported to another, more enduring machine. As the original brain ages or becomes injured or diseased, the mind can continue indefinitely, provided that its software is transferred to new, longer-lasting hardware whenever a breakdown occurs in the previous mechanical system.

Functionalism provides an ingenious solution to the mind-body problem. It makes sense of many facts about the mind, brain, and nervous system, as it rides the wave of new discoveries and inventions in computer and information-processing technology. Functionalism also advances an exciting research program for investigating psychological and neurophysiological phenomena in a rigorous scientific framework. Computationalism as a development of functionalism searches for the precise computational algorithms by which the mind performs particular cognitive functions. What, computationalists want to know, is the information-processing program by which the brain perceives the world, controls the motor activity of muscles, searches memory, integrates information from multiple sources to arrive at decisions, and performs all the other activities we associate with the mind? Interesting results have been discovered in this research program, lending further credence to functionalism as a comprehensive philosophical psychology. It is no exaggeration to say that functionalism is currently the most widely held theory of mind, popular not only with many psychologists and cognitive scientists, but also with a sizable number of philosophers. However, philosophical problems cannot be decided by vote or opinion poll but only through the critical consideration of arguments. Are the arguments in favor of functionalism satisfactory, or are there opposing arguments that might undermine the acceptance of the doctrine that the mind is a machine?

As with the materialist concept of mind, it may be worth remarking that, if functionalism is true, then all thought and action are fully determined. We cannot do otherwise than we happen to do if the mind is a machine.

Machines sometimes malfunction, but they cannot disobey the instructions in their programs or act of their own free will in defiance of the physical requirements of their hardware. If the mind is a machine, then it is equally subject to the deterministic laws of nature that govern the behavior of other kinds of machines. We might think that we can deliberate about a course of action that we are free to follow or avoid. But, if determinism is true, then episodes of considering what look to us to be alternatives that we could pursue or choose not to pursue and the final decision at which we arrive when we have made up our minds are all dictated by the functionalist program of input and output our brains are supposed to be implementing.

If determinism is true, then the decision-making process in which we consider whether or not to do something is merely an illusion. We are not free agents in control of our actions; rather, the outcome of our deliberations, given the information the brain receives for its calculations, is as fully predictable and as entirely predetermined as that of any other machine. Finally, since we do not hold machines morally responsible for what they do, if the decisions that we as living machines make involve no more free choice than do the operations of other kinds of machines, then it can be no more reasonable to hold ourselves or any other intelligent beings morally responsible for what we or they choose to do than it would be in the case of nonliving machines.

The problem of free will and moral responsibility for action is part of what is at stake in evaluating the truth of the functionalist theory of mind. As with other philosophical problems, we cannot disregard a theory if it is well supported by arguments just because we are uncomfortable with its implications. We must proceed much as we do in the sciences. In this case, we do so not by reaching judgments based on empirical evidence and observations for or against explanatory hypotheses. Rather, we need to consider the philosophical equivalent of scientific evidence in the form of arguments about the concepts of minds and machines. In this way, philosophical problems can be golden opportunities to clarify ideas about and the consequences of difficult concepts. Often we can do this by asking previously overlooked questions about aspects of a problem that are taken for granted in the sciences.

It is an interesting fact about functionalism that the exact hardware by which a given information-processing program is executed is largely indifferent to the machine's being able to achieve a certain state of mind. We know from using desktop computers that we can run a certain software package on different kinds of machines, provided that the machines have a compatible physical configuration and an operating system capable of implementing the program. At an even higher level of abstraction, the general way in which a computer program converts input to output in its mechanical functioning can generally be rewritten as the same basic information-processing design so as to operate even in quite different kinds of machine hardware with different computing protocols.

Thus, we can pop out the program for a particular task from one computer and run it on another machine, and sometimes on quite different machines. We can even simulate the functioning of an electronic computer on simpler kinds of machines. It is a standard engineering school exercise to devise a crude computer by means of tin cans and stones or by systems consisting of other physical objects that are capable of performing the basic computing functions of expressing, recording, and rigorously transforming information reducible to a code of two symbols (0,1; switch off, switch on), or the presence or absence of a single symbol by any method. Digital computers function at the most basic machine language level by rearranging strings of 0s and 1s used to represent any desired information, converting an input string of information to an output string by a definite set of rules. The outputs are then converted to signals to drive mechanisms that display a desired result on a screen or printer or move a robot's arm.

According to functionalism, as long as the same program is being implemented to transform the same input information strings into the same output information strings, the machines that perform these functions, regardless of how they accomplish the work, are functionally identical and, in that abstract sense, are the same machine. If, as functionalism teaches, the mind is also just an information-processing machine, then any machine capable of executing the same information-processing program as the mind is functionally indistinguishable from it. This means—again, *if* functionalism is correct—that the mind with all its special information-processing functions can be fully replicated by any information-processing machine capable of executing the same program for transforming the same abstractly coded input information into the same abstractly coded output information.

It follows, in principle, as a consequence of functionalism, that my mind could equally exist with all its memories, expectations, and generally all the aspects of consciousness that I consider to be my unique personality, in any functionally equivalent information-processing machine. Although my mind happens to be implemented on the hardware of my human brain and nervous system, according to functionalism, there is no reason I could not equally exist, instead, as the very same mind embodied and implemented in a system of tin cans and stones, following the same program for transformating input to output coded information strings as my brain now processes. As such, functionalism not only holds out the prospect of immortality—for at least as long as there are computing systems capable of carrying on a brain's program once it has become physically incapacitated—but also makes it possible in theory for the mind to be functionally cloned to coexist simultaneously on as many different information-processing machines as a person may care to inhabit.

Some critics of functionalism see these implications as among the theory's self-refuting consequences. But functionalists usually regard conclusions of this sort as interesting results of functionalism's novel explanation of the mind. The philosophical question underlying the dispute is whether thought can reasonably be understood as the dynamic interplay of coded information manipulated by an information-processing program, or whether thought itself, the content of which can be mechanically represented, is something different. An objection to functionalism that goes beyond conflicting intuitions about its implications complains that all methods of coding information for use by any type of digital computer are expressions of thought within the conventions of a language. If the distinction between intrinsic and derivative intentionality is correct, then thought is intrinsically intentional. The expression of thought in any language, on the other hand, including the binary code of 0s and 1s that computers use as information-processing machines, is at best the derivatively intentional expression of intrinsically intentional thought. Another way of putting the same objection is to say that, if thought is intrinsically intentional and if machines are essentially information-processing devices, then machines, however speedy and sophisticated, cannot think for themselves but, by virtue of involving the processing of information coded into a preformulated language, can at most represent the thinking of the intrinsically intentional minds that design, build, program, and operate them. According to this criticism, it is not the machine that thinks but, rather, the person who programs it as nothing more than a complex, derivatively intentional tool that combines language with electronics.

Thus far we have considered a standard objection to functionalism. What can the functionalist reply? One possibility is to distinguish between natural biological and conventional nonbiological languages. The brain might have its own internal coding of information that comprises a natural biological language, in which it represents facts about the external world, stores memories, and performs various information-processing algorithms. To say that language is at most derivatively intentional is true enough if we refer only to conventional nonbiological languages such as English, Russian, and Japanese, along with computer programming languages such as PASCAL, COBOL, FORTRAN, and BASIC. It might be objected that a language is, by definition, a system of symbols for communicating ideas and that ideas cannot be communicated unless they are communicated from one mind to another; however, if the brain's electrochemical signals cannot be translated into a conventional nonbiological language, then they cannot communicate ideas. If that is a requirement of language, then we cannot agree with functionalists who try to get around the problem we have been discussing by supposing that the brain, like a computer, must function by means of an internal system of natural signs or language of thought.

The brain's natural biological language is supposed to be intrinsically intentional, in the sense that it is naturally about or naturally intends or stands in abstract intentional relation to intended objects. Yet, even if this is true, it by no means logically follows that any and every reencoding of the brain's internal natural language in conventional nonbiological computer languages, or any imaginable more sophisticated and high-powered computer languages of the future, is guaranteed to have all the same properties as the internal language of the brain. Thus, if there is a distinction between the brain's natural biological language and conventional nonbiological languages, such that the brain's internal biological language is intrinsically intentional, whereas conventional nonbiological languages are not intrinsically but only derivatively intentional, then there is no reason to expect that the exact duplication of the brain's intrinsically intentional information processing by a computational information-processing machine will also be intrinsically intentional. If intrinsic intentionality is vital to the mind, as we have previously concluded, then two important consequences result. It follows, first, that the mind is not a machine and, second, that functionalism is false.

An information-processing machine is a device that converts coded input to output information in a rigorous, rule-directed way. Functionalism claims that two machines are functionally equivalent if and only if each is capable of the same information-processing functions. If the brain has a unique kind of natural biological language by which it encodes and processes intrinsically intentional information, then, contrary to functionalism's central and philosophically most important thesis, there is no information-processing machine functionally equivalent to the brain—or, as a result, to the mind. It further follows as an unexpected implication of functionalism that, if the brain has its own natural intrinsically intentional biological language, then, even if the brain is an information-processing machine, it is not identical to the intrinsically intentional mind, and the mind is not merely an information-processing machine.

FREE WILL VERSUS DETERMINISM

The objections to materialism and functionalism remove two theoretical threats to the freedom of will. But, even if these criticisms of deterministic theories of the mind are correct, it does not follow that the will definitely is free or that human minds can ever be morally responsible for what they choose to do.

There are several types of determinism, each of which, if true, would contradict the possibility of free will and moral responsibility. Determinism in its most basic form states that whatever happens in the universe cannot be otherwise. As applied to human thought and action, determinism implies that every mental occurrence, including decisions to do or not to do something, and the actions that issue from such decision making, cannot fail to occur in precisely the way they do. When I deliberate about whether to do something, I might imaginatively project the consequences of doing the act and compare them with the imagined consequences of not doing it. If I want to bring about those consequences, then I might decide and subsequently try to perform the action. On the contrary, if I want to avoid the consequences, then I might decide not to perform the action and try to prevent it from occurring. In the absence of compulsion to decide in one way or the other—and in particular, when I do not feel I must decide to act or not act beyond the reasons that might finally persuade me to act or refrain from acting—I ordinarily regard myself as deciding and acting or refraining from acting freely. Could this sense of freedom, about which I often experience a feeling of psychological certainty, be an illusion? Are we altogether deceived about having free will? Are our decisions and the actions that issue from them determined by forces that are beyond our control? If so, are we without moral responsibility for what we do?

Again, we have a deep sense and even psychological certainty that we are morally responsible for most of our actions. We also hold other persons morally responsible, except under extenuating circumstances, as we know from everyday ethics and the practice of law, in which persons are held accountable—rewarded or punished—for their decisions and actions. We raise children in such a way as to cultivate in them a sense of moral responsibility, as part of the socialization by which they learn to distinguish right from wrong. Are these activities philosophically well founded, or are they misguided? The connection between free will and moral responsibility is a bone of contention among philosophers. It is sometimes maintained that, if the will is not free, then, although we might go through the motions of deliberating about the actions we choose, what we eventually decide to do could not have been otherwise but, rather, is predetermined by whatever factors necessitate the decision and the actions that issue from the decision. If a decision to act and the actions that follow could not have been otherwise than they turn out to be, then they would have happened anyway and are not something over which we as agents exercise any effective control.

We are responsible for what we do only when we could have refrained from so acting. If we are determined to decide and to act as we do, then we as agents are not really in control and should not be held morally responsible. I am not morally responsible if a rolling stone strikes me and forces me to push a nearby victim off a bridge, like a row of dominos. Neither am I morally responsible when someone physically pushes me into another person and causes that person to fall off a bridge. If someone holds a gun to my head and credibly threatens to shoot me if I do not push a person off a bridge, then I may be judged to have no real choice in the matter. I do not act freely when I comply and push the person—in a sense, against my will—although I could choose to be shot rather than to obey the command.

The more clearcut case is that in which the stone strikes me and causes me to push the person next to me over the bridge rail. Here most people would probably conclude that I did not act freely and am not morally responsible for what I do. It might even be said that I did not really *act* at all but that I was merely passively affected or acted on by one event, which led to another event in which I did not choose, let alone freely choose, to act. If that is an unproblematic situation in which I do not freely choose or freely act, what should we say about the microscopic effect of a moving molecule, atom, or subatomic particle in my brain, in the neurochemistry that is physically related to the activity of my brain and nervous system? What if the movement of a microparticle in my brain results in a sequence of electrochemical signals that travels along the neural networks in my body and eventually causes a muscle movement by which I push the person sitting next to me over a bridge? If I am not morally responsible when a stone in motion pushes me and thereby indirectly causes me to push the victim in a large-scale sequence of macroscopic events, how can I be morally responsible if the same effect results from a tiny material particle in motion inside my brain that causally determines me to do the same thing as the outcome of a small-scale sequence of microscopic events? How could the size and relative visibility or invisibility by ordinary perception in the two cases make a philosophical difference in judging whether or not I choose and act freely? If moral responsibility is threatened when a sequence of events in my brain chemistry causes me to act in this way without freely deciding to do so, as a kind of unthinking muscular reflex or knee-jerk reaction, why should things be any different if the effect of a stream of moving material particles in the normal functioning of my brain chemistry causes me first to decide and then to act on the decision to push a person off a bridge? In any of these scenarios, it seems equally unreasonable to hold a subject morally responsible for what happens; yet, if determinism is true, then this is precisely the situation we are all in with respect to the decisions we make and the actions we perform.

The answer to the free will problem need not be tactically limited to the refutation of theoretical challenges to freedom. We can also say something more positive about the nature of mind to restore the intuitive belief that we ordinarily act freely when we choose what to do, in the strong sense that we truly could have done otherwise. What is the mind? We have asked this question before and have concluded that the mind is a source of intrinsic intentionality, in which thoughts essentially intend or are about something. In deciding to act, and thinking about whether and what to do, the mind more particularly intends a state of affairs that does not yet exist but is projected in thought as a goal to be achieved. The mind intends nonexistent states of affairs in contemplating actions, trying to decide whether to act and what to do, as a prelude to directing its energies in trying to bring about an as yet unrealized state of affairs.

There are some things we can reasonably intend to do and others we cannot. We do not usually form the intention to travel through time and revise the past. This is something we cannot do, although a very confused or mentally deranged mind might formulate even such a strange intention as this. We can, however, intend to do many things, such as tying a shoe, placing a telephone call, applying to law school, becoming president, going fishing, and performing Shakespeare in the park. Needless to say, we are not always successful in what we intend to do. We might not even succeed in accomplishing such mundane activities as tying a shoe if, for example, we are paralyzed, imprisoned in a full body cast, or suffering from acute arthritis. The point is only that, whenever we decide to do something, whether we succeed in doing it or not, we intend a nonexistent state of affairs that we choose to bring about. A decision to act is intentional; it is about, intends, or is intentionally directed toward an object—typically, a nonexistent state of affairs within the range of things an agent can causally accomplish. The decision to go to law school, for example, intends the currently nonexistent state of affairs in which I am enrolled in law school and working toward a law degree. If I am successful in accomplishing my purpose, then in the future I will have actualized the state of affairs in which I am enrolled in law school and working toward a law degree, thereby causing what was at first nonexistent to exist. Whether I succeed or not, my decision to act is an intention to do something. The decision to act, as the first initiating step of the action, intends a nonexistent object, a state of affairs that at the time of the decision, and typically through the first stages of the resulting action, does not exist, but that I hope will exist or I have chosen and have resolved to try to bring about.

The implication from what has gone before should now be obvious. We have seen that materialist and functionalist theories of the mind are false, precisely because they do not take into account the mind's intrinsic intentionality. By intending a nonexistent state of affairs as a goal for action, an agent is free in the sense of being capable of doing otherwise. The intention also makes the action free, in the sense that the agent could have refrained from doing it, because the decision to act at the initiating step of action is not causally determined. The decision to act and the action that issues from the decision, as we have seen, are not causally determined, because they intend a nonexistent state of affairs that cannot be fully explained or predicted in terms of determining causal factors. If the decision to act and the action issuing from it are free in the strong sense of not being causally determined, then they could have been otherwise. In particular, the decision and action could have been otherwise if the mind in its freedom and causal indeterminism had chosen differently, or, in other words, if the agent had made a different but equally free decision about what to do.

FREEDOM AND MORAL RESPONSIBILITY FOR ACTION

The freedom of the will is manifested in action. Suppose that I decide to order nachos from the appetizer menu in a restaurant. My decision is the first step in the action and can rightly be understood as an integral part of the action that results in my ordering the nachos. Could I have done otherwise? Not if all my actions are merely the mechanical effects of antecedent causal factors. If my decision is just a brain event, and if all brain events are necessitated by cause-and-effect relations that are not fully under my control, then my decision is also causally determined by the physical events that preceded the decision.

The decision to order nachos is a mental act that gives rise to other events, culminating in the action of my ordering the nachos. But the decision is not causally determined by the prior events in my brain and the external physical events that causally affect my brain. The decision to order nachos as opposed to egg rolls, buffalo wings, or stuffed grape leaves intends the as yet nonexistent state of affairs which is such that I have spoken or otherwise communicated with the waitperson to express my desire for nachos. When I do so, the world changes from one in which I have decided to order but have not yet ordered nachos to one in which I have acted on my decision and have actually ordered them. There can be no complete causal explanation and, hence, no causal determination of a mental occurrence that essentially involves reference to a nonexistent object, such as the nonexistent state of affairs of my ordering nachos when I have decided to order but have not yet ordered them. Causal relations can only actually exist between actually occurrent events. Since the decision to act occurs before the action is actualized, and since the decision to act intends an as yet nonexistent state of affairs, the decision cannot be adequately explained without including the nonexistent state of affairs that the decision intends. It follows that the decision cannot be causally explained, since causal explanations must be given entirely and exclusively in terms of existent physical events.

The decision to order nachos cannot be completely causally explained. If the decision cannot be completely causally explained, then it cannot be causally predicted. No brain scientist or cognitive psychologist could have predicted with the requisite degree of accuracy expected in such sciences as physics and chemistry what decision I would make. The best that could be done is to make a prediction on the basis of patterns of past behavior. If I order nachos whenever I go to a restaurant, or if I always order a Mexican appetizer whenever I go to a restaurant, and nachos are the only Mexican appetizer on the menu, then an observer might make an educated guess that I will probably choose nachos. Yet the remarkable thing about human decision makers is that they often express their freedom in unexpected decisions. The very fact that I have always ordered nachos might indicate that I want no more nachos, that it might be time for me to change my snacking habits and try something new. In any case, it is not possible to predict what I will do on the basis of the existent states of affairs prior to my acting on the decision, even for a perfect predictor who knows both all of these facts in the greatest detail and all of the relevant causal laws that would need to be applied in predicting how existent events will causally affect the future. Finally, if my decision cannot be causally predicted, then it is not causally determined. If an event such as my decision to order nachos is causally determined, then it is possible in principle to causally predict before I make the decision that I will, in fact, decide to order nachos rather than anything else. However, since we have just seen that my decision cannot be causally predicted, it follows that my decision is not causally determined. If my decision to act is not causally determined, then it is free. My will to act in deciding what to do and what not to do is free in the strong sense that I could have done otherwise. I could have ordered the egg rolls, buffalo wings, or stuffed grape leaves instead.

When applied to decision making about more important matters, it is easy to see that the same reasoning proves that the mind is free in a morally relevant sense. We are free to decide to do or not to do such things as lie, steal, or kill. Unless we are under unusual duress, or are subject to mental incapacity, our minds as sources of intrinsic intentionality in intending to bring about as yet nonexistent states of affairs are ordinarily free in what we choose to do. The mind's freedom from causal determinism is sufficiently robust, together with an undertanding of the distinction between moral right and wrong, to uphold our moral responsibility for the decisions we make, our actions, and the consequences of the actions that issue from our decisions. The mind, if psychological states are intrinsically intentional, is not merely a machine. By intending nonexistent states of affairs in deciding what to do, the mind not only is the living machinery of the brain and nervous system but also has intrinsically intentional properties that qualify the mind as something more than any machine or purely material or information-processing system. The brain is a machine, and the brain is evidently the body organ by which we think. But thought is not a purely mechanical phenomenon, because the mind's intrinsic intentionality constitutes a noncausal, nonmechanical property. The mind has both causal and noncausal and mechanical and nonmechanical properties, by virtue of which the mind is not simply the brain and is not simply a machine. The contracausal properties of thought, particularly those essentially involved in deciding to act, entail that thought and action are not causally determined, like those of an ordinary machine, and entail that we can be morally responsible for what we freely choose to do.

CAUSAL INDEPENDENCE OF THOUGHT

The analysis of the concept of mind and the intrinsic intentionality of thought that has been proposed raises questions about the nature of mental causation. Can thought, by intending as yet nonexistent states of affairs, cause other events to occur? If so, then we can readily account for the way in which decisions to act are related to other events that are supposed to happen in response to the mind's having reached a decision.

When a decision is made, there is a brain event that, in addition to possessing certain physical neurophysiological or electrochemical properties, involves an essential intrinsic intentionality. The decision is about something and, in particular, intends or is intentionally directed toward a nonexistent state of affairs, which the agent has thereby decided to try to bring about. The causal connections that exist thereafter in what the decision maker continues to do can be understood as occurring because of the physical neurophysiological or electrochemical activity in the brain.

If I decide to order nachos, then an event occurs in my brain that cannot be completely causally explained or causally predicted, and that in itself is therefore not causally determined. The events that are caused by the decision as intrinsically intentional brain occurrences are also, for that reason, not completely causally explainable or predictable and, in that sense, are causally free and undetermined. The decision subsequently causes other things to take place for which the agent can be morally responsible, as for the decision itself. The decision causes other thoughts to take place, including approval or disapproval evaluations and the like, and, more important, when the body is in normal functioning condition, produces a series of muscle activations and movements. When I decide to order nachos, I usually wait and occupy my time pleasantly until the waitperson appears and asks what I wish to order. I might then quickly review and confirm or alter the decision I reached earlier to order nachos. In either case, I might engage in such motor activity as handling the menu one more time or consulting my dining partners on their choices, then speaking the words, putting into action the complex muscles that move my jaws, mouth, tongue, and vocal chords to communicate the content of my decision, which may be to order nachos or to change at the last minute to order stuffed grape leaves.

All of these events have further consequences in the normal course of things. I will eventually taste the appetizers when they are brought and perform the other actions associated with having a meal, perhaps paying by withdrawing cash from my wallet and accepting the change or signing a credit card slip. There will also be other occurrences caused by my original decision to order nachos that do not involve further things that I do but, rather, things that are done or happen to me or that I suffer as passions rather than actions. These include such ordinary events as the digestion of the food I ordered and ate, which would have been different and would have had different overall consequences for my health and nutrition, given the substances they contained, if I had made a different free decision about a choice of appetizers. In this and many other ways, the decisions I make even about ordinary things can affect the future course of the world in interesting ways.

What is sometimes called mental causation is not a special kind of causation but ordinary causation that begins with a causally undetermined mental event of deciding to do something. After a decision is made, it initiates a sequence of causation that proceeds from event to event, leading eventually to the muscle movements described as the physical component of the action. This is the simplest instance of so-called mental causation, beginning with a mental event and ending with a muscle activation, which might involve a speech act of ordering nachos, the pulling of a finger on the trigger of a gun, or any of the other intentional body movements we characterize as actions. In reality, the situation is often more complicated. It is seldom that what we do involves only a direct path of causation from decision to action. Usually, we formulate a decision to act and then begin to do something that we believe and expect will eventually result in the action's occurring. Along the way, we monitor what is happening and try to control the outcome to agree with what we intend the end result to be by making continual adjustments in the ongoing action to make sure that it will take place, many of which may in turn require separate decisions about what to do.

Suppose that I decide to order nachos and am prepared to do so when the wait-person addresses me in Spanish and indicates an inability to speak English. The action I have decided to perform is ordering the nachos, and I am still committed to doing so. But now there is a practical question of matching means to ends, so that my purpose can be fulfilled. I must decide whether to trot out my rusty Spanish and try to make myself understood in that language, to point instead to a name on the menu, or to make a lucky guess that *nachos* is the same word in English and Spanish. Having made these intermediary decisions, I must further adjust my action response, so that whatever I do fits appropriately into the overall plan of action I am formulating in order to realize my original decision. There are countless adjustments that must be made along the way in trying to bring about the action I have decided to perform. Some of these adjustments are automatic, in that they involve only learned muscle movements that I do not need to think through consciously and make decisions about, whereas others might require that I make auxiliary decisions, the implications of which could ramify indefinitely. What if the waitperson is deaf? What if the waitperson cannot make heads or tails of my awful Spanish (mis-) pronunciation?

METAPHYSICS OF MENTAL CAUSATION

The freedom of will is not the only aspect of mental causation and the causal role of decision making in action. There is a problem in understanding the metaphysics of intrinsically intentional thought. How can some brain events have both material properties by which they are caught up in the causal nexus of physical cause and effect, and intrinsically intentional properties by which they exist contracausally outside of and beyond the causal nexus?

If we consider the complementary properties of derivatively intentional entities such as expressions of thought in language, then we can see the same sort of division there as in thoughts interpreted as intrinsically intentional brain events. The use of language to express ideas is physical, but not purely physical. When we write down sentences or disturb air molecules by projecting and shaping breath by controlling our vocal muscles, we create special kinds of physical objects. A written sentence is a physical entity in that it consists of a streak of ink, chisel marks in stone, finger or stick patterns in sand, or arrangements of magnetic particles on a plastic computer disk. A spoken sentence has less permanence, unless we record it on tape or film. But it is equally a physical entity when we think of it as a compression sound wave that radiates out from our vocal chords, through our mouths, and is received and understood by physical receptors, such as ears. Sentences are physical things, but they are not only physical things, because they also have properties that cannot be explained in purely physical terms.

Written or spoken sentences in a language also have meaning, just as thoughts do. The derivatively intentional meaning of language is not purely physical, for the same reasons we have already considered in the case of the mind's intrinsic intentionality. Language expresses ideas, and a language user's ideas expressed through language, produced as written or spoken sentences, can be understood only in terms of the objects and states of affairs that language users intend. Intended objects need not exist, so generally the derivative intentionality of language can no more be fully explained in terms of the physical properties of the ink, stone, magnetic particles, or air molecules in which ideas are expressed than can the intrinsic intentionality of the thoughts that speech acts express. This may be obvious enough when we reflect on the fact that we cannot interpret the meaning of a sentence written in a foreign language, if we lack facility in that language, just by understanding the physics and chemistry of the ink with which the sentences are written. If the physics and chemistry of the media of written sentences were sufficient to understand the meaning of sentences, then if we understood a sentence written in Russian in blue ink, we could automatically understand the meaning of another sentence written in the same ink in any other language. On such an absurd assumption, we could even conclude that any Russian sentence has the same meaning as any other sentence written with a substance having the same chemical properties as the medium in which the original Russian sentence was written

It is natural to object to the idea that the chemistry of ink or chalk marks alone is not the only relevant material property of a written sentence. A sentence also has a particular physical shape, which is a formal geometrical property of a written sentence, and for which there are analogous properties in the case of a spoken sentence. Such physical properties of sentences might also be invoked to explain the meaning of differently shaped sentences written in the same ink with the same chemistry. However, the physics as well as the chemistry of sentence inscription is still not enough to explain the meaning of sentences only in terms of their physical properties. First, we note that the chemistry of language use is not sufficient to determine meaning. The same thought can be expressed by means of a sentence written in blue ink or in red ink with a different chemistry. Second, it is important to see that, even if we take into account the shapes of the sentences, we do not yet have enough information to interpret their meaning. There are many different shapes in which the same letters of an alphabet can be written in many different typographical styles. Consider the difference in shape among English letters in ordinary type, boldface, italics, and any of the various fonts in which the language can be printed, not to mention differences in size, spatial separation and arrangement of letters, serifs, frills, and gothic curlicues. Even more dramatically, consider the differences between the way in which the same English sentence can be written in ordinary English, in Morse Code, or in the distribution of magnetic bits on a computer disk, which physically do not resemble one another geometrically.

Even if we were to group together all the alternative families of physical shapes in which the same sentences in a given language could be expressed, that would still not be enough to derive the meaning of a sentence from its chemistry and physics. The meaning of a sentence depends on its expression of ideas, and there is no basis in the principles of physics to determine, for example, that the word *raining* in the English sentence "It is raining" refers to or intends the occurrence of a state of affairs in which there is an atmospheric release of liquid water droplets from clouds. Consider the physics and chemistry of "It is raining" and the physics and chemistry of "Il pleut" (in French) and of "Es regnet" (in German), and ask what these shapes of symbols could have in common such that there might be general physical principles according to which they would all mean the same thing. The problem goes even deeper, because intentionality is not in any case a physical relation but an abstract relation that exists intrinsically between a thought and its intended objects and deriv-atively between the expressions of thought in language, art, or artifacts and their intended objects. As such, intentionality is not subject to physical forces and cannot be made the subject of a purely physical science—standing, as it does, outside the physical order of cause and effect.

Intentionality of the derivative rather than intrinsic sort is as much a basic prop-erty of language as the physics and chemistry of the medium through which a sen-tence is expressed. However, because the abstract relation of intentionality in lan-guage is not a physical property of the sentence but, rather, the aspect of a sentence by which it refers to the existent or nonexistent objects intended by the language user in writing or verbally uttering the sentence, the meaning of language cannot be understood in purely physical terms. The fact that a derivatively intentional expres-sion of thought in language involves both physical and nonphysical properties sug-gests that the intrinsically intentional thought it expresses also consists of purely physical neurophysiological properties and intrinsically intentional, physically irre-ducible properties, as an intrinsically intentional neurophysiological brain event.

When I reach a decision to do something, such as ordering nachos in a restau-rant, the mental event that constitutes my decision is a brain event, but it is not only a brain event. As a brain event, my decision is not totally uninfluenced by prior causal factors, even if it is not completely causally determined. I may choose nachos because I am influenced in my decision by the fact that in the past I have found their flavor pleasing, or because I have never tried them, but I have been partly conditioned by experience to want to try new tastes when given the opportu-nity. Being influenced to do something is not being irrevocably caused to do it and in no way deprives me of free will in choosing from the menu. After I have made my decision, the fact that my thought has physical properties as well as intrinsically intentional properties implies that my decision will also have a causal impact on what happens later. We have already seen how the decision to order nachos can cause other things to happen, such as actually placing the order, eating the food, paying for the bill, digesting the food, and so on. None of these things is physically caused by the intrinsic intentionality of my decision. They may be causally condi-tioned by the fact that I have made such a decision, because, if I had not so decided, I would not be in a position to order, eat, pay, or digest. Insofar as these subsequent occurrences are caused, they are caused by the physical properties of my thought as a brain event. By contrast, the intrinsically intentional aspects of my decision are best explained not in terms of physical causes but, rather, in terms of reasons that can incline me to do one thing or another by force of persuasion rather than physi-cal cause and effect.

Moreover, the intentional aspect of my decision contributes afterward to the chain of reasons that influences a continuing interaction between thought and action. I order the nachos after I have decided to order them not because a cause-and-effect connection compels me to do so. I am free until the last instant to adhere or not adhere to my decision, just as I am free in arriving at the original decision to make a different selection than I actually make, and to act otherwise than I actually do. I have reasons for choosing what I decide to do, but reasons are not physical causes. I order the nachos after I have decided to order them, because I have gone through the process of deciding what to order for the sake of arriving at an acceptable choice of what to eat. What sense would it make, unless I had had a last-minute change of heart, not to order what I had decided to order? Similar abstract logical and practical reasons rather than efficient physical causes lead me to eat the nachos once they are brought, and still other reasons persuade me to follow convention by paying for the nachos after I have eaten them, rather than trying to skip out on my tab. When these sorts of conditions are satisfied, then my decision to act, and the actions that occur as a result, are free in the strong sense that I could have done otherwise. They are also, therefore, decisions and actions, along with their direct and indirect causal consequences, for which I can be morally responsible.

MIND, BODY, AND MIND-BODY

The mind-body problem seeks an understanding of the mind and its properties as something exclusively mental, exclusively physical, or a combination of mental and physical factors. We want to answer the sojourner's question, so we need to know what kinds of beings we thinkers and knowers are. This chapter has explored the prevalent concept of mind as a material entity or biological machine, a living computer made of neurons and synaptic connections that processes information by input-output functionalities in much the same way as an artificial intelligence computer program.

The concept of the mind as a machine raises the issue of causal determinism. If we are causally determined thinking machines, then we are not morally responsible. The idea of choosing a course in life, then, also becomes meaningless; by implication, life itself might seem meaningless or absurd. This is why we have asked whether the mind is a machine and have criticized the implications of a mechanistic theory of mind. We have seen reason to reject exclusively materialist and functionalist explanations of mind as failing to do justice to the intrinsic intentionality of thought. Intentionality, in turn, is directly related to the problem of free will and to the philosophical controversy surrounding the commonsense view that people are ordinarily free and morally responsible for their actions, beginning with their decisions about what to do and how to act.

We have considered the argument that the intrinsic intentionality of mind in decision making relates thought to as yet unrealized nonexistent states of affairs. We have discovered that the decisions we make cannot be fully understood—and, hence, cannot be accurately predicted—without making reference to the nonexistent states of affairs our decision-making reasoning intends. However, since nonexistent objects do not enter into actual cause-and-effect relations, we cannot fully causally explain or accurately predict all of our decisions and actions. This conclusion implies that our decision making is not completely causally determined but is free in the strong sense that our decisions and the resulting actions could have been different than they happen to be. The decisions we make are often causally constrained, they have causal effects of many kinds, and they can be influenced by reasons, motivations, desires, hopes, and fears. Generally, however, people decide and act freely; they can choose to act and, consequently, act differently than they choose to do; and thus, they are ordinarily morally responsible for their decisions and actions.

If we look to the nature of mind, to what is to be a thinking thing, as a key to understanding the meaning of life, then in this discussion we have at least removed some of the philosophical obstacles to our ingrained sense of free will and moral responsibility that seem to follow from a causally deterministic materialist or functionalist philosophy of mind.

CHAPTER FOUR

Proofs and Disproofs for the Existence of God

GOD AND THE MEANING OF LIFE

Belief in God offers many people comfort and guidance in life. The idea that there is a supernatural all-powerful being that created and watches over the world and takes an interest in our welfare has been throughout history a very compelling concept. Different cultures have had different views about God or the gods, but most peoples have worshipped divine forces, entities, or persons that transcend life on Earth.

We must now investigate the philosophical assumptions of traditional religions that personify divinity, since belief in God might be thought to help answer the sojourner's question. Religion offers two kinds of solutions to the problem of the meaning of life. First, if God exists and is our creator, then the meaning of life may have something to do with God's will or God's plan for the universe and our place in it. Second, to the extent that many religions teach that there is an afterlife for the soul in surviving the death of the body, a believer may want to answer the sojourner's question by understanding all of life as a sojourn, a way station during which the soul is meant to prepare for a future spiritual existence.

The concept of God as a divine person, an intelligence in some ways like ourselves but infinitely greater in power, wisdom, and goodness, makes it possible to assume that what happens in the universe has meaning as the playing out of God's intentions. God intends whatever takes place, including all the daily events of our lives to which we attach importance, so that the occurrences that may otherwise seem random, absurd, and meaningless can be understood as the result of God's will. We may not—and, indeed, we need not—always understand the purpose of things that happen, especially when they run counter to what we take to be our personal interests. When we lose a loved one to death or suffer reversals of fortune, including the greatest of tragedies, we might fail to grasp why such disappointments occur. But some believers find solace by interpreting even the worst disasters as meaningful episodes serving a larger rational purpose that is part of God's grand design.

Can the meaning of human life be regarded as fitting into God's scheme? If so, then we might have an obligation to try to discover God's purpose for our lives and to conduct ourselves in accord with God's will. God may want us to be fruitful and multiply, to help others, to spread the Gospel, or to fight the Infidel.

There are many different religions representing many different opinions about God's intentions for human destiny. There are also serious epistemic difficulties about how we human beings could possibly learn who or what God is and what God's plan requires of us collectively and as individuals. Should we wait for a divine revelation? Some believers have claimed to receive communications directly from God, with specific instructions about what they should do. Yet such experiences are rare, they usually stand in need of interpretation, and various people who believe they have been visited by such revelations have reported quite different and sometimes contradictory conclusions about what God has told them. Moreover, we know that it is experimentally possible to duplicate some of the rapturous experiences of revelation that saints and mystics have undergone by such mundane physiological methods as fasting, drugs, sensory deprivation, social isolation, repetitive chanting, and even rapid spinning in a circle. We need not be religious skeptics in order to wonder whether it is really God or a person's own brain that is speaking to those who claim to have had revelations, as in the case of schizophrenics and others who claim to hear inner voices.

Another possibility is to discover God's will in the teachings of a holy text. The interpretation of literal or metaphorical meaning can be a further obstacle in discerning God's will. It is a commonplace in religious studies that the same writings have given rise to many different religious sects, some with radically different conceptions about what God intends. Then again, there are many different holy texts, including the Talmud, the Holy Bible, the Quoran, the Vedas, the Sutras, the Bardol Thödol, the Popul Vuh, the Book of the Great Awakening, the Book of Mormon, the Dead Sea Scrolls, the Analects of Confucius, and many others, including manuscripts that must have been lost to history and about which we know nothing at all. Which of these truthfully contain the will of God? How can we choose among them? We might adopt a syncretic viewpoint, according to which we should read and meditate on all of these works, with the hope that the more earnestly we study them the greater will be our understanding of God's plan for the universe. But the problem of interpreting any of these scriptures poses difficulties for arriving at a confident appraisal of the meaning of life, especially because together these holy writings have many points of agreement but in other ways contradict one another about very basic matters of religious doctrine.

WHY DO WE BELIEVE?

In practice, believers usually accept a particular text or set of texts as containing the religious truths they choose to follow. Such a preference is sometimes the accidental result of the fact that one body of writings rather than another was part of the religion in which the believers were raised as children at an impressionable age. If the same people had been raised as Zoroastrians rather than Christians, or as Christians rather than Zoroastrians, then, as we know from a comparison of world religions, many would be likely to remain faithful throughout their lives to one statement of doctrine rather than another.

This is also why religions devote extraordinary care to the education and religious indoctrination of the very young. For this is the time when religious attitudes take root and have the greatest chance of becoming firmly established for life.

Conversions from another belief or from nonbelief can also occur. But the question remains why one comes to accept one religion rather than another as an expression of the will of God or the gods and of why a believer comes to see one set of religious texts rather than another as offering insight into God's will. In most cases, a believer is simply drawn by compulsion or psychological necessity to regard a religion's teachings as true, without undergoing the equivalent of a scientific investigation and evaluation of options before choosing. In fact, religious believers sometimes speak of being chosen by a higher force rather than rationally choosing by their own judgment what to believe.

An important factor in the emotional and intellectual appeal of many religions is their narrative unity. We can think of religious views about human nature as a kind of story, with a beginning, a dramatic and sometimes tumultuous middle part, and an often satisfying, conflict-resolving conclusion. The first sentence of the book of Genesis in the Bible sets the stage for this kind of explanation of the world: "In the beginning, God created the heavens and the earth." That is literally the beginning of a very interesting story. Thousands of years after these words were written, we place ourselves in a scene of immediate action, in which we are currently engaged in making difficult moral choices in living our lives. Finally, the story has a definite ending, toward which we can see such events leading, such as a day of judgment followed by the eternal rewards of heaven or, in some religions, a reprieve from the endlessly repeating cycle of birth, death, and rebirth.

We know how to follow a story. To think of our lives as the enactment of a carefully scripted plot with a lively cast of characters, good and evil forces, justice, retribution, and a happy ending (we hope!) has a very strong appeal. All of the world's popular religions offer much the same three-part narrative movement, consisting of a supernatural origin of the world, conflict in our present existence, and extraworldly resolution as an explanation of the meaning of life. Explaining life as the unfolding of a religious epic tale can be extremely satisfying, because it describes our destiny as having closure, in which disharmonies are resolved, as in a great work of music or literature. It is easy to see why many people find such a unified account of where we come from, the significance of what is happening to us now, and how it is all supposed to conclude as more compelling than scientific or philosophical explanations. Religion has considerably more poetic license than philosophy or science to propound mysteries and concoct ingenious cosmological tales. It is as though traditional religions had adopted the line diagram we presented at the opening of chapter 1 to illustrate what we called the journey of a lifetime, but replaced the philosophical question marks with positive answers about the beginning and end of the world and our role in it that are not known through experience. If, however, we are to consider the truth of religious narratives about the meaning of life philosophically, then we must try to step back from the attractions of such an aesthetically pleasing and potentially psychologically comforting way of looking at human life, and ask whether there are good reasons to justify the religious stories we are told.

Regardless of whether and how God's will might be discovered, the belief that God exists and has a divine purpose for the universe can provide a satisfying answer to the sojourner's question. A major part of the question is to know whether life is meaningful or absurd and to know, if possible, that life is meaningful because the universe is the creation of a supreme intelligence, acting intentionally to bring about a certain order. If, as many religious believers accept, God is perfectly good, then the universe itself as a whole, appearances notwithstanding, is also perfectly good. This, then, must include all events that take place in all their ramifications for every individual human being, for whom there is a part to play in God's ultimate plan for the world. There is a difference, however, between believing that the existence of God makes life meaningful and knowing exactly what the meaning of life is by virtue of knowing exactly what plan or purpose God has for the world. We make progress toward answering the sojourner's question if we can at least know that there is a God and that God is a divine intelligence that is responsible for the condition of the universe. If we know that life has religious meaning, then we can sensibly go in search of it, to begin a quest for spiritual enlightenment that may eventually lead us to understand how we are supposed to act in accordance with God's will.

RELIGIOUS BELIEF AND THE SOJOURNER'S QUESTION

This conclusion, that if God exists then life might have a religious meaning, suggests another approach to the sojourner's question. A believer might accept a particular religious tenet, according to which life on Earth is a temporary state for the soul and life a preparation for a future state in which the person, self, or soul survives death to be resurrected in heaven, hell, or somewhere in between.

Some religions teach that the soul will be judged as worthy of eternal reward in heaven or damnation and punishment in hell. The basis for such a final judgment is a matter of dispute among religions. Some expect God to divide the chaff from the wheat according to whether a person has committed unrepented sins or certain kinds of sins or on the grounds of having accepted or having failed to accept the underlying beliefs of the religion. In some views, God as a perfectly benevolent being does not actually punish souls, or at least does not do so by means of the physical torments ascribed to hell as a lake of fire in Dante's *Inferno,* or by troops of little pitchfork-wielding demons, as in the apocalyptic paintings of Hieronymous Bosch.

Other conceptions of God see him (the male gender bias is an element of much of traditional religion) not as a loving, infinitely forgiving heavenly father but as a righteous, uncompromising, and even angry judge. Regardless of how these issues are decided by any given religion, the idea is that our life on Earth is a sojourn in which we are supposed to prepare ourselves for an act of judgment, after which our real existence will begin, according to a combination of our merits and God's justice or grace. The promise of heaven and threat of hell are sometimes prominent components in the motivation for religious believers to sustain the practice of their religion and to conduct themselves according to the principles of a moral code that is integrated with and may have its origins attributed to historical events in the religion's founding. This is true of the Ten Commandments in the Old Testament, which are supposed to have been handed down from God to Moses on Mount Sinai, engraved on stone tablets as the direct expression of God's will for the ancient Israelites as his chosen people. A moral code based on God's will in distinguishing good from evil behavior is generally known as a *divine command theory of ethics.* The meaning of life can be interpreted in a divine command ethical framework as acting according to what is perceived as God's moral law.

The fact that some people find it comforting to believe that, metaphorically speaking, the universe is in God's hands and that rewards and punishments are meted out to people based on their conduct during life—the fact that belief in God can provide one kind of answer to the sojourner's question—does not by itself show either that God actually exists or that belief in the existence of God can provide a satisfactory answer to the sojourner's question. To be adjudicated by philosophical criteria, these problems call for unflinching critical inquiry.

The intense conviction with which some people claim to believe in God's existence does not constitute philosophically acceptable evidence that such beliefs are true. We have already seen that psychological certainty by itself is no guarantee of the truth of any proposition. Some religious believers are so ardent in their faith that they claim to know the existence and nature of God with the same or even greater certainty than they know, for example, that they have two hands. However, it is easy, given how emotionally charged the topic of religion is, for most believers to confuse psychological certainty with solid epistemic justification. How can we distinguish between having good reasons for accepting belief in the existence and nature of God and engaging merely in wishful thinking? It is so satisfying for some people to believe that God exists and takes an interest in our welfare, that God can help us when we pray for assistance in time of crisis, and that God will distribute justice to people who have lived good lives or have held the right kinds of beliefs while handing out appropriate punishments to offenders in an afterlife, that religious believers are apt to conflate what they deeply want to be true with what they are epistemically entitled to believe.

REASON AND FAITH IN GOD

The importance of religious belief makes it imperative for philosophers to consider the reasoning by which the existence and nature of God might be justified. Such a stance raises an issue in the philosophy of religion about the relation between reason and faith. We often hear that belief in God is a matter of faith, which we must either accept or not accept, and that cold, hard, scientific or philosophical reasoning is irrelevant to religion.

This position calls for several types of response. If there is anything that characterizes a philosophical outlook, regardless of the details of the particular philosophy adopted, it is the commitment to pursuing reason wherever it may lead, without prejudging the outcome and without distorting the direction of arguments in order to arrive at conclusions that agree with preconceived beliefs. In science and mathematics, there is less temptation to bend the truth. There the truth or falsehood of a proposition is more likely to have tangible implications in the real world, so that making a mistake and twisting arguments to suit subjective ideological preferences is more likely to be discovered and corrected. In the case of religion, however, emotional investment is often so great, while the implications of taking a wrong turn in formulating and evaluating religious beliefs are virtually uncorrectable by practical checks on correct and incorrect inferences, that there is more opportunity as well as more inclination for some thinkers to try to make the outcome of arguments agree with their religious preconceptions. Arguments about religion that begin with false assumptions are less likely to be corrected, because they concern the existence of a supernatural being and what might happen to a person's soul after death, from which no one has come back to tell the tale, so-called near death experiences aside.

The thesis that religion can be only a matter of faith, to which reason in the form of philosophical argument is irrelevant, encounters another kind of objection. The plain fact, as we have already observed, is that various people, especially in different cultures, are often led by faith to accept totally different religious beliefs. Faith by itself is directionless. It does not contribute to the acceptance of any particular beliefs. Rather, faith is more like psychological certainty, and in some cases wishful thinking, which is no substitute for epistemic justification. Believers can have the same intensity of faith in contrary and even completely opposite and mutually contradictory propositions as logically inconsistent articles of faith. We know that this is true if, for no other reason, we study the religious wars that have occurred in history, fought with equal fervor on all sides by people of conflicting faiths. Buddhists, Christians, Jews, Muslims, Shintoists, Taoists, Zoroastrians, and all the various sects reflecting internal divisions accept the creeds of their religious divisions with the same intensity of faith and, in principle, exhibit the same degree of psychological certainty that only their religious beliefs are true.

Many people need an unshakable bedrock of true beliefs that explain the world and the purpose of human life. Some philosophers have controversially asserted that, when people are intellectually incapable of the abstruse metaphysical speculations of philosophy, they try to fill their need for an answer to such basic questions by fastening onto religious dogma, to which they pledge their undying allegiance in what is then called their faith in God. It can almost seem that the need for answers satisfied by religion is so deep that virtually any religious system will do, provided only that it offers the necessary psychological assurances that an individual requires and that the faithful can accept without question. However, since faith considered only in itself does not entail faith in any particular religious doctrine, and since people of comparable faith often radically disagree about matters of religious belief, it is essential to examine the content of religious teachings with the same healthy skepticism as any other subject, using the same tools of logical analysis.

It is sometimes claimed that everyone must accept some propositions entirely by faith. I do not know with certainty when I enter a building that the building will not collapse. I am not an architect or engineer, and even if I were, I would not ordinarily have occasion to investigate the structural soundness of every building before I venture in the door. In one sense of the word, my walking into a building is an exercise of faith. But is this the same kind of thing that is meant

by the concept of religious faith? There is an important difference between faith and trust. My attitude in entering the building, if I think about it at all, is something more like a combination of trust and hope. I certainly hope that the building will not come crashing down, and I trust that it will not. My reason for trusting that the building will hold is that I see the building standing solidly, and I have no grounds for doubting that it will remain standing during the time I expect to be within its walls. More important, I know that public buildings are built and inspected by professionals according to high standards of quality materials and workmanship that apply well-established principles of physics and related sciences that have been tested by years of experience in the construction trades. Although I may not take the trouble to think all this through, I implicitly accept with a high degree of objectively justifiable probability that the building will not collapse. I trust and hope that the building will not fall, but I do so for good reasons. I do not believe that the building will stay standing as an article of faith, and certainly not as anything comparable to an article of religious faith.

The difference is that, in matters of faith, I *cannot* scientifically prove or justify my belief. *Faith* is the word we use precisely when what we believe cannot be defended adequately by reason or empirical evidence. If I believe something by faith, then I believe it because or despite the fact that I have none of the sorts of proof that I otherwise consider necessary to give in support of my beliefs. When I trust something, I have or can have an objective reason for my belief. When I accept something on faith, I have nothing but the firm conviction of psychological certainty in the absence of any objective reason. If I were to have a reason for such a belief, I would not need to accept it on faith. Finally, when I believe something or act on hope and trust, I acknowledge the possibility that I could be wrong. I hope and trust that the building will not collapse when I am inside it, but I know that buildings do sometimes fall, so I recognize that there is a slight possibility that this could happen during my visit. But, if I believe something by faith, then I am unwilling to acknowledge even the remote possibility that what I believe could be false. To have faith is to put on the shining armor of the most invincible psychological certainty of which the mind is capable, but which, like any other form of psychological certainty, is still not necessarily true.

The need for philosophy to consider the reasoning that might be offered in support of religious doctrines must not prejudge its agreement or disagreement with beliefs accepted on faith. It is conceivable that philosophy might offer independent rational justification for beliefs that are previously accepted as articles of faith. Even if philosophy concludes that there are no satisfactory arguments to be given on behalf of the existence of God or other mainstays of traditional religion, it does not necessarily follow that faith must be abandoned in favor of a philosophical atheism or agnosticism, or that philosophers must renounce religious belief. On the contrary, if it could be shown that religion lacks adequate philosophical foundation, such a result might instead highlight the importance of faith in a religious believer's life. It would simultaneously reveal not only the limitations of religion as a system of beliefs that can only be adopted as a matter of faith rather than reason, but also the limitations of philosophy in the spiritual practice of religion.

IS IT SACRILEGIOUS TO ARGUE ABOUT GOD?

We are about to consider several proofs and a disproof for the existence of God. Before we begin, it might be worthwhile to address an objection that is sometimes raised against the idea of trying to reason about the existence of God. The emphasis on accepting God as an act of faith in some religions forbids any examination of the belief in God as blasphemous. Is it wrong altogether to consider arguments about whether or not God exists, or to ask whether or not human reason is powerful enough to prove or disprove the existence of God?

To denounce any inquiry into the existence or nature of God as impious overlooks the fact that many respected followers of traditional religions have also engaged in rational inquiry into the content of religious beliefs. It is an extraordinary presumption to suppose that we can know what God would find impious or blasphemous in our sincere curiosity and desire to know all that we can about God. If anything, it may be an even greater impiety to suppose that God would create rational beings and then disapprove of or be offended by our exercising this God-given reason by inquiring into God's existence and nature. It is also possible that those who try authoritatively to persuade us that it is morally wrong or offensive to God even to try looking logically at religion might be worried that their own religious beliefs will not stand up to philosophical scrutiny.

The very act of asking whether it is wrong to argue about God already applies reason to a considerable extent in trying to understand the concept of God. If we do not seek to clarify the concept of God, then our faith in and worship of God will be largely empty. For in that case we literally do not know what we are talking about in accepting God's existence and claiming to know God's nature and will. Thus, it may be unavoidable for even the most devout believer in God to combine faith with reason. If it is an act of impiety or blasphemy to exercise one's reason in thinking about the existence of God, therefore, it may be a problem for every religious believer as well as every unbeliever or religious skeptic.

We proceed by distinguishing two categories of proofs for the existence of God. These proofs are divided by the basic epistemological distinction between *a priori* and *a posteriori* knowledge. Attempts have been made to demonstrate God's existence from principles that are independent of experience and based on reason and as inferences that can be drawn from observable aspects of the empirical world. We will first consider several kinds of efforts to prove the existence of God from the standpoint of pure reason.

THE CONCEPT OF GOD

Although we have talked about God and the gods and have made reference to some of the major religious traditions in which God is worshipped, we have not yet tried to define the concept of God. This is an important step in understanding several of the most influential kinds of proofs for the existence of God that are supposed to follow from God's other properties. In the major monotheistic traditions of Judaism, Christianity, and Islam, God is generally said to be omnipotent, or all-powerful; omniscient, or all-knowing; and perfectly benevolent, or all good. As worshipped in these religions, God is assumed to be infinitely powerful, infinitely wise, and infinitely righteous. The definition of God in this conception is thus God =df an omnipotent, omniscient, and perfectly benevolent being.

It is sometimes said in attributing these characteristics to God that, if God were not to have these properties, then God would not be God, in the sense that no such being would be worthy of worship. If God is not infinitely powerful, then we cannot reasonably suppose that God is the creator of the universe, or that God necessarily has sufficient power to help us in time of need or to reward and punish forgiven and unforgiven sinners in an afterlife. If God is not infinitely wise, then we cannot reasonably suppose that God knows everything that happens—and, in particular, that God might not know whether or not we have lived a sufficiently good life to merit the eternal rewards or punishments of heaven or hell. God, in that case, need not know everything we do, or the intentions with which we do them and, so, cannot be a perfect judge of our actions. In that case, neither would God know whether or not we need help; our prayers for divine intervention might not be heard and would go unanswered. This would also fall far short of our concept of God as a perfect being. Finally, if God is not infinitely good or perfectly benevolent, then, again, God cannot be a perfect judge but, rather, might be evil or partly corrupt. If God has a moral personality like our own—that is, a mixture of good and bad—then it is unreasonable to suppose that God can judge us from a sufficiently high moral plateau to justly sentence us to eternal bliss or eternal damnation. In order to stand in judgment of human beings and rightly hand out such extraordinary rewards and terrible punishments with perfect justice, as God is sometimes supposed to do, God must be an infinitely morally more perfect being than those who are judged.

The definition is readily expanded to incorporate whatever other perfections might be attributed to God. Indeed, a simpler definition of God, which incorporates all of the properties we have now considered as part of the traditional concept, is of a being with all perfections, God =df the being with every perfection. The definition requires a little finessing, because we do not want to conclude that God has the property of being perfectly evil. To avoid this problem, we need an account by which, despite its misleading terminology, being perfectly evil is not a perfection but, rather, a defect of character, so that God as the being with all perfections could not be perfectly evil, or perfectly impotent, perfectly ignorant, perfectly incapable of creating the universe, or the like. Further clarification of the definition may take some work. But it should be possible to specify what is meant by a perfection, so that not every property taken to an infinite and, in that sense, perfect degree counts as a perfection in the intended sense. For the moment, we can dispense with this clarification and proceed on the intuitive understanding that a perfection is an infinite but specifically positive property rather than a negative or defective property, according to our perception of the distinction between positive and negative values.

ONTOLOGICAL PROOF FROM THE DEFINITION OF GOD

The definition of God we have developed provides the main assumption for an *a priori* proof of God's existence. There are many variations of the following inference, sometimes known as the *ontological argument* for the existence of God, of which we will consider two. We make use of a standard device for distinguishing the assumptions from the conclusions of an argument, in which we number all of the propositions and divide assumptions from conclusions by a short horizontal line. This method has the virtue of making all the parts of the argument explicit and of clearly showing the parts of the inference that are supposed to depend on others. We can then refer to each part of the argument by its corresponding line number. The first version of the proof from the definition of God is the following:

1. God =df the being with all perfections.
2. Existence is a perfection.
   _____
3. Necessarily, God exists.

An argument is *deductively valid* when, just in case its assumptions are true, its conclusions are true as a matter of logical necessity. A *sound* argument, by contrast, not only is deductively valid but has only true assumptions, thereby logically guaranteeing the truth of its conclusions. We test an argument by questioning the truth of its assumptions, and by granting the truth of its assumptions for the sake of argument, and asking whether, if the assumptions were true, the conclusions would also thereby necessarily be true. If not, then there is a counterexample, in which it is logically possible for the assumptions to be true and the conclusions false, which shows that the argument is deductively invalid.

The definition in assumption (1) in a way is true by stipulation. We can dispute a definition, as we did in the case of some of the proposed definitions of the concept of knowledge. A standard method is to look for counterexamples in which the *definiendum* and *definiens* do not exactly match. But the definition of God as the being with all perfections has the weight of history and tradition behind it; moreover, it makes sense as an explication of the concept of God that many people worship. Provided that we can define the concept of perfection with sufficient care to avoid attributions to God of any and every property taken to its infinite degree, then there is an obvious sense in which many religious believers, at least in the monotheistic traditions, conceive of God as the being with all perfections. However, the problem posed by the need for a precise definition of the concept of a perfection comes back to haunt us in the proof immediately thereafter in assumption (2). For now we are told that existence is a perfection. This proposition invites the objection that it is not necessarily perfect or a perfection for any and every thing to exist. Is it a sign of perfection that horrible, disfiguring diseases exist or that murderous fiends exist? Of course not—the implication is that existence is not always a perfection, or not a perfection *per se*. We can avoid such counterexamples by construing the concept of a perfection as a positive property, in the sense of being a property it would be better for the universe to instantiate than not to instantiate. Such an interpretation forestalls the counterexamples we have considered, because it would not be better for the universe to instantiate than not to instantiate infinite impotence, infinite ignorance, infinite evil, the existence of disease or homicidal maniacs, or any other bad thing to any degree.

Similarly, it might be objected that, if the argument were correct, then it would be equally possible to prove in parallel fashion that there must be a perfect summer cottage. The argument is that a perfect summer cottage has all the perfections necessary for a perfect summer cottage, including the ideal location, spaciousness, convenience, and the right sort of deck, loft, picture windows, and boathouse. It has no termites, it never needs painting, and the roof never leaks. But a perfect summer cottage would not really be perfect if, despite having all of these admirable properties, it did not exist. A nonexistent perfect summer cottage is hardly a perfect summer cottage, since we cannot actually stay there or make use of any of its supposedly wonderful amenities. If the argument for the existence of God from the definition of the concept of God as the being with all perfections were correct, then it would seem to be equally correct to prove by analogous argument that there must exist a perfect summer cottage and, by extension, a perfect mobile home, perfect dentist, perfect submarine, and perfect anything else. Since it is absurd to suppose that we could, by pure reasoning alone, prove the existence of a perfect summer cottage, it must be equally absurd to suppose that we could, by pure reasoning, prove the existence of God as the perfect being or the being with all perfections.

Without trying to define the concept of a perfection or perfect property more exactly, we might now have explained the idea well enough as a good quality it would be better for the universe to instantiate than not to instantiate. The account makes it possible to advance a less objectionable revision of the original inference that avoids these criticisms. The argument states the following:

1. God =df the being with all perfections.
2. For any being with all other perfections, existence is also a perfection.

3. Necessarily, God exists.

This version of the proof strengthens the second assumption to the point at which it represents a necessary implication of the concept of a perfection. If a perfection is a good quality that is better to be instantiated in the universe than not to be instantiated, then, although it is not a perfection for any and every imaginable thing to exist, for a being with all other perfections, existence is also a perfection. It is better for a being of infinite power, infinite knowledge, infinite goodness, and all other perfections to be instantiated rather than not instantiated in the universe. The universe is better by virtue of including, as opposed to not including, God or by virtue of being such that an existent God reigns rather than there being no God—or, as we might also say, the universe would not be better if it were presided over only by a nonexistent God.

There is something inherently suspicious about arguments that try to prove the existence of something from its concept or definition alone. Philosophers and theologians who have accepted a version of this kind of argument have usually held that God is the only entity whose existence follows logically by definition, or whose essence entails its existence. That God should be an exception to the rule for reasoning about other kinds of objects need not be surprising in and of itself, since, to say the least, God is metaphysically speaking an unusual kind of being. The proof that God exists from the definition of the concept of God as the being with all perfections demonstrates God's existence as a necessary being, not a mere contingently created entity like all the rest of the universe, including human beings. It might be said that the existence of a necessary being can be proved only as a logically necessary implication of its concept or definition. The acceptability of the proof depends, among other things, on whether it is reasonable to regard God as an exception to the usual rule that the existence of a thing cannot be proved merely from its concept, definition, or idea. If the concept or definition of God is subject to the same general limitation, then we might at best be able to prove that we must suppose that God exists or to recognize that the definition of God entails that God is defined as something that exists, from which alone it does not validly follow that God actually exists. By comparison, the definition of a winged horse entails that a winged horse has wings, but not that a winged horse exists or that any existent horse actually has wings.

OBJECTIONS TO THE ARGUMENT

What, then, can be said in criticism of the proof? The assumption in (2) in the preceding section is false and the argument unsound if existence is not a perfection. We have already seen that existence cannot be excluded as a perfection on the grounds that it is imperfect for bad things to exist. Yet there might be another difficulty with the premise.

Existence may not be a perfection even for a being with all other perfections. If a perfection is supposed to be a property that enters into the definition of an object in such a way as to determine its identity or that contributes to making an object the particular object it is, and if existence is not that kind of property, then a being with all perfections need not exist. The proof of God's existence from the definition, essence, or concept of God is problematic if it falsely assumes that existence is the kind of property that distinguishes God as a particular entity. There is a strong reason for rejecting assumption (2), on the grounds that, if existence helps define or identify any entity whatsoever as the particular entity it is, then it is logically impossible to ask of precisely the same object whether it exists or does not exist.

Suppose that we define an object in terms of the set of properties [P,W,G]. This may represent the properties of an object that is infinitely powerful, infinitely wise, and infinitely good. For such an object, so defined and identified, we can intelligibly ask whether it exists or fails to exist, which we can write in this notation as E![P,W,G] or Not-E![P,W,G]. The term *E!* for existence indicates by the exclamation mark that we are speaking of actual existence, thereby distinguishing existence as a special kind of property. If we try to include the property or perfection of existence E! as one of the defining or identifying properties of the object, then we must expand the set to include [P,W,G,E!]. In a way, it follows by definition that such an entity exists, since its properties include being actually existent, E![P,W,G,E!]. But we pay too high a price for this implication. For now, we cannot make sense of the false proposition that the identical object does not exist. The concept of a nonexistent infinitely powerful, infinitely wise, and infinitely good being that does not exist is not correctly written as Not-E![P,W,G,E!]. Rather, where nonexistence is as much a defining or identifying property of the nonexistent infinitely powerful, infinitely wise, and infinitely good being as the property of existence is supposed to be a defining or identifying property of the existent infinitely powerful, infinitely wise, and infinitely good being, we would need instead to express the nonexistence of the object in question as Not-E![P,W,G,Not-E!]. The notation we have adopted makes it clear in that case that we are not talking about the same object as existing or not existing, according to the two assumptions we are considering, since it follows directly from the identity principle we considered in discussing the mind-body identity problem that [P,W,G,E!] ≠ [P,W,G,Not-E!].

In order to make the proof work, we need to suppose that existence as a perfection is among God's defining or identity-determining properties; however, if existence is such a property, then so is nonexistence. The assumption is shown to be false as soon as we reflect that it precludes the possibility of asking whether or not the identical object exists or does not exist. The implication is that, although existence is a property, it is not a defining or identity-determining property that can enter into the definition of an object. If existence (or nonexistence) is not a defining or identity-determining property of any object, then assumption (2) of the first proof for the existence of God is false, and the argument as a whole is unsound and does not prove the existence of God as the being of infinite perfection.

The criticism confirms the thesis that it is generally incorrect to prove the existence of any object from its essence, idea, concept, or definition. The definition of an object is one thing, and its existence or nonexistence is another. The existence or nonexistence of any object, including God, whether or not God exists, is logically independent of the object's definition in terms of any set of identity-determining properties.

GOD AS THE GREATEST CONCEIVABLE BEING

There is another version of the argument that purports to prove the existence of God without violating the logical distinction between essence and existence. This formulation depends instead on the limitations of thought that entail a contradiction in trying to conceive of God as the greatest conceivable being which nevertheless does not exist. The idea of the proof is that, if God by definition is the greatest conceivable being, then we cannot conceive of God as not existing. The reason is that, if we assume for the sake of argument that God does not exist, then we can conceive of something greater than a nonexistent God—that is, something that has all the other properties of God and exists rather than fails to exist. The argument has this form:

1. God =df the greatest conceivable being.
2. Suppose for the sake of argument that God does not exist.
3. If God does not exist, then it is conceivable that there is a being other and greater than God (a being with all of God's other properties who also exists).

4. It is conceivable that there is a being other and greater than God.
5. God is the greatest conceivable being and God is not the greatest conceivable being.
6. Necessarily, God exists.

This style of argument is known as indirect proof, or *reductio ad absurdum.* It attempts to prove the truth of a proposition—in this case, that God exists—by assuming the opposite—here, that God does not exist in assumption (2)—and then deriving a contradiction, which is presented in conclusion (5). On the strength of the contradiction, the conclusion reflects back on the falsehood of the assumption, made only for the sake of argument. The assumption is refuted as false, and its negation is deduced instead, proving in (6) that God exists.

This form of argument is deductively valid, provided that the derivation of the crucial contradiction is deductively valid. The contradiction is that God both is and is not the greatest conceivable being. The first part of the contradiction, that God is the greatest conceivable being, follows immediately from the definition of God in (1), which is both reasonable and widely held by religious believers. In some ways, it is an alternative expression of the same thinking about God that underwrites the definition of God in the previous proof. If there is a difficulty in the argument, it must have to do with the other half of the contradiction, that God is not the greatest conceivable being. The inference is that, if God does not exist, then God is not after all the greatest conceivable being, together with the assumption made for the sake of argument that God does not exist. This, too, is deductively valid. But is it true that, if God does not exist, then God is not the greatest conceivable being? Can it be true that God does not exist but that God after all remains the greatest conceivable being?

The conclusion seems reasonable enough, but there is a hidden difficulty. If the assumption in (3) is true, then we are supposed to be able to conceive that a being other than a nonexistent God but with all of God's other properties exists. At one level of description, this appears easy enough to imagine. We must nevertheless remember the criticism of the previous proof. There we learned that existence and nonexistence cannot be regarded as defining or identity-determining properties. Here we are not asked in any obvious way to make such an assumption, but we are supposed to be able to conceive of a being that is just like God in every respect, except that the being we are imagining exists. The trouble is that, in order to conceive of such a being, we must not merely conceive of the being in question as different from God in existing rather than not existing. To do so would be to commit in another way the same mistake that undermines the inference of the ontological argument. The conceivably greater being is supposed to be different from God, but different only in existing rather than not existing.

If God is defined as in assumption (1), as the greatest conceivable being, then God has all perfections. To imagine a being different from God, without trying to make existence or nonexistence into a defining or identity-determining property, must then be to imagine a being that lacks at least some of God's perfections, such as being omnipotent, omniscient, or perfectly benevolent. If we conceive of a being that is other than God by virtue of lacking at least some of God's perfect defining or identity-determining properties, then in what sense can we be conceiving of a being that is greater than God? We will then be thinking of something existent rather than something nonexistent. But, if to be different from God means to have some difference in defining or identity-determining properties other than existence or nonexistence, then to conceive of a being different from a nonexistent God is to conceive of a being that has a different set of defining or identity-determining properties than God's possession of all perfections. However, to think of an existent but less than perfect being is to conceive of an existent but less than perfect being. It is certainly not to think of something greater than God, if God, whether existent or nonexistent, is by definition a perfect being. We already know of many existent things that fall short of our concept of God's perfection and as such are not the greatest conceivable, because they are not even as great in their defining or identity-determining properties as a nonexistent God.

If, despite appearances, we cannot conceive of an existent being that is other and greater in the relevant sense than a nonexistent God without violating the logical distinction between essence and existence, then this second proof for the existence of God from the definition and limits of conceiving an existent or nonexistent God is also unsound. The failure of the argument spells difficulties for *a priori* efforts to prove that God, by definition, necessarily exists. In these ways, at least, we cannot demonstrate that God exists from the definition or concept of God as a being with all perfections, or as the greatest conceivable being.

ARGUMENT FROM DESIGN FOR THE EXISTENCE OF GOD

We can now consider a different style of argument for the existence of God. Many believers maintain that we can know that God exists from our observation of the world, along with the inference that the order that prevails throughout the universe can be explained only by interpreting it as God's creation.

This type of proof is sometimes referred to as the *argument from design*. It tries to show that the universe must reflect the intelligent design of an infinitely powerful intelligent designer. We observe that the world seems to embody a kind of order or plan, from which we then try to reason that God exists, because only God could have brought about the existence of such a world. The insight that motivates this argument is sometimes informally expressed as the idea that the universe as a whole or an aspect of it of which we especially approve could not have happened purely by chance but must be the result of an intelligent plan, and, hence, of God as the architect and infinitely intelligent designer of the universe. The inference is often occasioned by a sense of awe at the vastness of the starry sky on an exceptionally clear night, or in admiration of a well-ordered natural part of the world, such as the marvelous adaptation of particular organs to their tasks, the beauty and functional structure of the eye, larger animal communities in their environments, or the movement of the planets in their regular geometrical orbits.

The argument can be formulated in several different ways, a typical example of which is the following:

1. The universe is well-ordered, like a gigantic machine.
2. Like effects probably have proportionately like causes.
3. The cause of well-ordering in humanmade, machinelike artifacts does not come about by chance, but is always the effect of an intelligent designer.

4. The cause of well-ordering in the universe is also probably the effect of a proportionately powerful and intelligent designer, known to most religions as God.
5. Probably, God exists.

It is appropriate for the conclusions in this argument to be probable rather than necessary or categorical. The inference is based on *a posteriori* evidence about the order and cause of order in humanmade, machinelike artifacts empirically perceived to exist in the world, as well as what is at most the contingently true principle that like effects have like causes. In this sense, the argument is more like a scientific demonstration of the existence of God, rather than a necessary proof by the definition or analysis of concepts.

The argument from design for the existence of God resonates with many believers who claim to be able to see God's handiwork in the beauty and order of the universe. There are also objections to the proof, however, which should be considered before we can accept the argument as proving even the probable existence of God. It is questionable, first of all, to what extent the universe is really well ordered. When we look at telescopic photographs of remote galaxies, they do not all appear to be structured in the same way but seem haphazard. The same is true when we look even at the surface of the moon, which is pitted by meteor and asteroid collisions, which must have struck its surface in the distant past. Many features of other planets also appear to be explainable as the result of random events, and we know that Earth, too, has been the scene of catastrophic astronomical occurrences, which have left traces on its geography and may recur in the future. The objection need not claim that God could not possibly be responsible for random events of this kind, but only that the existence of disorder alongside the order in the universe decreases the probability that the universe was created by a divine, infinitely intelligent, and infinitely powerful designer. When so much of the universe, on closer inspection, gives the appearance of resulting from unplanned, unintended accidents, it puts in perspective and diminishes the significance of other kinds of facts that are sometimes interpreted as evidence of intention, order, and intelligent design.

Similar remarks apply to alleged signs of order in the biological realm. Many living organisms and particular body parts suggest a natural fit and function that some would say could not be the result of blind chance. However, if we understand the processes of biological evolution, whereby environmental pressures to survive and reproduce tend to favor genetic adaptations that confer even a slight advantage on living things and are passed along to their progeny over long periods of time, then we can appreciate the contrary claim that the fitness we see can be explained adequately by natural selection.

The beautifully well-adapted creatures we observe in evolutionary theory, the best scientific account of the diversity of life, are the result of complex but unplanned selective forces. These forces eliminate unfit individuals and species that are less capable of competing for the requirements of life and reproduction, so that we do not experience them. Their elimination allows comparatively more fit individuals and species to flourish, which are the only ones we see in the brief span of recorded human history. Even so, fitness is a relative concept, and we cannot be said to discover in the world the perfect biological organisms that one might expect to be the creations of a perfect creator of the universe. It is obvious in one way that not all biological creatures are sufficiently adapted to their conditions of life, or no predator would ever be successful in capturing and killing any prey. The dilemma is that a successful kill indicates a well-adapted predator but an imperfectly adapted prey, while an unsuccessful kill indicates an imperfectly adapted potential predator and at least a comparatively better adapted potential prey. Other examples are familiar from our knowledge of human susceptibility to diseases, imperfect eyesight requiring artificial correction by lenses, and many other deficiencies, examples of which can easily be multiplied for non-human species as well as human beings. The world is marvelous, but it is not perfect; it does not necessarily present itself even to casual inspection as the handiwork of a perfect being, and the marvels it displays can be explained by natural processes according to scientific principles, without appeal to the existence and will of a divine supernatural entity.

We can try to reconcile traditional religious belief with evolutionary theory by supposing that God created evolution as part of the design for the universe, as a biological mechanism for the adaptation of species. This is an attractive way to avoid conflict between religion and science, and many religiously minded scientists and scientifically minded religious believers might see this as a good solution to the debate over evolution versus special creation. For present purposes, however, this mode of reconciling evolutionary science and traditional religion is not helpful, because it disables the argument from design for the existence of God. By recognizing evolution as the process by which species become adapted to changing environments, the account may be logically compatible with the existence of God as the author of evolution. At the same time, however, the proposal takes away the explanatory motivation for concluding that God must exist as the cause of order in the biological world. To say that God might have created evolution is not to argue that God must have done so, and, if the forces of evolution can explain biological adaptations without supposing that God exists as their inventor, but through natural selection operating on random genetic variations among individuals in populations of naturally developing living things, then the argument from design no longer proves that God is most probably the cause of the relative well-orderedness of the universe.

The biochemistry of life offers a plausible mechanical explanation of how organisms can arise through random combinations of the basic molecular building blocks of naturally self-replicating polypeptide chains of proteins, sugars, and phosphates. The argument from design for the existence of God with respect to the biological world requires not merely that it be possible that God's design is responsible for the well-orderedness of biological phenomena but also that God must be responsible for, or that only God's deliberate design can adequately explain, the well-orderedness of biological phenomena. The counterargument from evolutionary theory undermines the argument from design by proposing an explanation for the well-orderedness of the biological world, such as it is, independently of the existence of God or of God's divine design for the adaptation of biological phenomena.

Finally, if we were to conclude that the existence of God is the only probable cause of order in the universe, it still would not follow that the concept of God supported by the argument would bear any positive resemblance to the God of traditional religions. All that the argument from design for the existence of God is able to show is, at most, that there probably exists a designer or an architect of the universe. The argument does not show that the divine designer is perfectly benevolent, or even that the designer has any moral properties at all, let alone that the intelligent being responsible for order in the universe takes the slightest interest in what happens to human beings. The intelligent designer of the universe whose probable existence might be inferred in the argument from design can be shown only to be intelligent and a designer, but not necessarily to have any type of moral psychology.

If the order of the physical and biological universe can be scientifically explained without invoking the existence of God as a divine designer, then, even if God exists, there can be no logically valid argument for the existence of God that takes as its only evidence the machinelike order of the world. Such objections refute the argument from design for the existence of God and suggest that if there is a proof to show that God exists, it must come from a different direction and be developed along different lines. We have now considered several classical forms of *a priori* and one *a posteriori* argument for the existence of God, and we have seen that they are not decisive. We cannot examine every possible proof, but, since the ones we have evaluated are among the historically most influential efforts, we are in a position to conclude that the most famous attempts are inadequate as demonstrations of the existence of God.

Of course, even if we were to refute every conceivable argument for the existence of God, that would not disprove God's existence. God might exist even if God's existence cannot be proved. However, if in philosophy we are to proceed only on the basis of conclusions that are upheld by good arguments, then to the extent that standard proposals to prove the existence of God fail, we can begin to appreciate the difficulty, or even the impossibility, of demonstrating through reason and empirical evidence that God exists. If any and all such proofs are ineffective, then philosophy as a rigorous rational discipline cannot admit the existence of God or try to build any further explanations on the assumption that God exists. Again, this is not to say that philosophy is yet in a position to deny the existence of God, but only that the arguments we have considered so far do not successfully prove that God exists.

IF THERE WERE MIRACLES, WHAT
WOULD THEY PROVE?

The same kinds of objections apply to arguments that are sometimes given to show that God must exist in order to explain the occurrence of miracles. Here a major challenge the proof must face is skepticism about whether or not genuine miracles have ever actually occurred. We have reports of miracles in certain holy texts, but, if the problem of inquiry is to ask in an open-minded way whether or not God exists, then we cannot rely on the authority of any scripture as definitive testimony for the existence of miracles.

The reason is that, if we are not prejudging the existence of God, then we cannot automatically assume that any holy text is a truthful account of what it describes. If God does not exist, then holy texts are at least false in maintaining that God exists and, hence, might be false in other ways, too, especially in reporting what are supposed to be miracles. We know that not all holy texts can be true, because they contradict one another, and some people claim that even the most famous holy texts in the great Western religious traditions are internally self-contradictory. This objection has given rise to an exegetical industry of interpreting holy texts in what are often heroic efforts to reconcile apparently inconsistent passages and to arrive at logically coherent paraphrases of different parts of scripture. Beyond the testimony of ancient writings, some people claim that miracles occur even today. What do they mean by this?

There are several kinds of events that are sometimes referred to as miracles. One possible meaning is that a miracle is any highly unusual occurrence. If someone flips a coin and it stands on edge rather than landing heads or tails, or if someone recovers from what is statistically a fatal illness, with no obvious sufficient explanation of why this might have happened, then some people may speak of it either earnestly, metaphorically, or even in jest as a miracle. The word *miracle* is often used loosely, especially for anything fortunate, unexpected, or marvelous. If I get a letter containing a check just when I need it and without any expectation that it would arrive, then I might say, as I kiss the envelope and bless my good luck, that it is a miracle. But, if I were to stop and think about it, I would probably realize that there is an understandable chain of cause and effect that has resulted in my being sent the money, together with the coincidence of its arriving at a time of special need. In this sense, miracles are not evidence of any supernatural agency and, hence, are of no assistance to those who want to be able to prove the existence of God from the occurrence of merely unexpected, unexplained, or lucky events.

The other main category of what are popularly called miracles are happenings that are supposed to occur contrary to the laws of nature. Where miracles in this sense are concerned, there are several philosophical responses to be considered. In the first place, it is unclear whether, in fact, any such events have ever taken place. There can be occurrences that do not fall under any known laws of nature, but this might be because we do not yet know or understand all of the complex laws of nature. In order to verify a miracle in this category, we would need to know all of the laws of nature and that a particular occurrence actually violated all natural laws. If this seems to be too rigid a requirement, we might soften it a bit by allowing nonnatural miracles to be established whenever we have a clearcut documented instance of an occurrence that violates at least one well-accepted law of nature.

If a human being were to levitate without any artificial means in front of a large number of reliable witnesses, or survive hazards that would ordinarily destroy a person, then we would at least have a candidate for a credible miracle that could point toward the existence of a divine supernatural agency. Even so, it might be objected that any such miracle need not prove the existence of God as a perfectly benevolent creator of the universe but might equally support an inference to the existence of a supernatural evil being capable of reversing the laws of nature for something other than divine purposes. Further, we would need to argue that the laws of nature are never capable of exception without some sort of supernatural intervention. This would be a difficult conclusion to support, particularly when we consider that the merely statistical laws of modern quantum physics allow extraordinary anomalies to occur in physical phenomena, which are nevertheless supposed to fall within the regularities of natural law.

The suggestion is that belief in God may need to be a matter entirely of faith rather than reason. There is a sharp difference between the way in which we satisfy ourselves that other kinds of things exist, such as germs, genes, and distant stars and planets, whereby we accept nothing less than adequate argument based on sound reasoning and verifiable evidence, and the relatively widespread belief in the existence of God. Does this mean, then, that it is unreasonable to believe in God?

GAMBLING ON THE EXISTENCE OF GOD

There is an argument that does not try to prove that God exists but only that it may be reasonable to believe that God exists. The argument is presented in the form of a dilemma as a rational bet or wager. If God exists and I believe that God exists, then, according to traditional monotheistic religious teachings, I stand to gain an eternal heavenly reward. If God does not exist, it will not hurt for me to believe that God exists, so I might as well do so. If, on the other hand, God exists, then I might risk suffering eternal damnation and infinite punishment for failing to believe that God exists. The second horn of the dilemma also takes its impetus from traditional religions that project a final judgment in which all people will be rewarded in heaven or punished in hell for their religious belief or unbelief. It is reasonable and rational in the ordinary sense, other things being equal, for everyone to promote his or her own happiness and avoid unhappiness.

According to the dilemma, it is rational to believe that God exists, even if there is no rational demonstration of God's existence, and unreasonable not to believe. If I believe and I am right, I gain eternal happiness. If I believe and I am wrong, I lose nothing. But, if I disbelieve and I am wrong, I might suffer eternal unhappiness. The only remaining alternative is the one where I disbelieve that God exists and I am right—in which case I have the satisfaction, so to speak, of having known the truth. Although I lack conclusive justification during my lifetime, at least I will not suffer eternal punishment or unhappiness (or obtain eternal happiness) for my disbelief. The possible outcomes and the benefits and risks that attach to each suggest that, if it is rational for people to promote their happiness and avoid unhappiness, then it is rational to believe in God, even if the existence of God cannot be rationally demonstrated, and even if God does not actually exist.

The belief in God on this conception as supported by the wager is something like an insurance policy. I do not know that I will have a car accident, but I take out insurance to cover what could be potentially devastating expenses, just in case. I do not know that there will be a fire in my kitchen, but I keep the fire extinguisher in the cabinet charged with foam, just in case. Similarly, I may not know or be able to know that God exists in the sense of having a relevantly justified true belief that God exists. But, if I am wise and I want to maximize my chances for happiness and minimize my chances for unhappiness, then, since for all I know God might exist despite my inability to prove that God exists, I should believe that God exists, just in case. It is standard for believers in such contexts also to maintain that, after all, the human intellect is weak and cannot expect to fathom anything as great and conceptually overwhelming as the existence and nature of God. Thus, it should come as no surprise that we cannot rationally demonstrate God's existence by means of our ordinary canons of reasoning. It is rational to believe that God exists as a kind of insurance policy, even if I do not and cannot know that God exists, just as it is rational to have collision insurance or a functioning fire extinguisher on hand, even if I do not and cannot know that I will have a car accident or a kitchen fire. It is sound advice, wise counsel, and required by rational practical reasoning, to believe that God exists. I have everything to gain if I believe and I am right, nothing to lose if I am wrong, and everything to lose if I do not believe and it turns out that on judgment day, to my chagrin, I am wrong.

The dilemma has several interesting implications. We might raise doubts about its conclusions by reflecting on the religious tradition that is supposed to motivate the wager. Suppose that God exists and is a divinely righteous judge who will eternally reward believers and eternally punish unbelievers. It is part of the tradition that God judges individuals on the basis of their sincere beliefs and genuine acceptance of God's grace or, as we also hear, by looking into each person's heart and discerning his or her true attitudes of acceptance or rejection of belief in God. What happens if we try to rationalize belief in the existence of God as something like an insurance policy for heaven and against hell? Does this provide us with a sincere, genuine, and heartfelt acceptance of God that God would find sufficiently pleasing? Or is the wager a way of trying to outguess the possibilities without a deep conviction in the existence of God—so to speak, without a sincere love of God? If the wager puts us in the frame of mind only of someone who wants to have the equivalent of a judgment day insurance policy, then this strategy might simply backfire, because it might not provide us with the right attitude—which, according to traditional religions, will be rewarded by God. If our reason for believing in God is only to gain heaven and avoid hell and does not derive from a deeper acceptance of God, then God, who by reputation is not to be fooled about such things, may choose punishment rather than reward as the proper response to our rationalized belief. In that case, it would not be rational to believe in the existence of God on the basis of the wager. If we bet on God in the way proposed by the wager, we might be more likely to lose, even and especially if our calculations are correct.

There is a further problem, because it is not clear that belief is something we can control as the wager requires. It is one thing for an argument in support of a conclusion to compel belief when we accept the reasoning that the argument represents. If someone puts forward a proof to show that there can be no greatest prime number, then, if I follow the reasoning and accept the argument's conclusion, I may find myself compelled to believe that there is no greatest prime number. This is the way an argument usually drives belief. The argument is good, we accept it as correct, and as a result we modify our beliefs to absorb the new knowledge justified by the conclusion of the argument. But the argument of the wager is different. The wager does not purport to prove that God exists and then try, on the basis of its argument, to compel our belief that God exists. On the contrary, the wager assumes that there is no adequate proof for the existence of God. It proceeds from that assumption to argue that we ought nevertheless to believe that God exists, even in the absence of convincing argument, on the grounds that it might turn out to be better for our eternal welfare to believe than not to believe. This is a very different way of trying to compel belief. The wager encourages belief, not on the intrinsic merits of the proposition that God exists and what, if anything, we can know about the existence or nature of God, but because of the good or bad consequences that might occur as a result of believing or not believing that God exists. Yet it is unclear whether it is possible for belief to be manipulated by this line of argument.

As an analogy, imagine that I tell you that, if you do not believe that there is an elephant living in your television set, then I will arrange through my friends—a corrupt policeman and an even more corrupt district judge—for you to spend the rest of your life in a state prison, but that, if you do believe there is an elephant living in your television set, then I will arrange for you to receive $10 million tax free, with no strings attached. Can you do it? Presumably, you do not want to spend the rest of your life in prison, and, like most people, you might want the money offered as a reward. But can you believe on demand something for which you have no proof? You look into your television set and inspect the interior, but there is no elephant to be seen. Maybe you take apart some of the components of the television, trying to find a very small elephant, the picture of an elephant, or something of the sort that would help you make sense of the belief you are being asked to accept. When you inquire further, I tell you that you are not being asked to believe that there is a miniature elephant or a picture of an elephant. I repeat that, to avoid prison and earn the money, you must now believe that there is a full-grown wild elephant living in your television set, albeit one that you cannot see and for which you cannot expect any empirical evidence. You want to believe it, because you do not want to go to prison and you want the $10 million. But *do* you believe it? *Can* you believe it?

In thinking realistically about such an unrealistic example, what would probably happen is that you would either refuse to participate and accept whatever consequences were to follow, perhaps hoping that I was bluffing, or pretend that you believed, trying to convince me that you believed, like an actor or actress playing a part in a play. But pretending to believe and trying to convince someone else that you believe is not the same as believing. If this is the best you can do, if you cannot make yourself believe by the threat of bad consequences or promise of good consequences, then you must expect the worst to happen, provided that I have a way of telling that you are only pretending to believe. Pretending to believe in the existence of God, however, as in the original wager, will not enable you to prevail on judgment day against God's omniscience.

The analogy should be clear. The wager tries to compel our belief in the absence of sufficient evidence in support of the belief, on the promise of good consequences if we believe and the threat of bad consequences if we do not believe. This, however, is not how belief works. We cannot make ourselves believe in something when we have no adequate reason for accepting its truth. We cannot make ourselves believe; we can only make believe that we believe. In order to believe something, we must accept reasons that justify the belief on its own merits, not merely external motives for adopting or wanting to adopt a positive epistemic attitude about a proposition's truth.

If this is the correct philosophical reaction to the wager, then because of its likely ineffectiveness in the presence of an omniscient God and the objection that we cannot simply compel belief by external motivation, the wager does not actually deliver a rational motivation for believing in the existence of God in the absence of an intrinsically believable rational justification. If anything, we might do better if we are genuinely skeptical about the existence of God, even if God exists and judges us on a final judgment day—to heed Thomas Jefferson's advice at the opening of this chapter—by following what is our God-given reason as honestly and rigorously as we can, rather than pretending to believe something we do not actually believe for external motives in anticipation of the rewards of heaven or punishments of hell.

THE PROBLEM OF EVIL AS A DISPROOF
OF GOD'S EXISTENCE

We have critically examined arguments to prove the existence of God, as well as a dilemma involving external motivations to believe in the existence of God even in the absence of rational proof that God exists. But there have also been arguments to prove that God does not exist. We must now consider the most important of these, known as the disproof of the existence of God from *the problem of evil.*

The problem of evil is the contradiction that seems to arise on the assumption that God exists as the perfect creator of the universe, given that there is also natural evil in the world. The category of natural evil includes the occurrence of apparently unnecesssary pain and suffering. The usual examples emphasize the tragedy inflicted on innocent people through calamities of nature, such as disease, accidental injury, and cataclysmic events such as earthquakes and volcanoes. Natural evil is often distinguished from moral evil, whereby moral evil is the pain and suffering caused by the free will decisions of human agents who decide to hurt others. If human beings have free will, as we have argued in chapter 3, then we should not be too surprised if some people exercise their freedom in morally improper ways, resulting in the moral evil of inflicted pain and suffering. By contrast, natural evil occurs not as the direct result of any human agent deciding to act immorally but, instead, through the forces of nature without human decision or intervention. Why are some children born with terrible deformities? Why does it happen that people who, through no apparent fault of their own, are caught in natural disasters such as earthquakes and tidal waves, in which, irrespective of their morality and the good they might have to offer, are injured or killed?

The problem of evil suggests that there can be only three answers to questions about the existence of natural evil, all of which are incompatible with the assumption that God exists and is omnipotent, omniscient, and perfectly benevolent. The argument is that, if there is natural evil, then either (1) God does not know about the existence of natural evil, in which case, contrary to definition, God is not omniscient; (2) God cannot prevent natural evil, in which case, again contrary to definition, God is not omnipotent; or (3) God chooses not to prevent natural evil, in which case, again contrary to definition, God is not perfectly benevolent. If there is natural evil, the argument goes, God is either not omniscient, not omnipotent, or not perfectly benevolent. But, since God by definition is supposed to be omniscient, omnipotent, and perfectly benevolent, if there is natural evil, evil that cannot simply be blamed on the exercise of human free will, then God does not exist. The argument does not try to show unconditionally that God could not possibly exist, but only conditionally that God does not exist given the existence of natural evil. It would be possible for God to exist, according to the problem of evil, but only if God had created a world very different from the actual world, in such a way that it did not contain any natural evil. An entire branch of religious studies, known as *theodicy,* is dedicated to answering the problem of evil, and many ingenious solutions have been proposed. If all such solutions are inadequate, then the problem of evil provides a definite reason not only for doubting the validity of efforts to prove the existence of God but also for positively disbelieving in the existence of God. The argument has the following form:

1. God =df the being with all perfections—notably, omniscience, omnipotence, and perfect benevolence.
2. There exists natural evil in the world, evil that is evidently not the direct result of human moral evil.
3. If there exists natural evil in the world, then either God does not know about it, cannot prevent it, or chooses not to prevent it.
4. If God does not know about the natural evil in the world, then God is not omniscient; if God cannot prevent the natural evil in the world, then God is not omnipotent; if God chooses not to prevent the natural evil in the world, then God is not perfectly benevolent.

5. Either God is not omniscient, not omnipotent, or not perfectly benevolent.
6. God does not exist.

We cannot consider all of the responses that might be given to the problem of evil, but we can critically assess some of the most important replies and see whether they offer any relief for those who want to sustain at least the possibility of the existence of God, despite the argument.

One reaction is to distinguish between appearance and reality and to maintain that, although there appears to be natural pain and suffering in the world, it is merely an illusion. This is a difficult position to uphold, but some prominent philosophers have argued that the way the world appears to us is not the way the world is in reality. A variation on the theme is to claim that the world of experience is real enough but is morally and religiously less important than the world to come after judgment day. When the world is judged, the solution continues, the pain and suffering that occurred during the Earthly lives of all people will seem as though part of an unreal dream, left behind in the vastly more vivid and meaningful existence of the afterlife. The difficulty that remains for this solution to the problem of evil is that it does not explain why there should be even the illusion or comparative dreamlike existence of pain and suffering in the temporal world if God exists and is omnipotent, omniscient, and perfectly benevolent. Some religious thinkers argue that God's ways are inscrutable to human beings and even, as we noted before, that it might be a sign of impiety or blasphemy to ask or presume to judge why God does what God does. However, any such reply simply removes the interesting questions of religion from philosophical consideration and, so, cannot be a part of philosophical reasoning about the existence of God in light of the problem of evil. It has also been hypothesized that pain and suffering exist in the temporal world in order to test our faith, in which case those who accept the problem of evil as a disproof of the existence of God might be seen as flunking the test by preferring reason to faith.

Another possible answer is to suggest that natural evil is, after all, a consequence of moral evil. The Old Testament, as the holy book of Jews and Christians, indicates that Adam and Eve were created as perfect beings and only through their own free will decision to disobey God's will caused themselves to fall from grace. If this account of the origins of humankind and of Adam and Eve's transgression of God's law is taken literally, then all natural evil—the terrible pain and suffering that occurs in the world—might be the indirect result of human evil and would never have existed were it not for Adam and Eve's wrongdoing shortly after the dawn of creation. This solution, which has been accepted by some fundamentalist theologians and philosophers of religion, also has important drawbacks. The main difficulty is that the doctrine appears to impute a severe injustice to God that many religious thinkers regard as logically incompatible with God's perfect benevolence. It seems unreasonable for God to allow natural evil to be unleashed on the entire world, including countless generations of Adam and Eve's offspring, just because of what Adam and Eve as individuals chose to do. Am I morally responsible for the acts of a great-great-great-grandfather if he decided to kill someone many years ago? Am I responsible even for what my mother or father might have done? We do not ordinarily attribute sin to the children of people who have sinned, and we would regard it as an injustice to punish the children of a wrongdoer for what their parents have done. Yet this is precisely the situation we suppose God to be in if we try to solve the problem of evil by maintaining that natural evil is the result of original sin committed by our first ancestors.

The apparent injustice might be mitigated by other aspects of a religion like Christianity, in which God holds out a plan of atonement for human beings. However, these theological positions entail further philosophical difficulties of their own, and do not avoid the problem of why an omniscient, omnipotent, and perfectly benevolent creator of the universe would need to find a way to restore justice to the world after countless centuries of pain and suffering. The problem of natural evil remains real and unresolved by any of these proposals, as a serious philosophical obstacle to reason's acceptance of the existence of God.

GOD AND PHILOSOPHY

We might believe in God through faith, but some philosophers have argued that the existence of God can also be demonstrated rationally. The relation between faith and reason is an important topic for the philosophy of religion.

This chapter has critically examined some standard proofs and one disproof for the existence of God. The proofs include efforts to show that the definition or concept of God's essence as a perfect being implies God's existence, either because existence is a perfection, or because the idea of God is the idea of a being than which none greater is conceivable, in the ontological argument. Another attempt is made by the empiricist argument from design, by which the existence of God is said to follow as the highly probable cause of what appears to be the intelligently designed machinelike order of the physical universe. An effort to prove that God exists in order to explain the occurrence of miracles falters on the assumption that miracles in the required sense actually occur. The failure of these arguments suggests the difficulty or even impossibility of proving rationally that God exists. A wager that we ought to believe that God exists in order to maximize our potential happiness in heaven and avoid eternal punishment in hell is refuted as trying to compel faith by external motivation in the absence of intrinsically plausible grounds for belief—which, in any case, would not avail if cynically accepted as a judgment day insurance policy in the presence of an omniscient judge. The problem of evil—of how it is possible for God to exist as an omniscient, omnipotent, and perfectly good author of a universe in which there is also natural evil, apparently unnecessary pain and suffering—suggests a rational and thus far unanswered disproof of God's existence.

Problems about the limitations of reason in efforts to prove or disprove the existence of God lead naturally to more abstract metaphysical speculations. Why is there something rather than nothing? Is it necessary that God should have created a universe? Could the universe have existed by accident rather than as the artifact of a divine, all-powerful creator? The arguments we have considered in this chapter appear to discourage any prospect of answering the sojourner's question by finding common ground between philosophical reflection and religious faith. The idea that a reconciliation of philosophy and religion might nevertheless occur intrigues philosophers and theologians, who continue to search for new proofs, interpretations, and defenses of classical arguments for the existence of God, and to reach innovative understandings of the relation between reason and religious belief.

CHAPTER FIVE

Virtue, Morality, and Reasons for Choosing the Good

The essence of morality is a questioning about morality; and the decisive move of human life is to use ceaselessly all light to look for the origin of the opposition between good and evil.

—Georges Bataille
Critique (Paris, March 1947)

THE PROBLEMS OF ETHICS

If we could know that God exists and has a moral psychology, that God wills us to conduct our lives according to certain rules, and that God will reward or punish us for our behavior, then we would have a philosophically respectable answer to the two main problems of ethics: (1) What should we do? and (2) Why should we do it?

A divine command theory of ethics, by which all moral value depends on God's will, would inform us about how we ought to act and would provide powerful motivation for obeying a divinely ordained moral code. Who wants to spend eternity in hell? Who would not prefer to spend eternity with God in heaven? Some religions allow enormous tolerance for sin, if only we are saved by grace or accept salvation by repenting and acknowledging the main propositions of the faith. The promise of heaven and threat of hell are major factors in the popularity of traditional religions in enforcing a certain interpretation of ethical values. Some people see religion as a final bastion in stemming the tide of immorality and preventing the dissolution of society through moral anarchy. If God does not exist, some people believe, then any moral wrongdoing might as well be permitted, provided that discovery and punishment are avoided. However, it is perfectly possible for people who do not believe in God to be morally upright, whereas some have perversely used their belief in God to rationalize blatant immorality.

We have certainly not concluded that God does not exist. The arguments we have considered have shown only that the usual proofs for the existence of God are ineffective and that the problem of evil provides some philosophical grounds for doubting that God exists. The implication is at most the qualified one that, on the basis of our investigation to this point, we cannot build on the assumption that God exists in adopting a divine command theory of ethics as a source of ethical values or as a reason for obeying the principles of a religious morality. As philosophers, unless we can rationally uphold traditional religious beliefs, we cannot fall back on any religious system of morality as philosophically acceptable. We cannot avoid the hard work and sticky questions in thinking these things through for ourselves by relegating the problems of morality to religious leaders. We must inquire into the foundations of morality as independent of religion. We must try to arrive at a philosophically satisfactory analysis of the principles of ethics without religion, and to look for sufficiently motivating reasons to live according to correct moral precepts without assuming the promise of heaven or threat of hell. If we cannot do this, then we should admit that morality, like religious belief, lacks philosophical justification.

There is a difference between knowing what is morally right and actually doing it. By analogy, I may know all the rules of safe and legal driving, so that, if I am asked about them on a written exam, I can pass with a 100 percent grade. But knowing the rules by itself does not mean that when I get in my car I will choose to drive properly. It is one thing to know how I am supposed to drive and another to do it. It is also one thing to know what morality requires and another to choose to do it and carry through on my resolve by conducting my life in accord with the moral principles I accept. In the case of driving, there is ordinarily a strong incentive to drive according to the rules of the road. I recognize that the traffic laws exist in order to promote safety, and I do not want to be involved in an accident, because of the risk of injury or death, damage to my car, and increased insurance rates. Still, there might be situations in which I am tempted late at night with no other cars around to roll through a stop sign, take a turn without signaling, or the like. If it is easy and I think I can get away with it, I might try to bend or break the law a little if I can do so without suffering any bad consequences.

Where morality in general is concerned, should my attitude be any different? I might understand the principles of morality at an intellectual level, so that if I must take an exam about ethics I could pass with flying colors. Yet I might choose against acting, or find myself insufficiently motivated to act, in accord with the moral principles that I accept in theory when it comes to putting my beliefs into practice. If I allow myself to slide through some of the traffic rules when I drive, can I also do so where morality is concerned? If not, why not? If so, where should I draw the line? Is it ever ethical to lie to a friend in order to avoid hurting her feelings? Can it then be permissible to lie in order to obtain something I need or want, especially when I see other people doing so? Can there be circumstances under which it is morally permissible to steal or even to kill? How should I try to decide these matters? How do I know when to act and when not to act according to moral principles? Are moral principles absolute or relative to circumstances? If we can finally settle on a philosophically correct ethics, we must still try to find adequate motivations for morality, to ask and try to answer the equally fundamental moral question, *Why* be moral?

A code of ethics prescribes how we are to live and provides a guide to moral decision making. The meaning of life as an answer to the sojourner's question might be found in doing what is right, or acting in accord with moral principles. The meaning or purpose of life might be understood as trying to make ourselves good, a definite goal that can inform our daily activity with a reason to live. Life can have meaning when we see it as an unfolding series of choices we are free to make or not to make, in which we steer ourselves toward the goal of being good, of improving and perfecting ourselves morally at every opportunity as we strive to achieve moral excellence. This picture of the meaningfulness of life further presupposes that we can arrive at a philosophically correct understanding of moral principles and a reason for being moral. If we are to find meaning in being good and struggling to overcome what may be the contrary inclinations of human nature to make ourselves good, then we must have a particular moral code to follow as a guide to life, as well as a sufficient reason for choosing to live up to its requirements. To answer the sojourner's question by finding the meaning of life in morality, we must try to answer the two main problems of ethics.

TRAIN SWITCHING DILEMMA

Let us begin with a thought experiment. Suppose that you wake up to find yourself all alone in a railroad switching station. There is a single big switch with a handle in the middle of the floor. The purpose of the switch is clearly indicated in a set of simple directions printed above it, on a lighted panel that explains how the control can be used to redirect an oncoming train from one track to another. The blinking lights along one line of track on the panel show that a train is coming full-speed along the track toward the switching point where two tracks intersect. You look out the window and see that a train is barreling down on two automobiles stalled on the track. Each car has a single passenger trapped inside, each of whom is about to be struck and killed by the train, unless you pull the switch and force the train onto the other track. On the adjacent track, you see just one car with a single passenger trapped inside. As things stand, the person in the single car on the second track is not at risk, but will be struck and killed by the train if you choose to redirect it from the first onto the second track. The situation schematically looks like this:

TRAIN SWITCHING DILEMMA

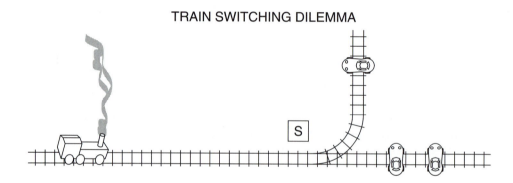

The problem is an unusual one that is unlikely to occur in real life. It also involves some oversimplifications, intended to bring out a contrast in the kinds of moral decision making we might be required to make in more realistic circumstances. We may further suppose, for simplicity's sake, that the people trapped in the automobiles on the train tracks are of precisely equal moral status. If we want to maximize their similarity, we can even imagine that they are morally indistinguishable triplets with the same genetic blueprint, who just happen to be caught in an awful predicament on the same day when you just happen to wake up in the train yard in the switching tower.

There are two problems to consider. The first is to decide what you would do in such a situation, and the second is to explain why you would do it. The first question is a practical problem in moral decision making. You can save a life by pulling the switch, causing the train to avoid hitting two stalled cars and killing two people. But you can do so only by diverting the train so that it hits another stalled car and kills another person. The catch is that, in order to save one life, you make yourself personally responsible for the death of a person who would not otherwise have died but for your decision to pull the switch. The second question is more theoretical. It calls for a philosophical justification of the decision you believe it would be right to make, and it asks you to reflect on the general principles you believe would justify your decision to pull or not to pull the train track switch. What principles would you be willing to affirm, say, if you had to defend your choice to the loved ones of those killed after the fact when they come to you and demand to know why you acted as you did? What reasons could you give to justify your decision in your own mind as you think about the incident and try to satisfy your conscience after the event?

The scenario is an interesting one, because doing nothing does not absolve us of responsibility. Here doing nothing is not pulling the switch, knowingly allowing two people to die. We have assumed that the people are all of equal moral value, so there is no basis for choosing some of the potential victims over others as morally more worthy to live. It is not as if the two people in the two trapped cars on the first train track are evil degenerates, who may be suffering from an incurable, agonizing disease and have tried unsuccessfully to commit suicide several times themselves, whereas the lone person in the one trapped car on the second track is a saint and scientist about to announce a secret cure for cancer that will otherwise be lost to the world. In addition to the assumption that all three trapped people are of indistinguishable moral quality, we can suppose that each would leave precisely the same number of loved ones behind to grieve if they should die, so that a desire to minimize the tragedy for the survivors is precisely equal for all three potential victims considered individually. If we can think of any other reason that would justify us in simplifying the choice of whether to cause one person to die instead of two, we will simply eliminate it by further supposing that the same properties are shared by all three people. In this way, for purposes of the thought experiment, we narrow down the choices unrealistically from an ethical standpoint, so that the only question is to whether to let one person die or two.

Once again, try to answer the two questions raised by the train switching dilemma. What would you do, and why do you think you should do it? The first question can be answered only by saying that you would either pull the switch or not pull the switch. The second question is open-ended, because in principle you could try to justify your decision to pull or not to pull the switch in many ways. However, if you are like most people who respond to this puzzle, you are likely to give one of two basic answers to the first and second questions, reflecting two radically different approaches to the problems of ethics.

CONSEQUENTIALISM AS THE GREATEST GOOD FOR THE GREATEST NUMBER

The first approach is to say that you would pull the switch and that you should do so because in that way you could save a life. The arithmetic is simple. If you do not pull the switch, two people die; if you do pull the switch, only one person dies. A good moral principle that many people accept is that we should try to make the world a better place by reducing the amount of unnecessary suffering whenever we can. By pulling the train track switch, we can prevent the death of one person. If, as we have assumed, there is nothing to distinguish the people in the cars by which to override the sheer difference in the number of people to be affected by the decision, then the morally right decision, perhaps the only morally justified decision, is to pull the switch, allowing only one person to die.

The first category of moral justification is known as *consequentialism*. The name is appropriate, because it judges the moral rightness or wrongness of an action on the basis of its likely consequences, in terms of the total happiness versus unhappiness the action can reasonably be expected to produce, when compared with the alternatives. The principle of consequentialism states that, of the actions we can perform, we should always prefer the one that will probably result in the most happiness over unhappiness. The *greatest happiness principle* is the view that our actions should aim toward increasing happiness and decreasing unhappiness for everyone concerned, the greatest good for the greatest number. In the case of the railway dilemma, the person in the switching booth has the clearcut choice of either allowing two people to die or doing something that will result in only one death. If we are supposed to act in such a way that our actions are likely to cause more happiness than unhappiness, then we are not only morally permitted but morally obligated to pull the switch, even though doing so will result in the death of a person who would not otherwise have died.

There are many situations in which we must make difficult choices, for which consequentialism provides a general moral justification in deciding what to do. A paramedic arriving at the scene of a disaster must quickly decide who is and who is not to receive assistance from a limited supply of professional help and resources. How should such choices be made? Emergency workers are standardly taught to *triage* the victims in such a scenario. They divide the injured into three categories, distinguishing people who are likely to live even if they receive no assistance, people who are likely to die even if they receive no assistance, and people who are likely to live if they receive assistance but likely to die if they do not receive assistance. The best that can be done is perhaps to minister to people in the third category who are in greatest need and for whom assistance is most likely to make a life or death difference. Someone who is in terrible pain but will live anyway, even if untreated, is not a priority for emergency assistance, even though the individual's suffering could be eased by medical attention. Similarly, a victim who is likely to die anyway should not be treated if there are others whose need is greater in the sense that they will die without help but are likely to survive if they receive care. A consequentialist would argue that the reasoning that supports the emergency health care strategy of triage should apply to all our moral decision making, because it promotes the same values of trying, wherever possible, to achieve the greatest happiness for the greatest number.

DEONTOLOGY AS RESPECT FOR MORAL RIGHTS

If that were the end of the story, then the only reasonable conclusion to reach about the train switching thought experiment would be to pull the switch in order to save a life, allowing only one person to die instead of two. In that case, there would be no philosophical interest in the problem. However, when confronted with this decision, some people have a very different idea about what would be morally right to do.

We have already seen that to do nothing in the train switching tower is to do something after all. Choosing not to touch the switch, but to walk away and ignore what is happening, is to avoidably condemn two people to die. Once we have understood what will occur if we do not pull the switch, we bear a moral responsibility for the outcome, regardless of whether we deliberately choose to divert or not to divert the train. Although it may seem evident that it is morally obligatory to pull the switch, as consequentialists believe, there are other considerations to take into account. It might be said that to pull the switch is morally wrong, because it entails a lack of moral respect for the passenger in the single car stalled on the second track. This is not merely a matter of disrespect in the sense of failing to show sufficient courtesy in interpersonal etiquette, but something morally much more important.

We must distinguish between *intrinsic* and merely *instrumental value*. Things that are intrinsically valuable have value in and of themselves, not merely as means to another end. We speak of intrinsically valuable things as being valuable as ends in themselves. For example, we generally suppose that being able to see is intrinsically valuable as a good in itself, not merely something that is good because of other purposes that being able to see helps us achieve. We would still value being able to see, even if we could accomplish the same goals in another way. Instrumental values, by contrast, are important to us only insofar as they make it possible to satisfy other desires. My automobile is valuable to me, but not intrinsically so; it is valuable only as a tool that enables me to do other things, to get groceries and carry my kayak. A good test of whether something is merely instrumentally valuable is whether and to what extent we would experience a personal loss if we were to replace the item with a substitute capable of performing the same actions and fulfilling the same means-to-end relations. If my car were to break down, I would have to decide whether it was worthwhile to spend the money needed to fix it, if it were even possible to fix, and if not, I would not hesitate to junk it and get another car.

The replaceability of an object of instrumental value by another of the same or greater instrumental value indicates that the thing in question is not intrinsically valuable as an end in itself, but only as a means to another end. We can often string together means-to-ends values in such a way that something valuable as a means to an end is valuable as a means to another means, and that to yet another means, and so on. It is valuable for me to have my car serviced, to change the oil and have the engine tuned periodically, in order for the car to run properly. This is a means to an end, in which the end is another means to another end. In some cases, purely instrumental means-to-ends relations can go on and on, but chains of instrumental means-ends relations must ultimately terminate in things that we do not do for the sake of being able to do something else but, rather, for the sake of something that is valuable as an end in itself, not merely as a means to another end. If not, then instrumental means-ends relations would continue indefinitely, with no reason to do anything except for the sake of being able to do something else.

In principle, we can treat other people either as means to an end or as ends in themselves. We treat other people as means to an end in many capacities. When I shop at the market, I am using the people who work there as means to an end. They provide a service that I need if I am to buy certain goods. I cannot simply walk into the store and take what I want, but I must exchange money for the things I need by trading with people who work in the store and are charged with the responsibility for making merchandise available to customers. In turn, I am used by them as a means to another end, since they depend on me and others who purchase what they sell as the ultimate source of their income, which they need to live. There are many ways in which people use each other as a means to an end in daily interactions, none of which by itself need be morally objectionable. What may be morally wrong, however, is to use other persons *merely* as means to an end rather than treating them as ends in themselves. When I go to the store, I use the employees there as means to another end, but I do not use them *merely* as means to an end. I treat them respectfully in subtle social ways that indicate my recognition of them, not only as replaceable instruments by which I hope to accomplish my purposes, but also as individuals with purposes of their own who have interests and desires of equal importance to them. My attitude toward another human being, another person as a center of intrinsic value, is markedly different from my attitude toward the things I am morally entitled to treat merely as instrumentally valuable means to another end, such as my automobile, my computer, and my clothes. The philosophical position that it is always wrong to treat other people as though they had merely instrumental value or only as means to another end, rather than as intrinsically valuable ends in themselves, is known as *deontology*.

If pulling the train switch in the tower entails using the person in the single car on the second track merely as a means to the end of producing the greatest good for the greatest number, or securing more total happiness than unhappiness in the world, then, according to deontology, by virtue of my attitude toward the victim, I am acting immorally. I should then refrain from pulling the switch, even if my decision causes two people instead of only one to die. Deontology holds that it is always morally wrong to treat other people as though they had merely instrumental value as a means to another end, instead of recognizing that they are beings of the highest intrinsic value as ends in and of themselves. If, when I look out the switching tower window, I see diverting the train toward the person in the single car as a way of maximizing happiness for others, then I might be treating that individual merely instrumentally as a means to another end, not as an end in him- or herself. In that case, a deontologist will regard my action as morally wrong, even if it results in one rather than two persons dying, and would urge me not to pull the switch.

SCAPEGOAT AND LIFEBOAT COUNTEREXAMPLES

If the deontological rationale for not pulling the switch in the train switching dilemma does not seem strong enough to justify the needless loss of two lives instead of one, consider the following general deontological objection to consequentialism. The criticism takes the form of a counterexample about a *scapegoat*.

Scapegoats are individuals who have not done anything wrong but are blamed for what others have done as a sacrifice to satisfy the public desire that someone be punished for an offense. The term *scapegoat* originated in the practice of ancient mid-Eastern cultures, in which the sins of a community were symbolically transfered to a goat, which was then killed, so that the real offenders could feel that the wrongdoing was somehow atoned. It is morally bad enough to punish an animal for the unethical behavior of human beings, who, unlike the goat, are moral agents who are supposed to know the difference and are able to choose between right and wrong. It is even more objectionable to treat other human beings as scapegoats, because to do so represents an extreme case of treating people as though they had merely instrumental value as a useful means to another end, instead of as intrinsically valuable ends in themselves. However, deontologists maintain, paradoxically, that this is precisely what consequentialism sometimes requires as morally obligatory.

Suppose that a heinous crime has been committed in a small, isolated town. The sheriff, who is charged with bringing the perpetrator to justice, does not know who did the deed but is holding a prisoner at the jail whom he knows could not possibly have committed the crime but on whom the crime might be blamed. The sheriff also knows that, if no one is charged with the crime, the local vigilantes will go on a rampage, and, if their past behavior is any indication of what is likely to happen again, there is sure to be considerable destruction of property and loss of life, perhaps as many as two or three people killed. Further suppose that, if the sheriff does things carefully enough, no one will ever discover his deception, so that there will be no erosion of respect for the law in the community. The sheriff, whom we may imagine to be a good consequentialist in his ethical outlook, now must consider whether or not to frame the innocent detainee in his holding cell. Should he do so? What does consequentialism require as the moral theory of the greatest good for the greatest number?

Deontologists argue that, in a case like this, the consequentialist is wrongly obligated to frame the innocent prisoner. The reason is that, by doing so, the sheriff knows he will probably avert the wanton loss of even more innocent lives by the vigilantes, who will kill at least two people. If what is important is the arithmetic that enters into applications of the greatest happiness principle, then the answer seems to be that the sheriff is not only morally permitted but morally obligated to frame the innocent person, or, as we can now also say, to make a human scapegoat of the prisoner whom he knows could not have committed the crime. Does this seem right? Imagine that you are the prisoner, perhaps awaiting a computer check to clear your bail after being arrested for a minor traffic violation. Would you be willing to accept the consequentialist verdict that you ought to spend the rest of your life in prison or possibly face capital punishment for a crime you did not commit, merely in order to assure that there be greater total happiness by preventing a riot of vigilantes? Or would you protest that this was a violation of your moral and legal rights, and that you were being used merely as a means to the end of bringing about more happiness for others, with no respect for your intrinsic value as an end in yourself?

If your intuition is that, in this case, the scapegoat is wrongly dealt with and morally mistreated, that the deontologist might have a point in objecting to consequentialism in all its implications, then you might be in a position to appreciate the conclusion of those who believe it would be morally wrong to pull the switch in the train track example. The application of the deontological respect for moral rights in that situation is much the same. A deontologist would argue that to pull the switch is to act without sufficient moral respect for the lone person in the single car on the second track, if the person is not being treated with proper moral respect as an end in him- or herself, but is being used merely as a means to achieve the end of providing greater overall happiness for others. This can now be seen as no different in principle than the scapegoat objection to consequentialism, because to pull the train track switch is, in effect, to make the lone passenger trapped in the single car a kind of scapegoat. By pulling the switch, although without actually blaming the person or trying to attach the sins of others to the passenger as such, we make that innocent person the accidental means to the end of saving another life. If we think that this is wrong in the sheriff-vigilante case, then it might also be wrong, as deontologists maintain, in the train switching dilemma.

The point is not that deontology is right and consequentialism wrong. The situation is more complex. There is a similar kind of objection to be made against deontology from the consequentialist side. Whereas consequentialism appears subject to the scapegoat counterexample, deontology appears subject to what we can call a *lifeboat* counterexample. Suppose that after a shipwreck there are eleven survivors in a lifeboat that can only hold ten. It is not that the lifeboat will merely be uncomfortable or leaky and dangerous if eleven people remain aboard but that it will actually sink, killing all eleven persons now inside. We may further suppose that the water outside is so freezing cold that not all eleven persons could survive by taking turns clinging to the ropes around the rim of the lifeboat until all are rescued. It is a simple life or death situation, in which, if one person is not ejected from the lifeboat, all eleven will die. Now, if someone volunteers to exit the craft, there is no problem. Similarly, there is no moral conflict if the group as a whole can agree to draw straws or accept another random procedure for choosing who is to drown, on the assumption that whoever is chosen in this way must then go overboard. But what if no one is willing to do so? A deontologist might interpret this scenario as one in which no one can rightly be singled out as a kind of scapegoat to be sacrificed for the benefit of others. The moral rights of each individual are sacred to the deontologist, in the sense that they can never be violated in such a way as to treat people as possessing merely instrumental value as a useful means to help provide for the welfare of others. However, if the deontological prohibition on treating other people merely as means to an end is applied in the lifeboat case, then everyone on board will die.

Thus, there is a moral standoff in the dispute between two radically different approaches to the problems of moral philosophy. Deontology and consequentialism each has an interesting point of view that captures some of our thinking about what is morally right and wrong, but each theory appears to lead to some morally objectionable conclusions. To act always to maximize happiness over unhappiness or the greatest good for the greatest number leads, in some instances, to scapegoat injustices in which some people are treated unfairly by being used instrumentally merely as means to another end instead of as intrinsically valuable ends in themselves. However, to act always in such a way that we respect the moral rights of people to be treated as intrinsically valuable ends in themselves and never merely as means to another end leads, in some instances, to lifeboat tragedies, in which everyone suffers an avoidable catastrophe in order to observe the moral principle that no one must ever be unfairly used in order to secure the happiness of others.

SYNTHESIS OF CONSEQUENTIALISM AND DEONTOLOGY

Is there a way to have the best without the worst of both worlds? Can we combine the positive features of consequentialism and deontology, while avoiding the implications that open each theory to counterexamples? One possibility is to say that we should generally try to promote the greatest happiness for the greatest number, except when doing so unnecessarily violates the moral rights of people to be treated as intrinsically valuable moral ends in themselves, rather than merely as instrumentally valuable means to another end.

If enough emphasis is placed on the qualification that the consequentialist greatest happiness principle should be followed except when doing so unnecessarily violates the moral rights respected by deontology, then we might be able to discern a philosophically relevant difference in the scapegoat and lifeboat cases. In the scapegoat case, the sheriff pins the crime on an innocent person in order to prevent the vigilantes from rioting and causing more unhappiness. But to have done so need not be judged as absolutely necessary under the circumstances.

The point is not just that creative police work might suggest a better way to thwart the vigilantes, such as using delaying tactics until their inflamed emotions subside, but also that it is not in any obvious commonsense way necessary to frame the innocent person for the crime. Rather, it takes only a bit of ingenuity and hard work to manufacture evidence and false testimony to make the scapegoat appear guilty. In the lifeboat case, by contrast, it is arguably more unavoidable that someone should be put overboard, if necessary, against his or her will. It is unavoidable for the survival of all concerned for someone's moral rights to be violated if no one volunteers in the lifeboat case; whereas, in the scapegoat case, it is not in the same sense unavoidable for the survival of all concerned for anyone's moral rights to be violated.

This compromise leaves it ambiguous how we are supposed to handle all imaginable cases of moral decision making. But it may be entirely appropriate, if, as some philosophers have maintained, ethics does not have the same degree of completeness and formal precision as logic, mathematics, and natural science. There may be situations for which we do not know exactly what the morally proper choice requires, and there may even be situations in which there is no completely satisfactory answer, for the simple reason that morality is not as cut and dried as other, more rigorous disciplines. Life is complicated, and theory inevitably oversimplifies. We should not be unduly puzzled or concerned if moral principles cannot perfectly settle every conceivable ethical problem. There may be irresolvable moral dilemmas, in which, no matter what we do or how we decide to act, we will be stuck doing something that is morally wrong, according to some reasonable ethical principle.

The ethical implications of the proposed synthesis of consequentialism and deontology offer a rough and ready basis for judging the morality of many kinds of decisions and practices. Even if the rule is not exceptionless, it is perhaps plausible enough to provide a platform for a continued discussion of the problems of ethics. We proceed here as we must in other areas. We do not know omnisciently with epistemic certainty that we have defined the concept of knowledge in an absolutely airtight way that will resist all logically possible counterexamples, that the mind is not after all a causally determined machine, or that there can be no philosophically satisfactory demonstration of the existence of God. We have only considered, critically evaluated, and gone forward as carefully as we can on the basis of the arguments that have seemed the most correct. As long as we are willing to backtrack if necessary and change our opinion in light of new arguments or new thinking about old arguments, this is surely the best we can do. Similarly, in the effort to articulate a moral philosophy, we can give only the most honest and thoughtful attempt to clarify the relevant ethical concepts and explore their implications.

What can now be said about the nature of ethics, from the standpoint of the principle we have provisionally adopted? We will tentatively judge actions as morally justified when, among the available alternatives, they promote the greatest happiness of the greatest number, except when doing so unnecessarily violates the moral rights of people to be treated as intrinsically valuable ends in themselves, not merely as instrumentally valuable means to another end. If the principle fails us, we will need to study apparent counterexamples and try to refine the principle so that similar objections can be avoided. For the time being, we can regard the theory combining consequentialism and deontology as offering the best insight into the nature of our considered moral judgments. There are still many other questions to be addressed. Does the principle apply to our treatment of nonhuman animals? Do we have moral obligations toward other species? If so, are they just the same as or somehow different from our obligations toward our fellow human beings? If not, why are animals different? In other words, can we perceive animals as having merely instrumental value, as means to our own ends, and not as possessing intrinsic value as ends in themselves? What are the implications of the principle for such thorny moral issues as abortion, censorship, gun ownership, drug use, sexual behavior, and all other topics of applied ethics?

THE ABORTION CONTROVERSY

It is not feasible to examine all moral problems in the detail they deserve. But we can provide a more complete sense of the theory under consideration by sketching a few of the results it entails for one of the most important ethical disputes of the day, the abortion controversy. This will offer an opportunity to consider the synthesis of consequentialism and deontology in application to an unresolved moral dilemma. The question of whether aborting an unborn fetus is ever morally permissible is a difficult problem with significant political overtones, in which many people have not only moral but religious values at stake. Our task is not to solve the abortion issue—for, in the end, it may be unsolvable—but to decide how the moral principle we have provisionally adopted might deal with the conflict of opinion that has arisen about the ethics of abortion.

The opposition between those who regard abortion as morally permissible under certain circumstances and those who believe that abortion is always or almost always morally forbidden reflects a fundamental disagreement about the nature and limits of moral rights and consequences. Consider a woman in the early stages of pregnancy who, for one reason or another, does not want to have a baby. The law in the country in which she lives permits her to have a clinical abortion in the first trimester, at any time in the first three months of a nine-month pregnancy. The reason she might not want to give birth to the child is not the concern of the law, but it could be relevant in judging the morality of a decision to have or not to have an abortion. We can simplify the discussion by setting aside as relatively uncontroversial the possibility that the woman chooses abortion in consultation with a physician whose professional medical opinion is that she will be at serious risk of life or health if she continues her pregnancy to term. It is unusual for even the most strident opponents of abortion rights not to make exceptions for such cases, possibly as a way, rightly or wrongly, of recognizing the rights of a biologically mature person as taking precedence over the rights, if any, of an undeveloped fetus; however, other reasons for choosing to have an abortion are well known. The woman might be too impoverished to raise a child, especially if she already has others to care for, or she may be at a point in her life when to raise a child would impose a severe burden, perhaps interfering with long-term career plans.

The difficulty is that the abortion issue concretizes a deep moral conflict between a woman's right to reproductive control of her body, which all but the most antifeminist, typically fundamentalist, religions respect, and the presumed but in many ways more controversial right to life of the unborn baby. The collision of values represented by abortion and antiabortion rights advocates is unresolved and perhaps unresolvable because of incommensurable differences between the nature of the rights of a pregnant woman and of the unborn. If the woman is unable to have a safe clinical abortion when she chooses it, for whatever reasons she deems important enough to make such a serious decision, then her presumed right to reproductive control over her own body is denied. This, many would say, is morally wrong—having or not having a baby, with all the consequences that follow, is a matter so private and personal that no one other than the woman, and possibly the father of the child, should have any say whatsoever in the matter. Otherwise, if a woman's right to reproductive control over her body is not respected, then she becomes a kind of slave, a mere instrument with only instrumental value as a means to another end of providing a maternal vessel or incubator in which a fetus can develop. Why should any woman have to undergo such a thing against her will, even if she becomes pregnant accidentally as a result of her own decision to have sexual intercourse?

On the other hand, when there is no medical reason for an abortion, the worst that the woman can expect to suffer is the usual pain and inconvenience of a nine-month pregnancy, followed by the potentially burdensome responsibility of raising the child or finding adoption for the child after birth. All of this is potentially painful, embarrassing, professionally problematic, and emotionally traumatic. Raising a child is a full-time job and an expensive proposition, as any parent can testify, which the woman for many legitimate reasons may not be prepared to undertake. Giving up a baby for adoption after it is born is a heartwrenching experience that most people would prefer to avoid. On the other hand, for the fetus, who may also have moral rights to take into account, abortion appears to be a much more serious violation of the right to life. For the unborn fetus, it is not just a matter of pain, inconvenience, emotional trauma, embarrassment, and the like—as it is for the woman—but of annihilation. How can we reasonably adjudicate between what the woman will suffer if her moral right to reproductive control of her body is violated by being denied access to abortion if she makes that choice, and the violation of the more basic moral right to life of the unborn child—if, indeed, the unborn have moral rights? What is pain, inconvenience, emotional trauma, embarrassment, and expense, compared with death, with never a chance to experience life outside the womb?

The conflict is complicated by the fact that the woman, unlike the fetus, is already participating in a moral community. She is a fully developed, biologically mature human being, whose rights are established and who has more definite interests; she already has a history, with memories and expectations for the future. By contrast, we do not suppose that an unborn fetus, especially in the first trimester of pregnancy, is in anything like the same situation. Here, too, there are important ethical conflicts at work in the opposition that occurs in the political sphere between abortion rights and antiabortion advocates. Does a fetus have rights at all? If not, then perhaps the abortion question can be settled straightforwardly and in keeping with the general ethical principle we have tentatively adopted. It is likely to produce more happiness in the world under the imagined circumstances to allow the woman to exercise her right to an abortion than the amount of suffering that an undeveloped fetus will briefly experience. So, is that what should happen?

There is some doubt about whether the fetus, especially in the very early stages of pregnancy, is capable of pain at all and, hence, about whether or not the fetus can reasonably be thought to have interests or rights. If a fetus is an unthinking cluster of cells, then what is the moral harm in aborting it before it develops a functional nervous system capable of pain? We do the same thing when necessary to cancerous tumors and other kinds of growths of tissue when it is expedient to do so. If the pregnancy continues long enough to the point at which the fetus develops a functional nervous system, then the moral situation—according to the synthesis of deontology and consequentialism that we have provisionally adopted—changes considerably. Even in this case, however, it might be decided on the basis of our ethical principle that the pain a fetus is likely to experience in the event of an abortion is less than the pain and difficulty the woman will experience if the pregnancy goes to term and beyond, and that, to procure the greatest happiness for the greatest number in this case, it is necessary to violate the fetus's moral rights. The crucial question is whether or not the fetus has rights; in particular, whether it has the right to life; and whether such a right outweighs the right of a pregnant woman to exercise reproductive control of her body.

CONFLICTS OF RIGHTS

How can we properly evaluate this conflict of rights and putative rights? An important consideration might be that the woman, as an adult, who is at least of sufficient reproductive maturity to become pregnant, has more at stake in continuing her life as she chooses than the unborn child has in beginning to live. The woman has already experienced much of life and has a more fully developed emotional range. In a sense, the woman is a proven quantity, whereas the fate of an unborn child is uncertain in many ways. The child might not survive to birth even if it is not aborted, or it might live for only a few days, weeks, months, or years. The woman, by contrast, is already living and experiencing life among other living, fully developed human beings who have survived to reach an intellectual and emotional status which the fetus has not and, even if not aborted, might never fully attain.

The incommensurability of rights of the woman and fetus are nowhere more clearly in evidence. The fetus does not yet actually have the same involvement in life and, hence, does not have the same interests as the woman. But the fetus, if aborted, will be totally destroyed and, so, will never have the opportunity to develop to the same level of experience and involvement in life with the same interests as the woman; whereas the woman, if denied the possibility of an abortion, will at most undergo pain, inconvenience, emotional trauma, embarrassment, and expense. Should the right to life outweigh every other right of every other person? Or should the right to life be qualified in certain ways, to take into account situations in which what would otherwise be judged as the lesser rights of another person take precedence even over the right to life?

The fact that a fetus is not able to speak up for itself and challenge attempts to violate its rights, whereas the woman can do so, is not necessarily enough to give more weight to the woman's right to avoid discomfort than the fetus's putative right to life. There are many cases in which we regard it as the moral obligation of people in a position to defend the rights of others to act on their behalf when they cannot do so. We do not suppose that it is morally permissible to use comatose patients as food or fertilizer, just because they are not able to stand up for their own rights. The weak, downtrodden, and otherwise physically vulnerable in a society are not, for that reason, deprived of rights and should not, we generally believe, have their rights violated, but should, instead, be protected by those who are stronger and able to help in any morally respectable civilization. It is a sign of our moral probity that we are willing to come to the defense of those who are wronged and cannot themselves seek redress of violations of their rights. This is presumably what many antiabortion activists believe themselves to be doing. Yet we should not suppose that extremists who bomb abortion clinics or threaten people involved in performing legal abortions with violence are morally justified in their acts of civil terrorism. The point is that there can be a legitimate moral disagreement about whether or not an unborn fetus has or does not have a moral right to life that outweighs or does not outweigh the moral right of a pregnant woman to reproductive control of her body if she chooses not to have a baby. As a result, if we are going to make progress in understanding the ethics of abortion, we can no longer avoid the philosophical necessity of defining the concept of a moral right.

One approach to the analysis of moral rights is to think of rights as arising through interests, and of interests as arising through having such a quality of life as to be capable of pleasure and pain. Or, as we might also say, moral interests might depend on the extent to which life can be made better or worse for a person as a result of what the person does or experiences. The individuals to whom we ordinarily attribute moral rights typically fit this profile and belong to this category. Not every living thing has moral rights, as we know from the counterexamples of plants, bacteria, and tumors. Only living things with special qualities have moral rights. We are wrong to treat people merely as having instrumental value as means to an end, because to do so is to disregard their interests. The interest that individuals with moral rights take in themselves and in what happens to them, in turn, appears to derive from the fact that they can experience pleasure and pain in ways that can add to or detract from the quality of their lives. I am interested in what happens to me only if what happens to me makes a difference in the way my life is lived, and for this I must not only be alive, but I must also be capable of experiencing pleasure and pain and of choosing pleasure and avoiding pain.

The first thing to notice as an implication of this definition of moral rights is that human beings are not the only individuals with moral rights. Any creatures capable of experiencing the difference between pleasure and pain have interests and, as such, have moral rights. Since nonhuman animals are capable of experiencing pleasure and pain, it seems to follow that animals also have interests and moral rights and should not be understood as having only instrumental value. We are not morally justified in using animals merely as the means to whatever purposes of our own we choose, but we should respect their interests and moral rights. Animals, perhaps in different ways or to a different extent, also belong to the sphere of our moral concern, just as other human beings do, as creatures with intrinsic value as ends in themselves, living lives that are as important to them as our lives are to us, even if they cannot think or express their feelings in anything like the way we human beings can. The topic of animal rights and of our moral obligations to animals is especially relevant on the present theory. If we do not want to consider nonhuman animals as persons, then we must amend the provisional principle of ethics we have been considering, so that it takes into consideration not only moral rights and the consequences of our actions for persons, but also the moral rights of and consequences of actions for any human or nonhuman beings that have interests by virtue of their ability to experience pleasure and pain. If even nonhuman animals deserve our moral respect as beings with moral interests and moral rights, then what about human fetuses, as unborn human beings? This line of thought takes us back to our earlier questions. Do fetuses have rights? Do fetuses, in particular, have a right to life? Does a fetus's right to life outweigh the rights of a pregnant woman who does not want to carry the fetus and give birth?

This is finally the hard question. An interesting answer that accords with actual legal practice in many countries, and that respects the moral rights of women to reproductive control of their bodies, is to say that in the early stages of pregnancy a fetus does not actually have moral rights, because, at that stage of embryological development, a fetus has not advanced far enough to be capable of experiencing pleasure and pain. This is a good approach to the problem in that it links in a satisfying way a woman's moral right to reproductive control over her body with a corresponding responsibility. The guideline makes a woman responsible for knowing as quickly as possible whether she is pregnant and, if she chooses abortion, obligates her to act quickly to minimize the fetus's suffering. If she is going to have an abortion by this principle, she must do so before the fetus develops a brain and nervous system capable of experiencing pain, and certainly before being able to experience a conscious awareness of injury.

The wish to avoid causing pain to a fetus is the humane rationale behind the limitation represented by this window of opportunity during which pregnant women can legally choose abortion in those governments that permit abortion in the early stages of pregnancy. The scientific question of whether the first trimester is a long enough time for a fetus not to have developed neurologically to the point of being able to experience pain remains open to debate. If abortion is ever to be morally justified, and if a fetus, like nonhuman animals, can have moral rights by virtue of having interests, then abortion can be morally permitted only prior to a fetus's having interests, interpreted here as any time prior to its having the capacity for pleasure and pain. With rights go responsibilities. If we believe that a woman has the moral right to reproductive control over her body, then we might also believe that a woman who chooses an abortion has the responsibility to do so early enough in the fetus's development so that it is incapable of suffering. In this way, the woman avoids causing the fetus unnecessary pain and may avoid violating the fetus's moral interests, by acting before the fetus has a moral right to life.

ACTUAL AND POTENTIAL MORAL RIGHTS

From a philosophical point of view, the trouble with this account is that it limits the moral rights of individuals to those times when they have interests in the sense of being capable of experiencing pleasure and pain. The interpretation excludes fetuses in the early stages of development from having moral rights, which might be a welcome conclusion for those who want to emphasize women's reproductive rights. In doing so, however, the proposal also overlooks what many defenders of the rights of the unborn consider in their antiabortion stance to be a fetus's *potential* rather than *actual* moral interests and moral rights. If fetuses at an early stage of development do not actually have the capacity for pleasure and pain, they will soon enough, if nature is left to follow its course. In a matter of days, weeks, or at most a few months, a normally developing fetus will be able to feel pleasure and pain and, so, is only a brief interval of time away from having the moral rights that would morally forbid its being aborted. But, then, where such important life or death ethical decisions are concerned, the antiabortionist argues, how can the difference in such a short amount of time make a difference in whether it is morally justified or unjustified for the life of a normal, healthy, and naturally developing fetus to be destroyed?

A further qualification about the concept of actual versus potential moral rights can be advanced to help support the conclusion that abortion can be morally justified, even for beings that potentially but do not yet actually have a moral right to life.

The basis for the distinction is that the fetus as a potentially but not yet actually sentient being is no different in principle from potentially but not yet actually conceived fetuses, considered as potentially but not actually fertilized ova, in all potential but not actually joined ova and spermatazoa. There is a potential fetus for every pair of vital human ova and sperm. But we do not suppose that we have any obligation to protect the potential moral rights of every potential fetus consisting of every potentially joined but actually unjoined male and female human germ plasms. It is implausible to think that the unjoined ova and spermatazoa of a random set of men and women have potential moral rights that must be defended against infractions. But, then, why suppose that the potential moral rights of potentially but not actually sentient fetuses are any different? Why suppose that potentially but not yet actually sentient fetuses have a moral right to life that would be violated by abortion?

The comparison between the potential but not actual moral right of unjoined ova and spermatazoa and the potential but not actual moral right of a potentially but not yet actually sentient fetus is instructive but flawed. There is an important difference between the potential occurrences in the two cases. We can identify a difference in degree of potentiality that can as easily be understood as a difference in kind. Consider the case of a normal, healthy fetus developing in a normal, healthy pregnant woman. At an early stage of development, the fetus is potentially but not yet actually sentient and, in that sense potentially but not yet actually, has interests that qualify it as potentially but not yet actually having a moral right to life. Compare this with the situation in which a single vital spermatazoan in a sexually fertile man living in a neolithic village in the Brazilian rain forest and a single vital ovum in a sexually fertile woman living in the Austrian Alps are described as potentially but not actually a fetus and, so, potentially but not actually sentient, potentially but not actually a being with interests, and potentially but not actually a being with moral rights, including a moral right to life.

There is a subtle but noteworthy difference even in the way in which the two cases are described. In the event of an already existent fetus, we find it natural to speak of the individual as potentially but not *yet* actually sentient, potentially but not *yet* actually a being with interests and moral rights, and so on. By comparison, in referring to the potentially but not actually joined ovum and sperm, we do not say that they are potentially but not *yet* actually a fetus and potentially but not *yet* actually a sentient being, with interests and moral rights, including a moral right to life. This apparently minor lexical difference reflects a significant distinction in the way we think about potentiality in the two cases. We say that the fetus is not yet sentient, because we know that, in the normal course of things, if the fetus is permitted to continue developing, it will soon become sentient, with all the other properties, including moral rights, that we suppose sentient beings to have. In the case of the unjoined ovum and sperm, by contrast, it is not a matter of their not yet becoming a fetus. There are too many obstacles and too many unlikelihoods in the way of the two germ plasms ever actually uniting in order for the sperm to fertilize the ovum and develop into a fetus. Is there even any strong probability or practical possibility that the man in the rain forest and the woman in the mountains will ever meet during their reproductively active years, let alone that they will have sexual intercourse at such a time and with such effect that the woman becomes pregnant?

Their ova and sperm are only in the weakest and most distant sense potentially a fetus, and they would first need to produce a viable fertilized ovum in order to speak in the same way of their containing between them a distributed or scattered entity, the egg and sperm, that is potentially sentient and that potentially has a moral right to life.

If we leave nature to its course, the already existent fetus will develop its brain and neurological system to the point at which the fetus will become sentient. This is not merely a remote possibility, as in the case of the rain forest man and Alpine woman, but something we expect to happen, as long as there is no fatal accident or interference. Indeed, nothing more has to occur for this to happen, except that nothing be done to prevent the fetus from developing into a sentient being; whereas, for the rain forest man and Alpine woman to make a baby, insurmountable odds would have to be overcome. In light of the enormous difference in degree between the potentiality of the occurrence of a being with a moral right to life in the two cases, someone might say that it would be better to speak of a difference in kind of potentiality. There is, then, an equivocation in the argument between two meanings of the word *potential.* We need not suppose that the potential but not yet actual sentience of a fetus in an early stage of embryological development is different in principle from the potential but not actual existence of a sentient fetus resulting from the logically possible but highly unlikely sexual union of the rain forest man and mountain woman. In recognition of the difference, we could distinguish between *strong* and *weak potentiality,* or between *naturally probable potentiality* and *merely logically possible potentiality.* If the distinction is accepted, then it seems reasonable to deny that a weak or merely logically possible potentially sentient fetus that would result from any unjoined ovum and sperm if they were ever to be united under the right conditions has a moral right or potential moral right to life. Eliminating moral rights for weakly or merely logically possibly potentially sentient beings does not diminish the plausibility of extending a moral right or potential moral right to life to a strong or naturally probable potentially sentient fetus. A potential moral right need only exist when we have good reasons to believe that a fetus will actually become sentient in the natural course of things in a relatively short time, if only nothing is done to prevent it from developing normally.

The effect of this counterargument is to emphasize the persistent difficulty of the abortion issue as a problem in applied ethics. We could solve the problem on philosophical grounds, although surely not to everyone's satisfaction, if we could wholeheartedly accept the general principle that only actually sentient beings have moral rights. It is not just the potentiality, but the strong potentiality of a healthy, normally developing fetus with its strong potentiality as a being about to acquire sentience, moral interests, and a moral right to life that sustains the abortion controversy, even among those who want very badly to respect a woman's sometimes conflicting moral right to reproductive control over her body. Legal and moral rights are not unqualified, but involve mediation in their exercise to avoid violating the rights of other people who also have interests that are not necessarily less important than our own. The philosophically intransigent and politically divisive controversy about abortion rights will not easily go away. To resolve it, if it can be resolved, will take a revolution in our thinking. But, by tracing out the major lines of argument in this bitter-tasting appetizer, we have come at last to an appreciation of how complex ethical problems can be, and of how differences of basic moral values in their interaction with scientific fact, metaphysical presuppositions, and common sense can result in enormous practical differences in the judgments reached by intelligent, conscientious, and open-minded moral decision makers.

We are now in a position to see how the synthesis of consequentialism and deontology applies to the abortion controversy. The principle tells us that, of the available choices, we should try to maximize happiness over unhappiness, except when to do so unnecessarily violates a moral subject's moral rights. It is for this reason that the conflict about the moral rights of pregnant women and unborn fetuses is especially relevant. The principle cannot be implemented unless we are clear about whether the individuals affected by an action have moral rights, which is precisely the focus of dispute in the problem of abortion ethics. The question of the moral rights or potential moral rights of a potentially sentient fetus in the early stages of development makes a difference in deciding whether a fetus can have its moral rights violated in a woman's decision to have an abortion. The implication is that the synthesis of consequentialism and deontology by itself does not solve every moral problem. We must know what the consequences of an action are likely to be and whether or not they will unnecessarily violate the moral rights of individuals touched by the action. Unresolved moral problems can persist, even if a correct moral ethical principle is accepted, when there are unanswered questions about whether the conditions of the principle are satisfied. By highlighting the issue of whether fetuses have moral rights as a basis for continuing disagreement in the abortion dilemma, we begin to understand why the ethics of abortion is likely to remain controversial.

VIRTUE ETHICS AS BACKGROUND TO CRISIS ETHICS

The problem of abortion is like many of the issues considered by moral philosophers. There is a tendency for ethical thinkers to overemphasize problems of moral reasoning in crisis situations, where an unusual set of circumstances requires a person to make a difficult but once in a lifetime moral decision.

What, if anything, should you do if you or a woman you know becomes pregnant but does not want to have the baby? What should you do if someone threatens you with physical violence and you need to decide whether to respond violently or to turn the other cheek? What should you do if you wake up in the train switching tower with the Cannonball Express bearing down on two stalled cars with trapped passengers inside, and you only have time to pull a switch that will divert the train? These are all emergency kinds of situations that do not often arise in life. Of course, we want to think about such possibilities, and about what we would and should do if they were to occur. Some situations (unwanted pregnancy) are more likely to occur than others (train switching dilemma), but all feature incidents that are rare and that, however they may call for clear thinking and good moral will, do not affect our day-to-day lives. This fact makes it important to distinguish between the moral decisions we need to make when a moral crisis arises from the principles by which we live our less turbulent everyday lives. Yet it is in living our ordinary lives that we need more general guidance, which, if successful and morally correct, may even help us avoid some kinds of moral decision-making crises. What can we say about the morality of everyday living when we are not confronted with moral decision-making emergencies?

Everyday morality requires virtue. We can think of virtue as a pattern of living in which we strive for excellence in all our activities. To speak of excellence in this way is to load the concept with ethical overtones. We do not speak, except ironically, of excellent liars or excellent thiefs, even if people who practice such unethical behaviors are especially effective and proficient in their moral wrongdoing. Virtue or excellence of conduct presupposes a positive ethical outlook and desire to do good. We are virtuous when we are willing to devote our energy to excel at bringing out the best human qualities in ourselves. This conception raises several issues. What is the role of intention in morality? What are the values by which we are to judge human excellence? Are there objective standards of morality, or is morality culturally relative or subjective? What are the proper motivations for acting morally? If we know what is right to do, but it is difficult or costly for us to behave morally, why should we put into practice what we believe in the abstract to be morally right?

Intention plays an important part in ethics. We have already seen that it is the intrinsic intentionality of thought—in particular, of our decisions to act when we choose or intend to do something—that makes our actions free in the sense of being such that we could have done otherwise. And we have seen that acting freely is a precondition of being morally responsible for our actions and their consequences. Even in the law, we do not usually hold people legally responsible for what they do if they have not acted intentionally. If an actor kills another actor unintentionally in the theater with a real loaded gun that has been accidentally substituted for a stage weapon, we would not generally hold the actor responsible before the law. To act is to do something intentionally, and we can only be morally responsible for our actions, for what we deliberately and freely choose to do.

There are theoretical conflicts in assessing the morality of agents acting with specific intentions as opposed to the consequences of their actions. Suppose that an evil dictator tries to send a boatload of political prisoners to an extermination camp, but the boat is swept along in a powerful current and, instead, ends up in a tropical paradise, where the prisoners enjoy a lifetime of happiness. We would not ordinarily credit the dictator with having done a morally good thing, even though what he did had a good effect, because the dictator's intentions were not good, and the good consequences that resulted occurred unintentionally, contrary to the dictator's intentions. If I see an unattended child drowning off the end of a pier at the lake, and I race down to the water to try to save the child, then ordinarily we would judge my decision as morally good, even if my action has the unforeseen and unintended consequence of knocking over two older ladies when I step on a loose board, catapaulting them into the water, where they drown. I intentionally save one person from drowning, but unintentionally cause two people to drown. By most ethical standards, I will have acted morally in intentionally saving the child but not immorally in unintentionally causing the two ladies to drown. In general, intending to do something for the sake of satisfying a moral desideratum makes the decision to act and the action that can reasonably be expected to issue from the decision morally justified, even if the unintended consequences of the action are unfortunate or regrettable, and even if the action does not actually accomplish the agent's intentions.

MORAL ABSOLUTISM AND MORAL RELATIVISM

What are the standards of moral right and wrong? What counts as a moral desideratum? Are moral values absolute or relative, objective or subjective? It is a familiar observation that what some people regard as morally obligatory, others see as merely permissible or even morally objectionable and forbidden. A classic example is the conduct of traditional Inuit or Eskimo tribesmembers, who send relatives off on an iceberg to drift away and die when they become too old to hunt or otherwise contribute to the tribal economy. This is considered not only morally permissible but obligatory and is accepted as such, even by the elderly or infirm who voluntarily participate in their own destruction. Such practices, however, are not considered morally correct in modern industrialized societies, in which banishing grandma and grandpa to icy deaths when they are too old or ill to work is not regarded as morally proper. There are many other illustrations of differences in moral attitudes and moral practices among different peoples and at different times. Some societies have practiced human sacrifice or exposure of children, leaving them to die; some societies have considered abortion morally permissible, and others have condemned it as morally wrong. The accounts of travelers to distant lands, and the field reports of anthropologists who have studied foreign cultures, testify to how different the ideas of moral right and wrong, of virtue and vice, can be among different peoples.

The philosophical question posed by these cultural differences is whether moral value is itself culturally relative, or whether there can be absolute ethical standards that hold universally, despite cultural differences in moral judgment and conduct. The mere fact that not all cultures accept the same moral values does not by itself entail that moral value is culturally relative. There could still be absolute moral values that some or possibly even all cultures do not understand or that they are unwilling to follow. If a thief breaks into your home to steal, you need not suppose that there are morally relative differences that distinguish the subculture of thieves from nonthieves, according to which thieves regard it as morally permissible to steal, whereas nonthieves believe that it is morally wrong to steal. A thief might even be convinced of the moral right to steal from others, as fully convinced and inspired with an attitude of moral righteousness about the moral permissibility of stealing as are others about the more conventional morality that forbids stealing. But the implication need not be that morality itself is relative. Instead, it could be that there are absolute moral standards and that the thief or the conventional moralist is simply mistaken in believing that stealing is morally permissible or that stealing is morally forbidden. How, then, can we distinguish between these possibilities?

An advantage of moral relativism is that it readily lends itself to an attitude of moral tolerance. But a standard objection to moral relativism is that, when taken to extremes, its implications concerning moral tolerance appear to be logically inconsistent. If we acknowledge that moral values are not absolute, then we may be less likely to try to impose our own morality on others. A typical example of the sort of moral intolerance that moral relativism might help alleviate is the superior attitude of religious missionaries from "advanced" societies, who, in visiting indigenous peoples in underdeveloped countries, compel the natives by force of arms or in other ways against their will into wearing clothes, practicing monogamy instead of polygamy, or adopting a religious and moral belief system different from or even incompatible with their own. This is the kind of behavior that is most prominently fostered by the preconception that one's own moral views are absolutely right and that the members of a particular social group are morally entitled or even morally obligated to require others to believe and act as they believe is right. Insofar as moral relativism contributes to a decline in the moral domination of one people by another, it might be judged as having a morally positive influence.

The problem with moral relativism is that it seems to preclude moral absolutism as absolutely morally wrong. That is, a moral relativist can tolerate any moral attitude except that of moral absolutism or moral intolerance. But why should moral absolutism be an exception to the wide range of moral standpoints a moral relativist is willing to tolerate? If all moral attitudes are justified relative to the cultural context in which they occur, how can moral relativists consistently object to the culturally contexted moral attitude of moral absolutists? The conclusion is that moral relativism may be logically inconsistent. Moral relativism allows any moral belief or practice to be morally justified relative to the cultural context in which it occurs, except moral absolutism. But, if moral relativism rejects moral absolutism as absolutely false or unacceptable, then moral relativism is not generally true; neither does it extend moral relativism and toleration to all moral beliefs and practices. If moral relativism admits any such exceptions, then it might as well allow others. According to moral relativism, if moral absolutism is absolutely morally wrong, then paradoxically there are at least some absolute moral values, whereby moral relativism is revealed to be logically incoherent.

Can a moral relativist consistently maintain that moral absolutism is justified within the cultural context in which it is practiced? This is an intriguing question, but the answer is "no," for two complementary reasons. First, according to moral absolutism, if an act or a judgment is morally right or morally wrong, then it is absolutely morally right or absolutely morally wrong, regardless of circumstance. This means that it is logically inconsistent to think of moral absolutism as confined to any particular social situation. It does not make sense for a moral absolutist to say, "Stealing is absolutely wrong, but only relative to a particular social group, such as the one to which I belong." Second, according to moral relativism, no act or judgment is absolutely morally right or absolutely morally wrong, but only relative to circumstance. This means that it is equally logically inconsistent to think of moral relativism in its full generality as allowing the possibility of moral absolutism even as confined to a particular social situation. It does not make sense for a moral relativist to say, "Stealing is never absolutely wrong, although it can be absolutely wrong relative to another social group to which I do not belong."

Moral relativism, however, ought to be committed to the conclusion that moral absolutism is justified relative to a cultural context, if moral relativism in its full generality is committed to the conclusion that any and every act or judgment is or can be morally justified relative to real or imaginable circumstances. For the same reason, moral relativism cannot accept moral intolerance as morally justified, even relative to a cultural context in which intolerance is cultivated as a way of life. Paradoxically, moral relativism must be morally intolerant of any moral intolerance, including its own moral intolerance of moral intolerance. This, finally, is what makes moral relativism in its full generality logically inconsistent.

The only remedy is to qualify moral relativism by modifying its full generality to admit certain exceptions for the sake of logical consistency. The trouble with this solution is that it compromises the generality of moral relativism, so that it is no longer true that all moral decisions are relatively morally right or wrong, and none absolutely morally right or wrong. The problem, then, becomes where to draw the line. If some decisions are absolutely morally right or wrong, even for the moral relativist, why not others? Why should we consider moral absolutism as opposed in principle to moral relativism, if logically there is no way to sustain a fully general relativism, but even the relativist must admit that at least some acts or judgments are absolutely and not merely relatively morally right or wrong?

If there are absolute moral values, and if moral relativism is self-contradictory, then the question arises as to how moral values are determined. It would be comforting if we could believe that moral values are objectively discoverable in the manner of scientific truths. What is troublesome about moral relativism, aside from its apparent inconsistency, is that it seems to imply a kind of subjectivism in the limiting case, in which the most narrowly defined subculture relative to which moral values can be justified converges on a single person. If moral relativism extends to each person, then whatever any person finds it morally permissible or obligatory to do is morally permissible or obligatory relative to that person's highly individualized personal subculture. But, when moral relativism degenerates into moral subjectivism, critics say, it is tantamount to moral anarchy, in which anything whatsoever can be regarded as morally right or morally wrong.

The antidote for the subjectivism of individualized moral relativism might be to restore objectivity to moral reasoning by following the model of the natural sciences. Unfortunately, there is an obstacle known as the *naturalistic fallacy* or *is-ought gap,* which implies that moral values cannot be defined correctly in terms of, or validly derived from, scientific facts. From the fact that my car has stalled, it does not follow that this is a morally good or a morally bad thing. It may be morally bad if it means that I cannot get to the hospital to take an injured person there, as I have promised to do. It may be morally good if it means that my car cannot be used as a bank robber had planned to get to the scene of a crime. Neither does it help to add facts in trying to derive the inferences. It may be morally bad if I cannot get to the hospital, specifically because it means that I cannot meet a moral obligation. It may be morally good if the bank robber cannot get to the bank, specifically because it means that the robber cannot do something that is morally forbidden. But it is only when the assumptions in moral reasoning embody moral obligations or prohibitions that it is possible to validly derive conclusions that also express moral values about what ought or ought not to occur or what should or should not be done. The is-ought gap implies that we cannot validly infer statements of moral value from statements exclusively of scientific fact. The world of facts is logically independent of the values moral agents might attribute to it, in much the same way that the existence of a sunset or waterfall is independent of the beauty a beholder might see or fail to see in it. The implication is that it might be hopeless to approach the objectivity of moral value in the same way as the objective truth of scientific fact.

If the world of facts itself is morally neither good nor evil but only in relation to the attitudes of a moral agent, how can moral value be objective rather than culturally relative or even personally subjective? The only possibility is if moral values can be justified by sound reasoning, but not as facts or derived from facts. Values need to be considered as belonging to a category of their own. This need not preclude values from the same kind of justification as other elements of our conceptual scheme. When we think about the train switching dilemma, we see two different moral perspectives in conflict. The arguments that might be formulated and evaluated concerning the morally right decisions and actions to be reached in such a case are not evaluated on subjective grounds but objectively, according to the same high standards applied in other rigorous scientific and philosophical thinking. It is part and parcel of the rigorous evaluation of these arguments that they must not be allowed to bridge the is-ought gap, by trying invalidly to derive statements of value from statements of fact. However, within this constraint, it is possible to put forward and accept or reject arguments about moral value by criteria of correct reasoning that are as objective as those involved in science, but are applied to questions of moral value rather than to matters of scientific fact.

If there are objective values in ethics, then what is the objectively correct solution to the problem about what to do in the train switching problem? So far, we have seen only an unresolved conflict of two moral perspectives reflecting opposed moral values, the deontological and consequentialist. We have seen that there are serious counterexamples to both of the extreme moral perspectives of deontology and consequentialism, the scapegoat objection in the case of consequentialism and the lifeboat objection in the case of deontology. Accordingly, we have proposed synthesizing the positive features of the two positions, in a moral principle that obligates us to promote whenever possible the greatest happiness for the greatest number, except when to do so would involve unnecessary violations of an individual's right to moral respect. We have observed further that it may not always be reasonable to expect that all moral decision making can be resolved neatly, but that the subject matter of ethical judgment might be less clearcut than that of scientific or mathematical reasoning.

For these reasons, it would not necessarily reflect negatively on the synthesis of deontology and consequentialism if there were no satisfactory answer to the train switching dilemma. That would be disappointing, perhaps, but it need not constitute a refutation of the theory. We have already encountered a problem of moral decision making that so far we have not been able to solve satisfactorily, in the controversy surrounding the moral permissibility or impermissibility of abortion. We are about to see that the solution of the train switching dilemma is not that far to seek within the framework of the principle we have considered. What is more important for the moment is to recognize that, in advancing alternative ethical viewpoints and evaluating supporting arguments and objections raised against them, we need not rely on subjective feelings about what is right or wrong. We can arrive at objectively justified conclusions about problems of morality, just as we can in mathematics and the natural sciences, by applying the same objective standards of argument and following the best arguments wherever they lead. In ethics, as in science, we begin with assumptions that are either accepted or rejected on intuitive grounds as pretheoretical starting points for theory construction, but that are no less objective for having to do with values rather than facts.

In the train switching dilemma, the synthesis of consequentialism and deontology suggests a course of action for the person in the tower. What should the agent do? Pulling the switch causes a person to be killed who would not otherwise die but, in the process, saves other lives. Of the available alternatives, pulling the switch is the only way to maximize happiness and minimize unhappiness. These considerations so far favor the consequentialist side of the synthesis and recommend the morality of pulling the switch. The remaining question is whether, by pulling the switch, the agent is avoidably treating the one trapped passenger without due moral respect. Here there may be room for disagreement and a continuation of debate about the morality of the situation for a clearly agonizing moral dilemma; however, in this case, there is no way to maximize happiness and minimize unhappiness except by treating the lone passenger merely as a means to an end, much as in the emergency lifeboat problem. If disrespect for the individual's moral rights in the situation is unavoidable in order to maximize happiness and minimize unhappiness among the possible actions available to the agent, then, according to the compromise moral principle we have tentatively adopted, it is morally justified to pull the switch and direct the train away from the two cars toward the single car, preventing the death of the two passengers in those cars, at the cost of causing the death of the individual in the other car. The solution is obviously not a choice with which every moral thinker will be entirely comfortable, but the decision can be defended as a conclusion arrived at by objective reasoning rather than by subjective feeling and, if it still seems objectionable, a conclusion that can be criticized and refuted, revised, or replaced on different but no less objective grounds.

WHY BE MORAL?

The remaining question to consider is why we ought to be moral. If we accept the proposition that there are absolute moral values, that in principle we can distinguish right from wrong by objective reasoning, then we might be able to arrive at a correct system of moral values. But even then we must answer the motivational question why we should be moral. Why should we act in accord, or actually put into practice or live our lives in agreement, with the principles we believe at an abstract or intellectual level?

We have already observed that it is one thing to know what we ought or are morally obligated to do, and another actually to do it. We might choose to do what we morally ought to do because we are afraid of the consequences of misbehavior. In extreme cases, we might go to jail or pay a fine, because there are legal penalties that sometimes come into play when we act immorally, where the law has an interest in reinforcing moral values and where the law is effective in punishing acts of moral wrongdoing as legal infractions. Or we might act morally because we are afraid of extralegal consequences, such as acquiring a bad reputation or being shunned by people with whom we need to do business or from whom we hope to obtain favors, which we will jeopardize if they come to believe we are not morally trustworthy.

Another motivation for morally proper behavior derives from the belief that God as a righteous judge will eternally reward morally good behavior in heaven or eternally punish morally wrong behavior in hell. We have provisionally concluded that philosophy has no adequate proof for the existence, let alone the moral nature, of God, and especially not for the specific content of any particular religious teaching about what might happen on a final judgment day. Neither can we accept the wager dilemma that it is rational to bet on the possibility that a final judgment might take place as a way of trying to make ourselves believe something for which we have no adequate independent justification. The religious motivation for morally proper behavior, however appealing it might be to people with religious predispositions, does not provide a philosophical solution to the question of why we ought to be moral. The argument from religion cannot motivate us on philosophical grounds to be moral unless or until someone discovers a philosophically defensible reason to believe in the existence and moral nature of God, as well as the proposition that God knows everything we do and will punish evil and reward good.

If there is no rational basis for belief in God, as chapter 4 suggests, then, many people have thought, there is equally no sound reason for acting morally. Why should we do what is ethically right? In particular, why should we do so when doing the morally right thing conflicts with what we want, or even with our happiness or welfare? What if we could make ourselves invisible by taking a magic pill? If we could do whatever we wanted without any risk of being caught or punished, would there nevertheless be a good reason for acting morally? The traditional religious solution to the problem is to invoke God's omniscience as including knowledge of whatever we do, even when our wrongdoing escapes the notice of our fellow human beings. The threat of God's punishment probably serves as a deterent for many people of religious faith, but we have seen that it is not a philosophically adequate way to explain why we should choose to act morally, even when the consequences might be unfortunate for us and even when we believe that we will never be discovered or punished for moral wrongdoing. If we do not believe in God or, if for philosophical purposes, we do not want to assume that God exists in the absence of proof, what reason can we have for acting morally? If we can take an invisibility pill and do whatever we want without fear of discovery or punishment, why should we not steal or kill, even when we know it is wrong? Why should we be moral?

Some philosophers have answered this question by saying that, when we do what is morally wrong, even if there is no God to reward or punish our behavior, we damage our souls, selves, or, if you prefer, our personalities. According to this solution to the problem, to act immorally is as inimical to our self-interests as it would be to deliberately injure our bodies so that we could not run, walk, or see. Even if we appear to escape retribution by human or divine justice, by acting immorally we corrupt our souls as badly as ingesting a poison damages the body, which no one would purposely do. By acting wrongly, even if we can get away with it in others' opinion and God's judgment, we injure what is most precious in and to us. We hurt ourselves in ways that are not adequately compensated by the benefit we appear to derive from the morally wrong acts we allow ourselves to commit. We will examine the way in which we injure ourselves, even without knowing it, when we act wrongly, as a reasonable philosophical motivation for putting moral principles into practice in our lives.

It might help to begin by distinguishing the reason for being moral from other kinds of internal motivations. It is not just a matter of wanting to avoid the psychological suffering that might result in a bad conscience when we do wrong. It appears that some people do not have a conscience at all. We might choose to pay the price of being nagged by occasional twinges of remorse for doing something unethical if the pleasure or selfish value that we obtain as a result is enough to make it seem worthwhile. A bad conscience also has a way of fading with time, as we become used to the idea of what we have done, and a bad conscience becomes quieted by repeated outrages, to which it eventually becomes accustomed. We might expect that, if we profit sufficiently by our wrongdoing, then, even if our consciences bother us for a while, eventually we will be able to sleep at night as well as anyone who is totally innocent of ever having done anything wrong. Independently of the opinions of others, of the external rewards and punishments we might or might not receive, and of our own opinions of ourselves as reflected in our idiosyncratic psychologies, we ought to be moral for another reason. We ought to be moral because, when we are not, even if we appear to avoid all punishment, including the self-punishment inflicted by an internal accusatory voice of conscience, we make ourselves unworthy of some of the best things life has to offer.

If we are social creatures, as commentators on the human condition agree, then our greatest good must revolve around our associations with other human beings. We want to have worthwhile associations with other people, not only for the sake of enjoyment in passing the time and establishing profitable business and other useful connections, but because it is intrinsically valuable to share their company. The highest type of social association to which we can aspire might be our greatest good and most important personal satisfaction; however, we make ourselves unworthy of the highest type of social association to the extent that we act immorally. After all, who would freely choose an evil person as a true friend?

We sabotage our self-interest whenever we act wrongly, because, through our actions, whether anyone knows it or not, we deprive ourselves of one of the greatest human goods. But what if no one ever discovers that we have done something wrong? Can we not then enjoy all the benefits of associating with the best, most accomplished, and most virtuous people? After all, by hypothesis, they do not know that we are immoral, perhaps because we have always used our invisibility pill to carry out our misdeeds. The answer has to do with the nature of moral virtue as the background morality by which we live our daily lives. Virtue is a matter of degree, and having done something morally wrong does not necessarily make us unvirtuous, if it has not become a habit or disposition that comes to define who and what we are. To err is human, and to rise above minor wrongdoing by acknowledging responsibility for it and to make amends, resolving to be strong and exercising control over our moral conduct, are among the ways we become increasingly more virtuous and increasingly more worthy of the highest type of associations with people of moral excellence. Acting responsibly is the primary way in which we can perfect ourselves as the subjects of objective moral judgment and action that we are capable of becoming by using our free will to choose what is morally right and refrain from doing what is morally wrong.

Could we also undertake truly heinous acts of wrongdoing and then return to our normal way of living in which we present a public image of moral good? This is a difficult question. Yet it seems that, aside from a temporary psychosis, the very decision to do something monumentally evil, arrived at by the usual process of morally responsible judgment of free will, can reflect only a morally corrupt character and, as such, could only be the act of someone who—regardless of how he or she is perceived by others and even if he or she performs only one terrible act of evil in his or her life—must be morally unvirtuous in a deep sense. If we are not talking about an occasional slip in doing something wrong, but an act of great immorality, then it is hard to see how the decision could be anything but the result of a morally evil character that has not previously surfaced in the person's public behavior. The virtuous can also make mistakes in accepting such people as friends, but we cannot expect them to remain good friends with people who are not and who probably will reveal themselves not to be morally good.

If we make a habit of moral wrongdoing, then our choices and actions become a more deeply ingrained part of our characters that begins to define who and what kinds of people we are. If we use our invisibility pill, not just as an experiment but in order to get away with deliberately chosen evil, then we soon become genuinely evil. An evil character or personality rooted in habit is practically impossible to conceal from others, so that people of virtue—those with whom it would be the greatest of human goods for us to associate—will discover our true attitudes and will no longer wish to associate with us. The dissociation of people of moral excellence from people of moral corruption is also part of the punishment that the law inflicts when it incarcerates criminals in prison and, in extreme cases of persistent antisocial behavior, in solitary confinement. Whether such punishments are morally justified is a controversial question. But the practice of isolating moral offenders from other people recognizes that social association is a natural good for human beings that is inextricably bound up with our most basic psychological needs, so that depriving a person of the ability to associate with others can be a meaningful penalty for legal and moral wrongdoing. Without sending moral offenders to jail, the decision simply not to associate with people whose conduct demonstrates a morally objectionable character enforces the moral preferences of the members of a social group. The natural desire to preserve the possibility of associating with individuals who are striving for excellence and who can help us achieve excellence in our own lives provides a powerful down-to-earth incentive for every person to be moral that is independent of religious presuppositions. It gives everyone a reason to cultivate a good moral character, even when it is possible to do wrong without the risk of being discovered. The idea is simply that everyone needs good friends, and that if we want to have good friends, we must try to be good people.

MORALITY AND THE MEANING OF LIFE

Is the pursuit of moral excellence the meaning of life and the answer to the sojourner's question? The challenge of achieving moral perfection can provide direction and purpose to life. Struggling to do what is morally right in developing a morally virtuous character is a full-time job. But not everything that occupies our attention is necessarily part of the meaning of life.

We need not doubt that following the path of morality is a worthwhile goal. It is at least as important to our lives as developing our talents, maintaining physical fitness and improving our athletic abilities, falling in love, raising a family, being successful in business, and participating in political affairs. All of these activities are vitally important to our lives, but are they themselves, the achieving or trying to achieve these things, the meaning of life? Is it the meaning of life to try to achieve moral excellence, or is it just one of many things we might choose to do in order to enhance our lives, without constituting their meaning?

The difficulty in trying to answer the sojourner's question in terms of moral conduct is that the meaning of life presumably ought to be an end in itself and not merely something done for the sake of something else. Can it be intrinsically valuable to be moral if the most reasonable motivation we can give for being moral—the reason we should try to do what is morally right, as we have now explained it—is for the sake of something else, in order to be worthy of associating with people of moral excellence? If we are to answer the sojourner's question, then, however important it may be to live morally, we might need to look beyond even the life dedicated to virtue and morality to uncover yet a different and more fundamental approach to the question of whether life is meaningful or absurd and, if meaningful, exactly where the meaning of life might be found.

CHAPTER SIX

Reflecting on What Philosophy Teaches

Philosophy is like trying to open a safe with a combination lock; each little adjustment of the dials seems to achieve nothing, only when everything is in place does the door open.

—Ludwig Wittgenstein
Personal Recollections, edited by Rush Rhees, 1930

METAPHILOSOPHY

In previous chapters, we examined some of the most important philosophical problems. But we have not explored the nature of philosophy itself—or considered the kind of study philosophy involves, its scope and limitations, purpose and methods. As might be expected, the nature of philosophy is as much a subject of philosophical controversy as any of the other subjects philosophy investigates. There is a philosophy *of* philosophy, or *metaphilosophy,* just as there is a philosophy of mind, philosophy of science, philosophy of moral conduct, philosophy of mathematics, philosophy of history, philosophy of religion, and philosophy of art.

The field of metaphilosophy has to do with the proper conduct of philosophy. What can and should philosophy take as its subject matter? How is philosophy different from science? Are there philosophical problems? If so, what are they, and how can we recognize them? What can and should philosophy try to accomplish? Can philosophical problems be solved? How should philosophy approach and try to solve philosophical problems? What value, if any, do its conclusions have? The answers to some of these questions might seem obvious, but philosophers have taken very different approaches even to such basic issues. To an extent, we can try to abstract answers to these questions from the practice of philosophy as we have now seen it in action. We must be careful, though, because, for all that we know, despite what might appear to be signs of progress in our proceedings, we might have been doing everything incorrectly from a proper metaphilosophical perspective. Now that we have done some philosophy, we are at last in a position to appreciate some of the concerns of metaphilosophy.

It will be useful to begin by considering a metaphilosophical position that is radically different from the one that has guided our inquiries up to this point. Then we can work back through some intermediary views to a metaphilosophy that agrees with and provides a theoretical framework to explain and uphold the way we have pursued our previous investigations of philosophical topics. As before, we must be prepared to rethink everything we have done so far from the ground up, if it should turn out that what appears in the end to be the proper way of doing philosophy contradicts our earlier efforts. If there is anything that philosophy teaches, it is to be uncompromisingly honest with ourselves, to inquire deeply and open-mindedly, and not to allow prejudices or emotions to control our thinking. We must be as critical of our own intellectual inclinations as of propositions we do not accept, rigorously following the best arguments to their conclusions, whatever they may turn out to be. Thus, it might be our first and most fundamental metaphilosophical principle to live by the rule of reason, even as we think about how to think about philosophy.

136

IS PHILOSOPHY POSSIBLE?

Some philosophers have claimed that philosophy is impossible. Philosophy is impossible if there are no philosophical problems, philosophical methods, or philosophical conclusions. One way in which such an extreme position might be upheld is by proposing an analysis of the meaning of language according to which only scientific statements of fact are meaningful. The preoccupation of philosophy with matters of value, and with metaphysical presuppositions that go beyond the empirical discoveries of science, suggests that the language of philosophy would not be meaningful under such a criterion.

Suppose that a metaphilosopher or meta-anti-philosopher were to advance a strong principle of meaning, according to which the only meaningful propositions are sentences that are true or false by virtue of the definitions of the terms they contain, or whose truth or falsehood can be confirmed or disconfirmed by a possible experience. Then we might extend meaning to all of science, true or false, and even to mathematics, if its axioms and theorems are interpreted as definitions or implications of the definitions of terms for mathematical concepts. We could also include as meaningful most of our ordinary talk in which we describe the facts of the world, including our psychological states of feeling happy or being in pain, our impressions of the weather, the facts that constitute a crime scene, the arrangement of furniture in a house, the history of politics, and many other things. But the putative propositions or pseudopropositions of religion, ethics, aesthetics, and metaphysics are not meaningful in this analysis of meaning, because they are not simply true or false by definition and are not confirmable or disconfirmable by experience.

If I say that God answers prayer, I am not claiming that God, by definition, answers prayer, for I assume that God chooses by divine free will to answer or not to answer prayer. Neither am I maintaining that I can experimentally verify or disprove God's answering prayer. The reason is that, even when what I pray for happens to occur, I cannot scientifically distinguish between God's causing this to happen and the desired events' happening by chance or their being such that they would have happened anyway. God, if God exists, is a supernatural being, so propositions about God's properties are not subject to scientific check. Similarly, if I say that killing is wrong, or that Jan Vermeer's painting *De Keukenmeid (The Kitchenmaid)* is the most beautiful artwork of the seventeenth century, my pronouncements do not automatically follow by definition, neither can they be empirically confirmed or disconfirmed by experience, observation, or scientific experiment. It is not just that someone might disagree with what my statements purport to say, but also that, when anyone does disagree, there is no way, even in principle, to decide whether either of us has said something true or false. If there is no way to determine the truth or falsity of a statement, then in what sense can the statement be said to have meaning at all? The *verification criterion of meaning* excludes all such sentences as pseudopropositions that, despite appearances, are literally meaningless and have no truth value.

The same might now be said about the pseudopropositions of philosophy. Philosophical pronouncements about ethical or aesthetic value, about the existence or nature of God, or about the meaning of life, among other traditional philosophical themes, are meaningless, according to the verification criterion of meaning. The idea of philosophy as an inquiry into a special subject matter, such as that of the sciences, but with different questions and a different methodology, is likewise misguided. Anyone who adopts this metaphilosophical perspective rejects inquiry into any philosophical problem as nonsense, refusing to admit there are any genuine philosophical problems and, hence, that there are no legitimate philosophical methods leading to meaningful philosophical concepts or conclusions. The most that we can do in philosophy, then, is to explain precisely how efforts to make philosophical pronouncements or to engage in philosophical inquiry are inherently meaningless, and to recommend that those who are interested in knowledge concentrate, instead, on science as the only sphere of meaningful questions and answers.

The verification criterion of meaning historically has had a salutary effect in eliminating much admitted nonsense in many areas of thought and discourse, including excesses in certain ways of doing philosophy. There is every reason to be suspicious of high-flown metaphysical speculations that try to explain the world by misapplications of metaphors or by means of vague and poorly defined but impressive-sounding terms that substitute literary flourish for good reasoning. However, we should not judge too hastily all such efforts as philosophically worthless until we have entered more sympathetically into the standpoints from which they are offered and have made sincere efforts to understand why particular concepts have been introduced and what philosophical purposes they are meant to accomplish. In any case, in keeping with our general metaphilosophical principle of considering all things critically but open-mindedly, we should not dismiss any philosophical enterprise by sweeping critique, without considering its merits seriously on its own terms. If we adopt the verification criterion of meaning and, on its strength, eliminate all philosophical traditions, then we may be overlooking important insightful ideas. Philosophy is not party politics but, rather, the desire to know, to attain wisdom, without preconditions about how inquiry should proceed and where it will end up. We must be prepared to follow arguments wherever they lead and to not close ourselves off from any potential source of understanding without a fair and an impartial hearing. This is not to say that there are no meaningless philosophical pseudopropositions, unworthy philosophical systems, or invalid modes or methods of trying to do philosophy. We should nevertheless be cautious in adopting any metaphilosophical position that overturns all philosophy from the standpoint of what must itself be a philosophical position.

There are also serious difficulties in the verification criterion of meaning as a metaphilosophy that would undermine all of classical philosophy. One embarrassing question for the verification criterion is whether the verification criterion itself is supposed to be true by definition or by scientific confirmation. It does not seem to be verified, or even verifiable, in either of the ways the criterion narrowly prescribes. This is a problem for the theory, because it suggests that there can be exceptions. If the verification criterion as a kind of metaphilosophical principle is not subject to its own requirements, then why not suppose that other propositions—including those of religion, ethics, aesthetics, metaphysics, and philosophy generally—cannot also be meaningful, despite not satisfying the verification criterion? The fact is that we do know reasonably well what we mean when we say such

things as God answers prayer or that Vermeer's *De Keukenmeid* is the most beautiful painting of the seventeenth century, even if we do not suppose that these pronouncements derive their meaning from definition or experience. If we did not
know what they meant, we could not dispute them—as when skeptics reply that
God does not answer prayer because God does not exist, because God does not
have a humanlike moral psychology, because God is too busy or uninterested in the
fate of human beings to answer, or because God is a transcendental entity outside
of physical space and time and cannot causally interact with the created universe.
All of these statements make sense, and we can attribute meaning to them readily
enough. They are not like nonsensical fabrications of nonwords, such as *Dreebel
moop,* or grammatical but otherwise obviously meaningless sentences, such as
"Blue concepts sleep furiously."

What is even more disastrous for the verification criterion is that it logically
depends on a false and oversimplified model of how science is actually done. Science does not advance by the old textbook method of collecting observations and
organizing them in ways that suggest hypotheses to be confirmed or disconfirmed
by further observations or experiments. That some of the observation-hypothesis-
experiment structure takes place in science cannot be denied. But observations are
already theory-laden and are virtually valueless in scientific discovery if they are
naively collected with no prior theoretical purpose or principle in mind. Moreover,
there is a framework of historical background, a sociological context in which scientists are trained and taught to find certain kinds of problems interesting and other
kinds uninteresting, together with aesthetic standards that dictate the kinds of
hypotheses to be considered and the types of experiments designed in order to test
them. Scientific hypotheses do not come from nowhere but, rather, are the result of
creative thinking by scientists that does not simply conform to the verification criterion of meaning. Scientists, like others who try to explain things, tell a story about
the world, in the course of which, they make use of language that in many ways
does not fall under the two verificationist categories of sentences that are true or
false by definition or true or false by virtue of being confirmable or disconfirmable
by possible observations or experiments. This is part of what scientists do, but only
part. The attempt to make philosophy scientific, and to bring to philosophy the
same kind of methodological discipline that characterizes the most successful work
in natural science, cannot simply try to impose the verification criterion of meaning on philosophy, because the verification criterion does not even completely and
correctly describe what scientists actually do, or the ways in which scientists mean-
ingfully use language.

SCIENCE AND PHILOSOPHY

If the verification criterion of meaning is unacceptable, then we need not seriously
consider its metaphilosophical implications for the meaninglessness of philosophy.
The meaning of philosophical language can be at least as rich and diverse as scientific language. But there are other attempts to argue that philosophy is very different in purpose and methodology from the natural sciences.

Let us examine the choices for a less radical metaphilosophy. If philosophy is not simply nonsense, or at least not nonsense because of the verification criterion, then the scientific model for philosophy could still acknowledge a similarity between the ways science and philosophy identify problems and work toward solutions. There is a good rationale for this characterization, because the natural sciences originally developed out of, and, at a point in their history, broke away from, philosophical inquiry. As recently as the mid-nineteenth century, what we now commonly refer to as scientists spoke of themselves as natural philosophers and of their work as making contributions to natural philosophy. The institutions of modern science were separately pursued as such only quite recently in history, as they defined more specialized subject matters and introduced experimental techniques that justified distinguishing themselves from philosophy. The separation of science from philosophy left philosophy as a more humanistic pursuit of wisdom and understanding of value and the world. However, because science is an offshoot of philosophy, there need be no logical incompatibility in regarding some styles of philosophy as scientific in the contemporary sense.

What would be a scientific approach to philosophy? Science identifies theoretical and practical problems, things to be explained and ways of controlling limited parts of the world in order to satisfy human needs. Science clarifies problems and formulates hypotheses to explain phenomena and to help discover ways to engineer the world. Science considers how observations and experiments can confirm or disconfirm these hypotheses, which it then proceeds provisionally either to accept and put into practice or to abandon or refine in an ongoing search for the truth about publicly observable aspects of experience. There is often a complex interaction between the theory and the practice of science, such that practical applications of science derive from theory, whereas theory is also shaped, corrected, and checked by its success or failure as it is applied in practice. To what extent can metaphilosophy profit from this way of understanding the purpose and methodology of science? There are similarities as well as differences.

We can think of philosophy as being like modern science in articulating problems. If philosophical problems are not nonsense, as the verification criterion would have it, then we can regard philosophy as identifying a special area of philosophical problems that are different from those in which scientists are interested but that, similarly, can be divided into purely theoretical and practical categories. Philosophers, like scientists, want to explain things, albeit different kinds of things, and to put their ideas into practice. At least if we accept at face value what philosophers say about their work, they are engaged in a process of trying to explain, among other things, the meaning of language, the rightness and wrongness of certain actions, the beauty of nature and art, the relation of body and mind, the conditions of free action, the identity of objects persisting through change, and the concepts of space, time, and causation. Science asks such questions as, Why does iron rust? Why do birds migrate? Why do the stars and planets appear to move in an arc across the night sky? By comparison, philosophy asks, Why is there something rather than nothing? Why do causes precede effects? Why do we ordinarily hold people morally responsible for what they do?

There is a parallel kind of interaction between theory and practice in philosophy. Whereas some scientists want to apply the findings of theoretical physics to build bridges, design telescopes, and diagnose and cure diseases, some philosophers want to apply the answers to philosophical problems to practical concerns, such as implementing morally correct principles in legislation, introducing new concepts of mathematical proof, contributing to the reform of methods in the natural sciences, and offering philosophical foundations for art and literary criticism that can directly affect the practice of music, literature, and the plastic arts. Like the interaction between theory and practice in the natural sciences, the attempt to put philosophical ideas into practice can reflectively transform philosophy, especially when theory does not agree with practice, and practice reveals problems and intricacies that philosophical theory did not previously take into account, as the requirements of practice reveal the need for adjustments in theory.

There are points of similarity between scientific and philosophical theory and practice, but there are also differences that should not be downplayed or underemphasized. It is obvious that science uses certain more specialized methods than philosophy, although philosophy also has special methods. As a first approximation, we can say that philosophy generally relies more on arguments and critical evaluation of the logic of arguments, whereas science makes greater use of empirical observations and experiments. Yet even this distinction requires clarification. Philosophy is not indifferent to the facts of the world as discovered by scientific observations and experiments, and much of philosophy takes its point of departure from an understanding of the universe it shares with modern science. Science, for its part, cannot proceed without using and critically appraising rational arguments, which drive much of scientific inquiry in analyzing data, constructing hypotheses, interpreting results, and deciding what to do next. The emphasis on shared facts and similar methods is nevertheless more important to science than to philosophy. By contrast, concepts, insights, and arguments in the abstract are more central to philosophy than to science; in a sense, they are all that philosophy as philosophy has to work with. Observations and experiments often provide important subject matter for philosophers to philosophize about, but it is not part of philosophical method as such to gather information about the world in the same way as empirical science.

Philosophers, as philosophy has come to be practiced, do not rely primarily on publicly testable hypotheses and their confirmation or disconfirmation by further observations and repeatable publicly observable experiments. Scientists, although they also define concepts and formulate arguments, typically do not limit themselves to deciding important scientific questions in the way that philosophers try to solve philosophical problems by clarifying concepts and working out the conclusions of good arguments. Scientists, like philosophers, use thought experiments as well as real physical experiments and are concerned about counterexamples to their definitions and arguments. But philosophers as philosophers have only thought experiments, which do not require physical equipment of the sort scientists use, for deciding philosophical questions. The differences between the way in which scientists approach scientific questions and the way in which philosophers approach philosophical questions are not so strong that we cannot conceive of science as the continuation of philosophy by other means. This, again, reflects the history of their relationship, of science as a continuation of the philosophical search for truth applied to a special set of problems. At least we can understand philosophy and science as grading off imperceptibly into one another at points of contact where the two disciplines have a similar agenda.

WHAT IS A PHILOSOPHICAL PROBLEM?

There is a difference in the overall project of philosophy that distinguishes it more sharply from any modern scientific study. Philosophy makes it its business to investigate the underlying assumptions and presuppositions that are generally taken for granted in other specialized fields of inquiry.

This methodological commitment makes philosophy stand out as radically different in comparison with the natural sciences. In classical physics, for example, scientists do not ask whether or not all events have causes. Instead, they presuppose that all events have causes and proceed to determine, by observation and experiment, the cause of this particular event or type of event and that particular event or type of event. Philosophers, by contrast, are interested in the longstanding metaphysical question of whether all events have causes, or whether there can also be uncaused events. They try to answer such distinctively philosophical questions, not by observation or experiment, although they may regard such information as relevant to their inquiry, but by reflecting on and sometimes trying to refine the meanings of concepts in analyzing ideas and exploring their implications in ordinary and thought experiment contexts, arriving at an understanding of the problem by articulating the best, most reasonable arguments that survive the best, most rigorous and penetrating criticisms.

When philosophy turns to other sciences, to the arts and politics, and to other human endeavors, it raises a distinctive kind of question about matters that these subjects and practices take for granted. The philosophy of mathematics asks such questions as, What is the metaphysical status of mathematical entities such as numbers and geometrical archetypes? What, if anything, is special about mathematical knowledge and mathematical truth? What constitutes a mathematical proof? The philosophy of art asks such questions as, What is an artwork? Is photography art? What are the identity conditions for replicated artworks, such as the multiple performances of a symphony? Is there an objective distinction between good and bad art? The philosophy of law and political philosophy asks such questions as, What is the meaning of justice? Can citizens be morally obligated to obey the law when the law disagrees with morality? Is it possible for there to be a morally justified war?

What is a philosophical problem in general, and where do all these philosophical questions come from? How can we recognize a philosophical question and think up new philosophical questions of our own? These are all metaphilosophical questions. One, perhaps too easy, answer is to say that philosophical and metaphilosophical questions ultimately derive from the same source as scientific questions—human curiosity. We desire to know why sunsets are beautiful, just as we desire to know why iron rusts; we desire to know whether two objects can be in the same place at the same time, just as we desire to know whether rats can learn to run a maze more quickly after increasing their intake of vitamin A. But curiosity is too general an answer to the metaphilosophical question about the nature and origin, specifically, of philosophical questions, as opposed to scientific, historical, religious, and other kinds of questions. What is unique about philosophical questions is that they raise conceptual difficulties about the underlying assumptions or presuppositions of other disciplines and, in the case of metaphilosophical questions, about the underlying assumptions or presuppositions of philosophy. The sign of a philosophical question is that it arises in response to a conceptual confusion, a kind of tension or conflict in thinking, that occurs when we ask about the deepest and most fundamental beliefs on which another discipline or human practice or endeavor ultimately depends.

A philosophical question is most often expressed in the form of a conceptual puzzle or paradox, a contradiction in matters that we would otherwise have thought unproblematic. We have seen examples in every previous chapter of this book. It is not until we reflect on many things around us—including the science, history, and religion we are taught, the politics that shape the institutions in which we live, and the art, music, and literature we admire—that we discover such problems. A philosophical education is partly a sensitization to the existence of philosophical questions in areas where we would not previously have imagined there were difficulties. The conceptual puzzles and paradoxes of philosophy often take the form of surprising inconsistencies among seemingly innocent concepts.

As a classic example of a philosophical paradox, consider the common assumption that every proposition is exclusively either true or false. The very concept of a proposition might be defined by this characterization of its possible truth values. However, if every proposition is exclusively either true or false, what shall we say about the truth value of what appears at least to be the proposition "This proposition is false"? If the proposition is exclusively either true or false, then we are faced with a dilemma. If the proposition is true, then, since it says of itself that it is false, it is true that it is false. But, if the proposition is false, then, again since it says of itself that it is false, it is false that it is false—in which case, it is true. The proposition paradoxically seems to be true if and only if it is false, an evident contradiction. As an illustration from the philosophy of mind, consider the seemingly innocent assumption that only the person who is experiencing a sensation can be certain of it. I alone can know in this strong sense that I am in pain; you can only infer that I am in pain with a lesser degree of certainty in drawing inferences from my verbal and other kinds of external behavior. All this may appear obvious; however, when we inquire more deeply into the concepts of sensation and knowledge, we might conclude, as some philosophers have proposed, that only another person can know that I am in pain and that I can never know it, let alone know it with certainty. The philosophical reason, it has been argued, is that we cannot know something unless we can also doubt it, and no one can doubt that he or she is in pain or undergoing any other sensation.

The sign of a philosophical problem is typically that we feel drawn in two directions by equally compelling but contrary positions. That there are good arguments on opposite sides of a question usually suggests that there is an underlying conceptual conflict to be explained or resolved. We gain philosophical understanding when we clarify the ideas that give rise to such puzzles and paradoxes. The clarifications that ideally are achieved in the process of philosophical analysis can then be put to use in solving philosophical problems and avoiding related kinds of confusion in other areas of thought. A philosophical system can be built up out of such integrated discoveries, united by a common method, with applications to many domains. It is an oversimplification, but we can describe a major part of the difference between philosophy and science by saying that philosophical problems are primarily conceptual conflicts indicated by puzzles and paradoxes in the basic assumptions or presuppositions of a theory or practical activity, including philosophy itself, and that philosophical methods are primarily dependent on the critical evaluation of arguments.

PHILOSOPHY AS A CONVERSATION

Another respect in which philosophy is different from science is that philosophy is a conversation in dialogue with its own history. Philosophy, frequently but not inevitably, takes its point of departure from the discussion of philosophical problems that philosophers have dealt with in the past. Although scientists sometimes take an interest in the history of science, scientists are usually satisfied to move ahead with currently accepted scientific theory and methods, and do not feel the same compelling sense to look backward at their history and begin their inquiries by considering what their predecessors have had to say about the same topics. Some philosophy is detached from the history of its subject in much the same way as science is, but, in characterizing philosophy as a whole, it is a conspicuous feature of the way that philosophy is often done to take its history into account not merely as an interesting curiosity, but as an essential foundation for continued work toward the clarification of philosophical concepts and the solution of philosophical problems.

To this point, if we have correctly described the main differences between science and philosophy, then this fact should be easy to explain. Whereas science is interested mostly in developing and applying theories to arrive at a correct understanding of the world and, where possible, to achieve engineering control over natural forces, philosophy is engaged in a conceptual inquiry into the meanings of ideas that shape human thought. All science as science really cares about is getting the right answers about how the world works and about how we can make use of the laws of nature to bring about desired results. For such an enterprise, the history of science is usually irrelevant. We do not, therefore, expect to see modern-day chemists seriously researching the history of alchemy as a normal part of their scientific inquiry. For contemporary chemistry, the efforts of alchemists to transform so-called base metals such as lead into gold are an amusing historical footnote but are by no means a part of the science today, even though, by blundering along with mistaken assumptions in pursuit of a physically impossible goal, the alchemists managed to discover some interesting things about the chemical properties of certain physical substances, along with the useful beginnings of crude laboratory methods. Neither do we expect present-day biologists to devote any of their energy to the study of spontaneous generation, vitalism, inherited acquired characteristics (Lamarckism), or any of the other discredited ideas that once held sway in the early history of science.

In philosophy, the situation is very different. It is by no means uncommon for contemporary philosophers investigating problems in any area to go back even to the earliest recorded philosophers from ancient Greece or the non-Western traditions, and everything in between, as a living source of problems and inspiration for solutions. Philosophy's dialogue with its history is not merely a procedure for prudently avoiding the mistakes of the past and the wasted effort of reinventing the wheel, but is also a rather more essential element of philosophical method. The reason is plain to see when we recall the interpretation of philosophy as a conceptual inquiry. Philosophers rightly perceive that, in order to understand the concepts we have today, we must understand their origin and development. Thinkers from philosophy's past are in the best position to comment on the state of conceptual problems in their own time from the standpoint of their cultural milieu. There are opposing viewpoints about the philosophical significance of philosophy's history, as there are about almost all matters of philosophical investigation. But one plausible answer is that the history of philosophy is timelessly relevant to the practice of philosophy, because some perennial aspects of the human conceptual framework remain relatively constant over time, whereas other aspects undergo interesting and potentially enlightening transformations.

The point of describing philosophy as a conversation is not merely to emphasize the dialectical nature of philosophical exchange. Philosophers often, but not necessarily, talk to each other. Some of the most famous philosophers devote much of their best energy to writing ideas in notebooks that are not even shared with other thinkers during their lifetimes. It is true that great schools of philosophy have flourished in an environment in which gifted teachers met to discuss the problems of philosophy with a few devoted students. It is also true that philosophers tend to be gregarious, meeting whenever they can to discuss their ideas and to argue, debate, ponder, and fret about questions that do not seem to engage the rest of the world. But contributors to other disciplines also find it important to talk to one another, and there is a deeper sense in which philosophy is a conversation. Philosophy is an activity in which minds meet across vast distances of space and time. The reader of a great work from the history of philosophy is virtually in direct touch with an author from centuries or even millenia in the past, as well as from remote civilizations that may have since become extinct.

When I pick up a work of philosophy from an important thinker, I enter into the thoughts of someone who has reflected on ageless topics of concern to the human spirit, about logic, morality, religion, art, history, science, and the practice of philosophy. The fact that the author lived more than 2,000 years ago or is still living today need not make any difference in the way that the thinker speaks to me personally about the problems of philosophy, about concepts that we share or that have changed from time and place to the present day. Philosophy is a conversation we can have among ourselves, and with other thinkers elsewhere or long since dead. Through their writings, we can come to know the ideas of these philosophers, all of whom have something of value to say to us, no matter how the current facts of the world economy, technology, and political circumstances have changed.

It is the importance to philosophy of argument and the criticism of argument that makes philosophy a conversation. In trying to understand a great philosophical text, we are necessarily drawn into a discussion, at least with ourselves, but usually with the author of the work and with others with whom we may wish to share our ideas. We might be intrigued, or we might be shocked and outraged by what we read. We might accept or doubt the truth of what is said. But it is almost impossible to read philosophy without becoming personally involved. It is when philosophy hooks us in any of these ways that we enter into the conversation about topics that began in ancient times and continues even more actively today. We want to argue with the author of a philosophical work. In a sense, we want to argue with the book, but also with ourselves, our teachers, and our friends. For it is by argument that we come to grasp the issues, and it is only by argument that we can hope to understand.

Despite its involvement with its own history, there can sometimes be progress in philosophy. New philosophical problems and methods arise, even as a result of philosophy's dynamic dialectical interaction with its history. There are dramatic revolutions in philosophical attitudes, solutions to longstanding questions, new trends of thought, and heroic figures who break new ground and defy the authority of conventional wisdom in order to take philosophy into uncharted territory. Philosophy feeds and grows on the identification of conceptual problems and the clarification of thought that comes about by argument and counterargument, definition and counterexample, thesis and antithesis, problem and solution, and criticism in an upward spiral through history that brings together curious minds in each generation to contribute to philosophical enlightenment. The philosophical thought handed down in philosophers' writings and other cultural traces is a precious legacy that can help us understand some of the greatest enigmas of human existence. These are problems that were known in different guises to thinkers in every age, and their insights can fuel our own desire for a kind of wisdom that cannot come from the special sciences, religious faith, or any other discipline or method of inquiry except philosophy.

FLYING SOLO IN PHILOSOPHY

The nature of philosophical study as a quest for personally satisfying answers to life's mysteries is the flip side of philosophy as a conversation. Although the practice of philosophy is a participation in the ongoing arguments that have preoccupied philosophers at all times, it is also an individualized activity of making ideas and conclusions one's own by accepting and being able to provide reasons for them that are not merely borrowed from others, but are admitted into one's philosophical stance only after being thought through and assimilated.

This feature of philosophy marks yet another difference between philosophy and science. It is not a hard and fast distinction, but one that allows points of contact between philosophy and its historical offshoots in the natural sciences. It explains why philosophy, much more than science, is usually the product of individual minds working individually, rather than of scientific research teams. By contrast, science, despite its reliance on individual genius, lends itself more easily to collective endeavor, while philosophy is a more personal quest for understanding. The personalization of philosophy does not preclude the possibility of philosophical schools and circles of thought among thinkers of similar interests, or those who agree with one another methodologically. Although philosophers share ideas and collaborate on research and writing projects, it is more common for great figures in the history of philosophy to be solitary in the development of their philosophical systems. The reason is that philosophical, as opposed to scientific, understanding arises from a particular kind of curiosity that can be satisfied only by a personally conducted inquiry that ends in personally approved clarifications of ideas and solutions to problems.

The justification for a scientific discovery is, so to speak, bigger than the individual scientists who make the discovery. But the point of philosophical reflection is usually more to satisfy oneself at a very personal level that one's concepts have been set in order and that the conceptual puzzles and paradoxes that occasioned one's philosophical doubts and perplexities have been untangled. It is for this reason that, although we find great individual thinkers in the history of philosophy and science, it is a remarkable feature of modern science that it pursues its investigations of the natural world by virtually anonymous teams of researchers for whom method is more important than insight, whereas philosophy has largely continued its individualized search for personal understanding. This is why we speak of the *science,* not the *sciences,* of chemistry and why, by contrast, we speak very naturally of as many different philosophies and alternative philosophical systems as there are philosophers advancing distinctive visions of philosophical problems.

It is not just that philosophers love to argue and, so, are reluctant to agree with one another merely for the sake of keeping age-old philosophical controversies alive. Rather, philosophers by vocation are involved in a project that is not validated by public agreement. In a way, this is also true of science. Many scientists, like philosophers, have upheld their views despite widespread opposition and institutional harrassment. A scientist, like a philosopher, can be right in maintaining a conclusion, even if no one else agrees. The difference is that, in science, we assume that, if those who now disagree with a scientific conclusion were to set aside their prejudices and consider the facts objectively and open-mindedly, then they would accept the same results. While such consensus would not be a sure sign that the scientist had gotten things right, it is a possibility that needs to be described against the background assumption that, where scientific facts are concerned, people can disagree, but it usually makes sense to expect a right answer. In philosophy, by contrast, many different philosophical perspectives are possible, because many more assumptions are open to question. As a result, among most philosophers, even when they argue most passionately for what they believe, there is not the same presumption as in science that there is only one correct conclusion. The achievement of popular agreement in the marketplace of philosophical as opposed to scientific ideas, if it were to occur, would not necessarily be understood by philosophers as indicating the value of a philosophical system, in the same way that it is standardly thought to be a goal for and indication of success in the natural sciences.

PHILOSOPHICAL OBJECTIVITY

The difference is not that science is objective and philosophy is subjective. There are subjectivists in philosophy, and even philosophical subjectivists. But philosophy can be just as objective as natural science in its rigorous reasoning and critical evaluation of the logic of arguments. Moreover, philosophy is often as interested in the objective facts of the natural world as the natural sciences are, although usually in a different way.

Rather, the difference that allows multiple philosophical perspectives and alternative philosophical systems is that philosophy, unlike science, does not presuppose a single starting point for its investigations, a common set of existent facts or assumptions. Philosophy, by contrast with natural science, considers everything as up for grabs, and requires each thinker to decide on the best and most appropriate way to begin philosophical inquiry. Science, broadly construed, has a common methodology. It assumes that the physical world exists, that when we observe things by means of the senses we are or at least can thereby acquire true information about real existent entities and states of affairs, that time and space are real factors, and that causal connections in the future are likely to resemble the causal connections of the present and past. In philosophy, all these and every other proposition on which a scientist might seek to build an explanation of the world are called into question, and must stand the test of philosophical critique undertaken from many different philosophical starting points. It is the uninhibited intellectual freedom of philosophical inquiry that finally characterizes the distinction between the methods of philosophy and science.

Although some philosophers may decide to accept the same basic assumptions as natural science, there is no obligation for other philosophers to do so. Hence, there is no guarantee that different philosophers, even if they were to follow the same rigorous methods of argument and analysis, would necessarily arrive at the same philosophical conclusions. This is to say nothing of the fact that different philosophers, as expressions of the radical difference in the starting places they find most satisfying or correct, all apply the same techniques of reasoning. Philosophers even disagree about the criteria for correct logical inference, the methods by which arguments are constructed and criticized, and generally about anything else that contributes to the evaluation of arguments. It is the lack of a universal common ground that makes philosophy exciting, personal, and innovative. Philosophy is an arena in which ideas are challenged in every conceivable way from every conceivable perspective, and in which new and unexpected concepts are encouraged to come forth. If philosophy is nevertheless a rigorous discipline, it is because philosophers, having laid down preferred principles for philosophical inquiry, even if other thinkers do not agree, are willing to follow good arguments relentlessly to see where they lead.

Science, as understood and practiced today, has no comparable free rein to define its methods, to conclude that the world of experience does not exist or that causation is nothing but an illusion, or to reach other positions that some philosophers have seriously and influentially, if notoriously, maintained. A scientist as an individual thinker might arrive at such beliefs, but not as a result of scientific reasoning. Science is a theoretical research discipline that takes certain assumptions about the nature of reality as its ground rules, along with a general framework for considering and testing hypotheses by observation and experiment that are not open to wholesale revision by scientists. Compare the situation of the scientist with that of a games player who chooses to move a knight diagonally like a bishop on the chessboard. Nothing physically prevents the games player from moving the piece in this way, and nothing physically prevents the scientist from refusing to consider observations or experiments as relevant to the truth of a scientific theory. It is just that, by doing so, the games player is no longer playing chess but is playing either no game at all or an improvised game, similar in some ways to but obviously different from chess. Likewise, a scientist who breaks the rules of scientific investigation is no longer practicing science but is either doing philosophy, is not engaged in any kind of inquiry at all, or is making up new rules for a previously unrecognized kind of intellectual endeavor.

What we call natural science, although no more rigorous and in some ways less critically reflective than the most radical philosophy, does not, by its ground rules, have the same freewheeling freedom to inquire critically into any topic and raise difficulties about any assumptions. The natural scientist makes valuable discoveries about the physical world by presupposing answers to some of the questions that philosophers are intellectually committed to investigating as undecided, the solutions to which might point in many different philosophical directions. Although in some ways philosophy sets the standards for investigative rigor even as practiced by mathematicians and natural scientists, philosophy does not have the luxury of building on presuppositions it is not obligated to question. Philosophy, unlike natural science, is entitled to accept assumptions provisionally, if at all, only after they have passed muster in an analysis that seeks to identify, understand, and if possible resolve conceptual puzzles and paradoxes.

WHY IS PHILOSOPHY DIFFICULT?

The tasks of philosophy are formidable. This is why some philosophical texts are so difficult to understand. The authors strive to take nothing for granted, but to proceed only in the most intellectually circumspect way. Such philosophers propose to secure the ground of their own enterprise, beginning with the most minimal assumptions and building only on propositions that have been validated by philosophical criticism.

The less a philosopher allows philosophical inquiry to begin with as a starting place, the more tentative and resourceful its investigations must be. By inquiring into the presuppositions of all disciplines, including philosophy, philosophy sets itself a daunting task, in which it is hard to make smooth or rapid headway. Of course, another reason some philosophy is difficult is that, as in other disciplines, some philosophers are simply not very good writers, and they produce works that are compositionally clumsy expressions of their ideas. It is usually worthwhile to struggle even with slow-going philosophical texts of this kind for the sake of the insights they contain.

The problems in developing a minimally presuppositional philosophy make several alternative options attractive for metaphilosophy. Some philosophers find the prospects of a radical philosophical inquiry into the basic assumptions of philosophy itself to be impossible or unintelligible, and, in response, prefer to proceed in somewhat the same way as science. They accept certain propositions as a philosophical starting place, on the grounds that any starting place will do. If there is no definite way to validate or invalidate a starting place, then we might as well begin with assumptions that either seem intuitively correct, agree with science, or are presupposed by science. If we relax the requirement by which philosophy must try to account for everything, including its own methodology, then various strategies for developing a philosophical program suddenly become available, each supporting a different way of doing philosophy, potentially identifying a different philosophical problem, and calling for a different kind of philosophical conclusion.

TWO TYPES OF METAPHILOSOPHY

We can think of two very different basic types of metaphilosophy. One begins with accepted or otherwise independently justified theories or practices—science, mathematics, ethics, aesthetics, history, or religion—and works toward whatever must be presupposed in order to uphold these theories or practices in whatever form they exist. The other approach to metaphilosophy examines the basic assumptions of a discipline first, and allows only the conclusions or implications that follow from premises to be accepted in the superstructure of a theory that stand up to the most rigorous philosophical scrutiny. It is a difference of what metaphilosophy is to take as a starting place for philosophy, marking a fundamental distinction in the method and ideology of philosophy. These two metaphilosophical alternatives can be described as *transcendental* and *foundational metaphilosophy*. They are represented in the following diagram:

Two Types of Metaphilosophy

Transcendental Metaphilosophy	Foundational Metaphilosophy
Independently accepted theory	Theory supported by assumptions
⇓	⇑
Assumptions required to uphold theory	Independently accepted assumptions

In transcendental metaphilosophy, we start out with a more or less uncritical acceptance of beliefs that have proved their usefulness. Then, taking these received views as already justified, we try to uncover the underlying philosophical principles that are indispensable in order for the beliefs to be true. The philosophical presuppositions that are found to transcend science, mathematics, and other disciplines or belief systems just as they exist can be either relatively simple or sophisticated.

We might begin with mathematics as mathematicians have developed it, and as scientists use it in theory and practice. A transcendental metaphilosophy might need to suppose, among other things, that there are infinite sets and series of mathematical entities, along with all that this presupposes or entails. If there are no infinities, then certain parts of pure theoretical and applied classical mathematics do not make sense. But we want these parts of mathematics to make sense, because, if they do not, then we cannot rely on them in the applications we require in physics and other natural sciences, in algebra, trigonometry, and calculus. We use the axioms of classical infinitary mathematics in building bridges and rocketships and we get satisfying results; the bridges withstand weight and the rocketships find their targets in outer space. From this, we conclude that the mathematics must be right, and we proceed from there to ask what indispensable philosophical principles must be true in order for the mathematics to work. The same is true with respect to the philosophical principles that might be uncovered by a transcendental approach to metaphilosophy in uncovering the underlying assumptions of science, ethics, aesthetics, history, and religion.

The second type of metaphilosophy, as the name *foundational* metaphilosophy suggests, is more radical. It does not grant permission to take received belief systems at face value as though they were independently justified, even if they appear to be so useful that we can hardly imagine doing without them in our practical lives. What we must do, instead, is to undertake a careful investigation of fundamental philosophical principles, and not allow ourselves to build on them unless or until we are fully satisfied that they are philosophically acceptable. Afterward, if we can restore classical mathematics, science, and other disciplines on solid philosophically secure foundations, well and good. But, if we discover difficulties in the assumptions that are supposed to ground these subjects, then, on this metaphilosophical model, we must be prepared to reject any theoretical and practical superstructure that depends on faulty foundations, regardless of how useful they appear to be. This method is potentially more extreme, because it can lead us to reject well-received and widely used disciplines if their underlying principles cannot be adequately justified.

To continue the example about the philosophical foundations of classical mathematics, according to foundational metaphilosophy, if we cannot independently justify the concept of infinity, then, if higher mathematics depends on the existence of infinite sets and series, we must also reject classical mathematics, including calculus, regardless of how essential it appears in physics and the other natural sciences. If the foundations are faulty, then they cannot adequately uphold the superstructure—in which case, we must either work out alternative foundations or, to be consistent, abandon the superstructure as insupportable.

The distinctions between these two metaphilosophical approaches to philosophy are pervasive. They make an enormous difference in the way philosophy is done, in the kinds of problems philosophy recognizes, and in the kinds of philosophical conclusions that can be reached. There are advantages and disadvantages in both types of metaphilosophy. To begin with received belief systems and work toward the underlying assumptions that are indispensable to them is to start out with something that has already proved its worth in the world of practical affairs. We must be doing something right in physics if we can successfully build bridges and send rockets to the moon. Thus, we might well proceed metaphilosophically by accepting the sciences as justified by their effectiveness in predicting and controlling events in the world, and by working backward to the assumptions that must be true in order for such higher-level beliefs and practices to exist. We have to start somewhere in philosophy, as in anything else. Why not begin with something like natural science, which has established itself as valuable to human interests? Then, whatever else must be presupposed in order for science to proceed, the metaphysics of science, mathematics, or another discipline, can be adduced as vital to philosophy. The aim of philosophy includes identifying and trying to solve philosophical problems that arise in the effort to clarify whatever assumptions are needed to make sense of the mathematics, science, or other theories or practices that are justified by virtue of their usefulness.

The main disadvantage of transcendental metaphilosophy is also connected with its apparent advantage. By using the success of natural science or another discipline as a starting place for philosophy, we might after all be starting with something that, despite its usefulness, is theoretically mistaken or confused. We know from the history of science that what sometimes passes as a correct theory of the natural world is later rejected, whereupon the need to revise or replace previously accepted scientific principles is recognized. Scientists used to believe that the health of the human body was governed by four humors—blood, lymph, white bile, and black bile—and that, as a hydraulic system, the body occasionally needs to have its liquid pressure adjusted by bleeding with lancet or leeches. Today, this way of thinking about the body is no longer accepted. Yet, despite being overturned as a false science, the theory had a certain usefulness in the treatment of disease and cannot be dismissed as total medical quackery.

It is one thing to reflect on the quaint beliefs that previously held sway in natural science, and another to acknowledge that contemporary science might seem just as quaint from the standpoint of future scientific discoveries, which might eventually replace what we now believe to be true. Other examples can easily be multiplied to include illustrations from almost any area of scientific inquiry, in physics, chemistry, biology, geology, astronomy, and even the higher principles of mathematics. According to the model of transcendental metaphilosophy, if we conceive of philosophy as beginning uncritically with science in whatever state we find it and working out its indispensable underlying assumptions or those that must be true in order for science to be correct, then we risk uncovering only the mistaken assumptions presupposed by a mistaken science. In that event, philosophy becomes infected with the same errors as the science with which it begins. However, some philosophers have understood the purpose of philosophy as offering an independent intellectual perspective from which other disciplines, such as science, religion, history, and art, can be critically assessed, rather than merely accepted at face value as an acceptable starting place for philosophy.

The alternative extreme is foundational metaphilosophy. The approach is more radical in not accepting any received discipline as a starting point for philosophy but, rather, beginning with a thorough critical investigation of the assumptions that might be adopted in building a belief system. The advantage of the foundational model is that, in this way, philosophy avoids inheriting the errors of a potentially false or conceptually confused science. By contrast with transcendental metaphilosophy, foundational metaphilosophy forbids us from making further progress in philosophy unless or until we have satisfied ourselves that our assumptions are correct and that they provide a sound foundation on which to build. Accordingly, the method offers the promise of philosophical adequacy throughout our belief systems from the ground up, by beginning with the most basic assumptions, assuring that they are correct, and allowing inferences and theoretical and practical developments to be accepted only to the extent that they can also be found to satisfy the requirements of philosophical justification. The metaphilosophy of going from bottom to top, and making sure everything in between is correct, might appear more likely to assure epistemic certainty than going from top to bottom, as in a transcendental metaphilosophy. A radical metaphilosophy permits several ways of considering the usefulness of scientific, ethical, aesthetic, historical, or religious theory and practice, without uncritically supposing that the practical value of a discipline entails its suitability as a starting place for philosophy.

We return for a moment, then, to the usefulness of physics in predicting and engineering events in the physical world. The foundational metaphilosopher need not deny the value of physics. One philosophical question is whether the usefulness of physics and mathematics in physics is real or apparent, and whether or not the usefulness of physics is attributable to the truth of the principles of physics, or whether its uses can be separated as independent of its truth or falsehood. Many false principles can be useful. It can be useful in measuring time, for example, to speak of the interval between sunrise and sunset, even though the sun does not actually rise or set, and the sun does not move around the Earth but, rather, the Earth rotates on its axis as it orbits the sun. To invoke another astronomical example, science found it useful for centuries in predicting the motion of stars and planets to suppose that the Earth was the center of the universe and that all other bodies in space move in perfect geometrical circles. But today we know that the Earth is not even the center of our solar system, and that other satellites move in elliptical orbits determined by a complex adjustment of gravitational fields throughout the universe. The usefulness of a theory can often be independent of its truth or falsehood, and usefulness by itself is not generally an adequate basis for judging truth. But, if a theory is not true, despite being useful, then beginning with a useful theory without being in a position to judge its truth, or even its conceptual coherence, and working backward transcendentally to uncover the theory's underlying philosophical assumptions, risks identifying only philosophically mistaken assumptions. To take a more dramatic example from the philosophy of religion, consider that, if God does not exist, then beginning as a starting place for philosophy with the usefulness of traditional religion in explaining certain aspects of the world and the history of humankind, or in offering psychological comfort to believers, is likely to uncover false presuppositions about the existence and nature of God and, thereby, to infect the resulting philosophy with falsehood.

The disadvantages of foundational metaphilosophy, somewhat like the disadvantages of transcendental metaphilosophy, also derive from its advantages. What makes foundational metaphilosophy attractive is its promise of never taking any theoretical step or authorizing any theory-based practice without first establishing its philosophical credentials. This method holds out the possibility of developing a belief system that is epistemically certain, with no point of entry for falsehood.

The trouble is that, if everything must first pass scrutiny according to the most rigorous philosophical criticism, then how do we ever start the process? In order to positively evaluate a starting place for philosophy, to give approval to our basic assumptions before trying to build any sort of superstructure on its foundations, we need a secure way of justifying the assumptions. To do this, in turn, we must apply a method of justifying the assumptions, which requires that the method of justifying the assumptions itself be justified, so that we apply only correct standards. Now an obvious regress threatens. We need correct methods to justify foundational assumptions, but methods for justifying foundational assumptions must themselves be justified, for which we require justified methods for justifying methods. The situation is similar to but importantly different from the problem of the criterion or diallelus. The challenge here is not to overcome or break out of a circle but, rather, to find a principled way of halting an infinite regress of increasingly more basic principles needed to justify less basic principles justifying more basic principles. For, when we speak of basic principles, we already refer to the most fundamental principles of any belief system. The regress entailed by the problem of explaining how radical philosophy is to get started in certifying assumptions as philosophically acceptable might show that the very concept of a basic principle is logically incoherent.

There is bound to be disagreement among philosophers about the right metaphilosophy. Metaphilosophy is so important and fundamental to philosophical outlook, and has such large implications for the conduct of philosophy, that many of the most fundamental philosophical disagreements, when pursued to their origins, ultimately depend on differences of metaphilosophy.

SYNTHESIS OF FOUNDATIONAL
AND TRANSCENDENTAL METAPHILOSOPHY

If these problems cannot be settled satisfactorily by invoking a universal logic that all philosophers agree to follow, what hope is there, then, for a foundational metaphilosophy? Since transcendental metaphilosophy appears to suffer from disadvantages as devastating to its program as foundational metaphilosophy, what hope is there for metaphilosophy in general? By implication, what hope can there be for any philosophy, or for philosophy as a way of inquiry?

We might try to develop a compromise position. What if we were to propose a modified but less than absolutely foundational metaphilosophy to consider critically all assumptions except those connected with logic or the standards of philosophical criticism? Philosophers frequently criticize each other's conceptions of logic and standards of philosophical criticism, so that any metaphilosophy that ignores this aspect of philosophy cannot provide a complete theory of philosophical practice. The idea of a foundational metaphilosophy that does not go all the way is a contradiction in terms. But how can there be any compromise with a radically foundational metaphilosophy? Any addition to or deletion from a foundational metaphilosophy, by definition, makes the result nonradical or, in any case, less radical. The only choices are to defend one type of metaphilosophy against the other or to find a third category, and argue that the two extremes we have considered are false alternatives.

Nevertheless, it might be possible to achieve a synthesis of foundational and transcendental metaphilosophy, similar to the synthesis of deontology and consequentialism we examined in solving the train switching dilemma in theoretical ethics. Let us first explore the principles of a transcendental metaphilosophy that establishes a set of ground rules for evaluating philosophical arguments. The idea is to uncover the basic principles by which philosophers discuss philosophical problems. A transcendental explication of the requirements for philosophical argument can be worked out in several ways. One possibility is to identify logical principles that cannot be denied without nullifying the effort to advance or refute any philosophical argument. Such principles can be defended as indispensable to reasoning, without which the prospect of considering the merits of any argument would be unintelligible. If we cannot defend or object to an argument without making use of certain logical principles, then those principles can be transcendentally inferred, at least contextually, for use in evaluating the argument and its counterarguments as we find them in actual philosophical discussion.

Having articulated the ground rules of philosophical argument as the basis of a transcendental metaphilosophy, we can then apply the principles to give a further evaluation of inferences for or against particular philosophical positions. When we have settled on a system of logical guidelines, we can use them to work toward a radically foundational metaphilosophy in support of a correct philosophical superstructure. If we further stipulate that the assumptions of a belief system can be foundationally metaphilosophically cross-checked in terms of their higher-level consequences, then we may have provided a sound working synthesis of transcendental and foundational metaphilosophy.

The hybrid metaphilosophy does not diminish the radical nature of foundational metaphilosophy, for it allows even the ground rules of philosophical argument to come under scrutiny while they are being used. Whatever reasoning is indispensably involved in bringing a philosophical argument under foundational metaphilosophical review, in criticizing the argument and trying to refute it, can be introduced as part of the transcendental metaphilosophical basis for evaluating the argument's logic. The way in which the hybrid metaphilosophical ground rules come into play is that they are introduced only when eliminating them would make it impossible even to raise objections. If the ground rules are wrong, then we cannot even make sense of efforts to criticize any philosophical arguments that presuppose them. At any time a provisionally accepted choice of rules is in place, we can avail ourselves of a set of logical principles for the foundational metaphilosophical evaluation of philosophical arguments. The principles, although derived transcendentally, involve a bare minimum of philosophical commitment, in that they include only rules that cannot be rejected without making nonsense of any argument, even in support of a decision to reject them. By judiciously applying the rules of philosophical argument, we can radically scrutinize the underlying assumptions presupposed by any discipline, including the transcendentally deduced rules with which we begin. In keeping with the rigorous methodology of foundational metaphilosophy, as we proceed, we can agree to accept only the basic assumptions that satisfy the most demanding standards of argument.

When we try to apply the hybrid metaphilosophy, what conclusions do we reach? The answer, in part, is contained in the philosophy we have explored in the preceding chapters, as well as in the comparative study of alternative metaphilosophical positions just described. This is what we should expect, because the metaphilosophy that has been proposed is the philosophy of philosophy that has been explored in these philosophical tidbits. A different approach to philosophy leading to a different selection of philosophical answers to the same questions would reflect a different metaphilosophy. There is a critical interaction between philosophy and metaphilosophy, by which we can improve our philosophy by reconsidering its principles at a higher metaphilosophical level, and improve our metaphilosophy by learning from our successes and failures at a lower philosophical level. By working back and forth from philosophy to metaphilosophy and metaphilosophy to philosophy, we can refine both our philosophy and our metaphilosophy, using each to develop criticisms that might lead toward improvements in the other.

RETURN TO THE SOJOURNER'S QUESTION

We are now in a position to answer the sojourner's question. It is not the kind of solution that will satisfy everyone, and certainly not every philosopher. But it is an answer that is compatible with the methods of philosophy and metaphilosophy we have practiced in all our preceding discussions.

The meaning of life brings many people to philosophy. The sojourner's question is an invitation to embark on a difficult and highly personal pilgrimage. It is one of the most important kinds of inquiry we could undertake, because it goes to the heart of who and what we are, and how we are to live, whether we can reasonably conclude that our lives have meaning, and, if life is not absurd, whether the meaning of life can be found in life itself or must be sought in something beyond.

Is there a meaning to life? Can we have knowlege, and if so, what kinds of things can we know? How can we discover and validate knowledge? If we can know some things, can we know about ourselves—what kinds of things we are? Are we living biological machines or something more? Do we have free will—the freedom, in a meaningful sense, to choose what we do—and can we be morally responsible for our actions? Or are all our decisions and actions causally determined, like the properties of any other physical system? Is it possible to demonstrate by reason that God exists or does not exist? If we could prove that God exists, would that help answer the problem of the meaning of existence? If we can know that we are capable of free will decision making but we cannot prove that God exists, what are the implications for ethical judgment about what we ought and ought not to do? What are the principles of morals, and, if we can agree on a correct moral theory, why should we act according to its requirements? Why should we be moral? Finally, what is the nature of the peculiar inquiry known as philosophy that we engage in when we ask and try to answer these kinds of questions? Is philosophy possible? What is it to develop a philosophy? What is a philosophical problem, and what is a philosophical solution? Do philosophical questions make sense? How are they similar to, and how are they different from, scientific questions? What is the value of philosophy? From the standpoint of a proper metaphilosophy, what is the proper method of philosophy?

By sketching answers to problems in all six chapters, this book has not merely offered a plate of philosophical hors d'oeuvres. Rather, the arguments we have considered constitute an incomplete but connected theory of knowledge, and they explore the metaphysics of thought and mind, the freedom of will, the concept of God and the relation of reason and faith, the pursuit of virtue and morality, and the nature and relevance of philosophy in a systematic exposition of philosophical ideas that circles back to the problem of the meaning of life with which we began. Along the way, we became skilled in some of the most important methods of philosophy. We learned how to construct and critically evaluate definitions of concepts by means of counterexamples, to consider thought experiments, to develop arguments for and against philosophical positions, to apply identity criteria for objects, and many other things, as we built up a useful vocabulary of philosophical terminology.

Understanding what can be learned and expected from the study of philosophy suggests that the practice of philosophy itself provides an answer to questions about the meaning of life. Whether or not thinking about the problems of philosophy is part of the solution to the riddle of life's meaning and whether or not the practice of philosophy explains the meaning of life, philosophy as a method of inquiry about existence, meaning, and values may offer the only possibility of reaching an intellectually satisfying answer to the sojourner's question. Life has no meaning if we do not try to discover for ourselves whether it has meaning and what meaning it may have, if we do not inquire into its meaning with sufficient rigor to appreciate what it means for life to be meaningful or absurd. Philosophy enables us to do this; rather, philosophy is the name we give to our reflections about beauty, truth, and the good, as well as the meaning of life and the meaning of questions and answers about the meaning of life.

The sojourner's question asks who and what we are, whether life is meaningful or absurd; and, if life has meaning, what its meaning is. We have seen that the meaning of life cannot be philosophically justified as dependent on the existence of God or of God's plan and purpose for the universe. Yet we can take comfort in our philosophical analysis of the concept of knowledge whereby in principle we can come to know the answers to these and other important questions. The theory of knowledge entails the possibility of knowing about the meaning of life, and settling other philosophical problems as well, provided that we can arrive at relevantly justified true beliefs. The philosophy of mind offers insight into the nature of thought and helps explain who and what we are, while holding out the possibility of free will and morally responsible decision making. The study of moral philosophy enables us to judge critically the principles whereby we distinguish between ethical right and wrong and plan a life of virtue as moral excellence. It can also provide us with philosophical reasons and motivations for deciding to do what is morally right, even if God does not exist or cannot be proved to exist, and even if doing what is morally wrong is easier or more profitable than doing what is morally right.

The philosophical problems we have considered along the way suggest a purpose and direction for life. We can choose to lead a life of moral excellence, not because we fear God's wrath or desire a heavenly reward or because we think that by doing so we participate in God's divine plan for the world, but because philosophy teaches that this is the best way of improving our lives. We can find meaning in life through philosophy by adopting as our goal the purpose of trying to make ourselves the best human beings we can, according to what philosophy reveals about the possibilities for moral perfectability.

However, this is not the only or even the most important way in which philosophy suggests an answer to the sojourner's question. We have sampled a variety of the aims and rewards of a philosophical way of life. When we think about our problems philosophically, we engage in ongoing consideration of some of life's greatest enigmas. We may thereby come to see philosophy as an intrinsically valuable end in itself, and as a way of coping intelligently with the difficulties posed by the challenges of trying to understand the meaning of life. Thinking philosophically can be the answer to the sojourner's question, if in philosophical inquiry, in a contemplative attitude abstracted from the usual distractions of daily living, we discover that a higher purpose in life is satisfied by philosophical reflection. We may come to appreciate philosophical reasoning as a worthwhile process and activity in itself, as it leads us in the search for answers to philosophical questions, in which we develop our critical capacities and work toward perfection as thinking moral beings. It is the philosophical sojourn itself that provides the solution to the sojourner's question. The activity of questioning, rather than any particular answers, may help us discover the meaning of life. We should not be surprised to find that the meaning of life for self-conscious beings such as ourselves is to become as fully self-conscious as possible. If this is a worthy goal, it suggests a purpose for life in which philosophy—as the disciplined contemplation of existence, meaning, and value—can be the most helpful method in reaching greater self-awareness along life's journey.

If you share the sense of importance in questioning the meaning of life, and if you have absorbed the main lessons of these appetizers, then you may find yourself dissatisfied with their solutions to philosophical problems. The success of a philosophical exchange among several thinkers, including an author and reader, is measured by improvement in understanding, not necessarily by agreement on substantive conclusions. Philosophy, as stressed throughout, is a conversation. If you have whetted your appetite for philosophical problems as a result of these first studies, then you may be prepared to continue the dialogue in a new direction, in your own voice and in your own way. You can do so by challenging the answers offered here with doubts and criticisms that may have occurred to you during your reading. In carrying on the philosophical investigation of these questions, you may decide to reject the positions that have been defended in these chapters, and to refine or replace them with others you find more acceptable. That, in a sense, is the most important idea of philosophy.

A philosophical outlook requires following the best arguments, especially when we disagree about which arguments are best. In philosophical reasoning, even as you approach problems open-mindedly and try to learn from the criticisms and contrary opinions of others, you must listen to and learn to trust your own good judgment, against which, in the end, in your own thinking and for your own purposes, there can be no higher court of appeal. Other people's ideas can provide a useful starting place. But no one, not even the most prestigious professional philosophers, can do this thinking for you. This is not to say that philosophy is subjective, but there is no escaping the personal touch in philosophical inquiry. Even if you come to share the position of someone you take to be an expert in philosophy, you cannot do so—you can only pretend to agree with another thinker's ideas—if you do not at least personally understand the conclusions you have decided to accept. In coming to understand a philosophical position, in turn, you cannot avoid working through the same reasoning or arriving at the same destination by your own route. In the process, it is impossible to grasp the inferences from step to step without deciding for yourself at each point whether or not you agree with the arguments and their conclusions. It is precisely in this activity of thinking through philosophical problems and their solutions, in which individuals participate in personal reflection, that the ongoing philosophical conversations that began in ancient times continue today.

The study of philosophy teaches us to inquire open-mindedly into the most basic assumptions of theory and practice. Philosophy is the most general abstract inquiry into the fundamental problems of meaning, and it is the most rigorous effort to use reasoning and argument critically and self-reflectively in order to comprehend the significance of all aspects of human experience. Philosophy is not only a subject to study in books or to think about in moments of idleness, but also a way of life. It is literally a way of life for professional philosophers, for those who have devoted their thinking lives to the problems of philosophy. But it can also be a way of everyday life for people who are not full-time philosophers, but who need to consider the questions of philosophy as part of their intellectual development and have a desire to understand the kinds of issues explored in these appetizers concerning the meaning of life, the possibility of knowledge, the concept of mind, the existence and nature of God, and moral conduct and virtue in the pursuit of excellence. For philosophical sojourners, the meaning of life, in large part, is to seek the meaning of life.

Index